W9-BWF-116

AMERICAN V·A·L·U·E·S

OPPOSING VIEWPOINTS®

AMERICAN
V·A·L·U·E·S

OPPOSING VIEWPOINTS®

David L. Bender & Bruno Leone, *Series Editors*

David L. Bender, *Editor*

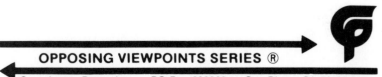

OPPOSING VIEWPOINTS SERIES ®

Greenhaven Press, Inc.   PO Box 289009   San Diego, CA 92128-9009

Library of Congress Cataloging-in-Publication Data

American values : opposing viewpoints / book editor, David L. Bender.
    p.   cm. — (Opposing viewpoints series)
    Includes bibliographical references.
    Summary: Various authors debate what Americans value in politics, society, business, and religion; what patriotism is, and how to improve our culture. Includes critical thinking skills activities.
    ISBN 0-89908-411-7 — ISBN 0-89908-436-2 (lib. bdg.)
    1. United States—Moral conditions. 2. Social values. [1. United States—Moral conditions. 2. Social values. 3. Critical thinking.] I. Bender, David L., 1936-   . II. Series.
HN90.M6A45   1989
306'.0973—dc20   89-36526
                                                                CIP
                                                                 AC

"Congress shall make no law... abridging the freedom of speech, or of the press."

First Amendment to the US Constitution

The basic foundation of our democracy is the first amendment guarantee of freedom of expression. The *Opposing Viewpoints Series* is dedicated to the concept of this basic freedom and the idea that it is more important to practice it than to enshrine it.

Contents

Why Consider Opposing Viewpoints?

"It is better to debate a question without settling it than to settle a question without debating it."

Joseph Joubert (1754-1824)

The Importance of Examining Opposing Viewpoints

The purpose of the Opposing Viewpoints Series, and this book in particular, is to present balanced, and often difficult to find, opposing points of view on complex and sensitive issues.

Probably the best way to become informed is to analyze the positions of those who are regarded as experts and well studied on issues. It is important to consider every variety of opinion in an attempt to determine the truth. Opinions from the mainstream of society should be examined. But also important are opinions that are considered radical, reactionary, or minority as well as those stigmatized by some other uncomplimentary label. An important lesson of history is the eventual acceptance of many unpopular and even despised opinions. The ideas of Socrates, Jesus, and Galileo are good examples of this.

Readers will approach this book with their own opinions on the issues debated within it. However, to have a good grasp of one's own viewpoint, it is necessary to understand the arguments of those with whom one disagrees. It can be said that those who do not completely understand their adversary's point of view do not fully understand their own.

A persuasive case for considering opposing viewpoints has been presented by John Stuart Mill in his work *On Liberty*. When examining controversial issues it may be helpful to reflect on this suggestion:

> The only way in which a human being can make some approach to knowing the whole of a subject, is by hearing what can be said about it by persons of every variety of opinion, and studying all modes in which it can be looked at by every character of mind. No wise man ever acquired his wisdom in any mode but this.

Analyzing Sources of Information

The Opposing Viewpoints Series includes diverse materials taken from magazines, journals, books, and newspapers, as well as statements and position papers from a wide range of individuals, organizations and governments. This broad spectrum of sources helps to develop patterns of thinking which are open to the consideration of a variety of opinions.

Pitfalls To Avoid

A pitfall to avoid in considering opposing points of view is that of regarding one's own opinion as being common sense and the most rational stance and the point of view of others as being only opinion and naturally wrong. It may be that another's opinion is correct and one's own is in error.

Another pitfall to avoid is that of closing one's mind to the opinions of those with whom one disagrees. The best way to approach a dialogue is to make one's primary purpose that of understanding the mind and arguments of the other person and not that of enlightening him or her with one's own solutions. More can be learned by listening than speaking.

It is my hope that after reading this book the reader will have a deeper understanding of the issues debated and will appreciate the complexity of even seemingly simple issues on which good and honest people disagree. This awareness is particularly important in a democratic society such as ours where people enter into public debate to determine the common good. Those with whom one disagrees should not necessarily be regarded as enemies, but perhaps simply as people who suggest different paths to a common goal.

Developing Basic Reading and Thinking Skills

In this book, carefully edited opposing viewpoints are purposely placed back to back to create a running debate; each viewpoint is preceded by a short quotation that best expresses the author's main argument. This format instantly plunges the reader into the midst of a controversial issue and greatly aids that reader in mastering the basic skill of recognizing an author's point of view.

A number of basic skills for critical thinking are practiced in the activities that appear throughout the books in the series. Some of the skills are:

Evaluating Sources of Information   The ability to choose from among alternative sources the most reliable and accurate source in relation to a given subject.

Separating Fact from Opinion   The ability to make the basic distinction between factual statements (those that can be demonstrated or verified empirically) and statements of opinion (those that are beliefs or attitudes that cannot be proved).

Identifying Stereotypes   The ability to identify oversimplified, exaggerated descriptions (favorable or unfavorable) about people and insulting statements about racial, religious or national groups, based upon misinformation or lack of information.

Recognizing Ethnocentrism   The ability to recognize attitudes or opinions that express the view that one's own race, culture, or group is inherently superior, or those attitudes that judge another culture or group in terms of one's own.

It is important to consider opposing viewpoints and equally important to be able to critically analyze those viewpoints. The activities in this book are designed to help the reader master these thinking skills. Statements are taken from the book's viewpoints and the reader is asked to analyze them. This technique aids the reader in developing skills that not only can be applied to the viewpoints in this book, but also to situations where opinionated spokespersons comment on controversial issues. Although the activities are helpful to the solitary reader, they are most useful when the reader can benefit from the interaction of group discussion.

Using this book and others in the series should help readers develop basic reading and thinking skills. These skills should improve the reader's ability to understand what they read. Readers should be better able to separate fact from opinion, substance from rhetoric and become better consumers of information in our media-centered culture.

This volume of the Opposing Viewpoints Series does not advocate a particular point of view. Quite the contrary! The very nature of the book leaves it to the reader to formulate the opinions he or she finds most suitable. My purpose as publisher is to see that this is made possible by offering a wide range of viewpoints which are fairly presented.

David L. Bender
Publisher

11

Introduction

"Every effort to confine Americanism to a single pattern, to constrain it to a single formula, is disloyalty to everything that is valid in Americanism."

Henry Steele Commager, *Freedom, Loyalty, Dissent*

Among the larger nations of the world, there are two factors which distinguish America. The first is its relative youth. Americans trace their heritage as a sovereign nation not to the landing of the first English settlers in 1607 but to George Washington's inauguration as president in 1789, only 200 years ago. The second factor is the unique complexion of its inhabitants. Indeed, the pageant of American peoples boasts an ethnic, racial, and religious mixture virtually unmatched by any contemporary nation.

These two factors combine to create an American value system that is both uniform and mosaic. Democracy, the belief that power should arise from those over whom it is exercised, has provided and continues to provide the uniform footings from which America's social and political institutions have grown. At the same time, America's immigrants have brought to its shores more than the wish to participate in the democratic dream. By bequeathing such a diversity of cultural ideas and objects, they have forged America's singular "melting pot" experience.

By chance and design, America thus has become a land of contrasting values—a place where, as historian Henry Steele Commager implies, conformity and disloyalty are synonymous. And while this phenomenon is not exclusively American, few other peoples have elevated the "agreement to disagree" nearly to a religious article of faith.

This anthology of opposing viewpoints attempts to portray the diverse nature of Americanism as reflected in its value system. The viewpoints purposely focus upon issues which have been argued as far back as the fledgling days of the nation when its survival was often little more than a wistful hope. It is remarkable and telling that they are still being debated today with similar constancy and urgency. Debated are, What Are America's Political Values? What Are America's Social Values? What Are America's Economic Values? What Are America's Religious Values? What

13

Is True Patriotism? and What Does America Need?

Because values evolve, contemporary ideas add a vital ingredient to this third edition of *American Values: Opposing Viewpoints*. Some of the viewpoints, however, were chosen for the timeless nature of their message. For example, Robert Bellah's description of America's civil religion, although stated over 20 years ago, remains a powerful argument today. If the reader completes this anthology sensing the complexity and uniqueness of the American value system, this book will have served its purpose.

1 CHAPTER

What Are America's Political Values?

Chapter Preface

This chapter explores the political values that form the basis of American democracy. The first two viewpoints explore the foundation of America's political values. The last four warn of dangers confronting these political values and the remedies for these dangers.

Today, many Americans are disaffected and experience a sense of hopelessness about their political institutions. Many of these Americans argue that the best remedy may be to rediscover America's political heritage. The political values discussed in these viewpoints and articulated by the founders of our country may still possess the vitality to invigorate today's generation of Americans.

"I have given you in brief outline what I call 'The American Canon,' the canonical scriptures of true Americanism."

America's Values Are Found in Its Documents

Daniel L. Marsh

Daniel L. Marsh, a former president of Boston University, believes that it is important for Americans to have clearly stated values to which they can profess allegiance. He identifies seven documents from America's past that form the canonical scriptures of Americanism, much as the Bible represents Christianity. He identifies these seven documents as the Mayflower Compact, the Declaration of Independence, the Constitution, Washington's Farewell Address, the "Star-Spangled Banner," Lincoln's Second Inaugural Address, and a 1923 speech by Woodrow Wilson. The following viewpoint is taken from a speech delivered by Mr. Marsh on May 7, 1942.

As you read, consider the following questions:

1. Why does the author feel it is important to have a "Bible of Americanism"?
2. What was his reasoning for choosing each of the seven documents that form the American bible?

Daniel L. Marsh, "The American Canon," *Vital Speeches of the Day*, June 15, 1942, pages 524-29. Reprinted with permission.

17

Why is it that we do not have something to which every American can give allegiance? If you ask a member of a religious organization for the source of his authority, no matter whether he is Roman Catholic or Protestant—Methodist, Congregationalist, Episcopalian—he always will name the Bible as the source of his faith. The Hebrew will date his religion back to the Old Testament; the Christian, to the Old Testament and New Testament; and they will say that the canonical scriptures contain the authoritative rule of their faith and practice.

So I said to myself: "What canonical scriptures of Americanism are there that correspond in patriotism to the Bible in religion?" Then, upon my own account, I started out to discover them. I did not say much about it, but I kept on working at it in odds and ends of time for some 20 years, and in the course of that time, I read an enormous number of speeches and papers of one kind and another. . . .

In the course of my study I kept sifting out, applying my own canonical rules to ascertain whether the document really could be classified as part of the Bible of Americanism. Would a particular document stand the canonical test? Could it become a part of the authoritative rule of American patriotism? In the course of study, I selected seven documents. So far as my own judgment goes, there is no eighth. Then, just to carry out the whimsical notion I had, and to add a little to the interest of it, I gave them certain scriptural connotations. I have the Genesis of American Democracy; the Exodus; our Book of the Law; our Major Prophecy; the Psalm of Americanism; the Gospel of Americanism, and the Epistle to the Americans—those seven. I have not found an eighth. I have thought that if we could rear a generation of Americans who would be intelligent concerning those seven, and the conditions of the times out of which they grew, the historical background and implications of them, we would have a body of intelligent patriots. We would give our allegiance to something that was fundamental in democracy. For, in a democracy it is a great deal harder to focus loyalties than it is in a totalitarian system. In a totalitarian state you precisely focus your loyalties upon a person, and you yield your allegiance to the person. In Nazism it is to Hitler; in Fascist Italy it is to Mussolini, and in Communism, it is to Stalin; but when you come to a democracy, if you are going to have an intelligent democracy perpetuated for the future, you will focus your loyalties upon a set of ideals, and you will yield your allegiance to a set of ideas and ideals.

So, we must have an intelligent comprehension of the ideas and ideals that underlie our American democracy. I hold we have them in these seven documents. Let us look at them very quickly.

Genesis: The Mayflower Compact

First of all, the Genesis of our American Democracy is in the Mayflower Compact. . . .

By 1620, the little band in Holland decided that they did not wish to stay there. They did not want their children to become Dutch, and did not like the worldly surroundings, so they made plans to go to America. They managed to get a charter allowing them to settle in Virginia—they expected to land no further north than the Hudson River. They had enormous courage. They had not only the actual hardships of a long voyage, but they were told things which they had no reason to disbelieve, which were even worse than the actualities. For instance, they were told that the savages would capture these white people and bind them to a stake. Then, while they still lived, they would cut out steaks and chops from them and broil the steaks and chops before the eyes of the victims. Nevertheless, they came.

A Body Politic

In the name of God, Amen. We whose names are underwritten, . . .having undertaken, for the glory of God, and advancement of the Christian faith, and honor of our king and country, a voyage to plant the first colony in the northern parts of Virginia, do by these presents solemnly and mutually in the presence of God, and one of another, covenant and combine ourselves together into a civil body politic for our better ordering and preservation.

The Mayflower Compact, September 11, 1620.

It is an interesting story as to how they got started, trying this and that until the Speedwell and Mayflower groups were formed. The first land they sighted in November 1620, was what we now call the tip of Cape Cod at Provincetown.

Before they landed, they found they were off their course. They were far north of where they intended to land. Some of the persons they had recruited in London were impatient with the restraints imposed by the leaders of the Pilgrims, and said, "When we land, we will do as we please, for here nobody has authority over us." And they were right. But when the leaders of the Pilgrim band heard this, they assembled all the adult males except two (who were sick) in the cabin of the Mayflower, and, using Miles Standish's sea chest as a desk, they then and there drew up the first written compact by which any group of people upon earth ever agreed to govern themselves. That Mayflower Compact is the Genesis of American democracy. . . .

We come to the Exodus—the going out from the land of tyranny and bondage to the Promised Land of liberty and self-government. No matter by which nation the different colonies were formed, it was not long until they all came under the control of England. By 1670, persecutions and oppressions had begun; by 1760, life was almost intolerable. George III had come to the throne. George III was young, only 22 years old; he was dull, stupid, uneducated, arrogant, bigoted, bullheaded, and finally, crazy. His mother had dinned into his ears the dictum, "George, be King!" He accepted the then prevailing philosophy that a colony existed for the enrichment of the mother country. He saw an opportunity to get money to carry on his European wars; and by 1774, the colonies could endure it no longer, so they called a Congress to meet in Philadelphia in September of that year.

Exodus: The Declaration of Independence

They met as Englishmen to defend their rights as Englishmen. They drew up a letter which they addressed to their King, and the King refused to receive it. When they adjourned, they adjourned as Englishmen to reconvene the following May as Englishmen for the redress of grievances as Englishmen. But before they met in May 1775, the sod of Lexington Green had soaked up the first blood shed for American independence, and at Concord. . . .

Although they met as Englishmen, it was not long until they saw that there were other rights than those of Englishmen which they had to defend, so, by June of 1776 there was introduced into Congress a resolution that "these United Colonies are, and of rights ought to be, free and independent states." Then Congress appointed a committee of five men consisting of Jefferson, Adams, Franklin, Sherman, and Livingston, to draft a Declaration of Independence. They thought that a decent regard for the opinion of mankind would require them to tell the world why they were going to war. The committee designated Jefferson to draft the Declaration. He had a reputation for a felicitous style and a facile pen.

Jefferson—handsome, tall, democratic, a lawyer from Virginia, red-headed, with a fine literary style—sat down in his room upon the second floor of the little lodging house at the corner of 7th and Market Streets in Philadelphia, and in one half day, without looking at either pamphlet or book, wrote the Declaration of Independence—our great national symbol, the Exodus of American democracy. . . .

Book of Law: The Constitution

We come quickly to our Book of the Law. Of course, you would know at once that that which corresponds to the great Mosaic code in the Old Testament is the Constitution of the

United States.

In American history, between the ending of the Revolutionary War and the adoption of the Constitution of the United States, there was practical anarchy in this country. The colonists had been held together during the war by their fear of the British Redcoat, but as soon as he was withdrawn, they feared each other more than anything else, and they were especially afraid of a strongly centralized government. There were 13 different states, and those who could see beyond the then immediate present, knew that there was developing upon these shores, 13 jangling, jarring, jealous nations. . . .

A More Perfect Union

We the people of the United States, in order to form a more perfect Union, establish justice, insure domestic tranquility, provide for the common defense, promote the general welfare, and secure the blessings of liberty to ourselves and our posterity, do ordain and establish this CONSTITUTION for the United States of America.

Constitution of the United States, September 17, 1787.

In this period certain wiser heads like George Washington, Benjamin Franklin, James Madison, and Alexander Hamilton, advised the calling of a Constitutional Convention, which met in Philadelphia, May 5, 1787, and remained in session until September 17 of the same year.

I give it to you as my calm and deliberate judgment (I speak carefully as a student of history) that I do not know anywhere in the story of the onward movement of the children of men, any other gathering that can compare with this Constitutional Convention for a self-effacing, disinterested devotion to the cause which had brought them together. There was no lust for the limelight. There was no self-interest to serve. Those men had in mind only one thing—the preservation of the Union with the liberties which had been won upon the field of battle, and in handing the blessings on to posterity. . . .

Note how ours is a government of laws; and when you become acquainted with it and with its implications, I swear no one then will wish to scrap what we have for some uncertain figment of the imagination.

In the Mosaic code you have Ten Commandments. The American counterpart of those Ten Commandments are the first ten Amendments to the Constitution of the United States. We call it our Bill of Rights. The Constitution could never have been adopted if the leaders had not promised that as soon as it was adopted, they would adopt the Bill of Rights as the first ten

21

Amendments. Of course, they were adopted, and as soon as they were adopted they became a part of the Constitution. Some people draw a thin line of distinction between the Constitution and the Amendments, but in reality as soon as an amendment is adopted, it becomes a part of the Constitution just as much as any other part of the Constitution.

Those ten Amendments are like the Ten Commandments of the Mosaic Code, with this difference: that the Mosaic Ten Commandments issue their "Thou shalt not's" to the people, while our Ten Commandments issue their "Thou shalt not's" to the government. In our case that Bill of Rights protects our fundamental freedoms. . . .

Prophecy: Washington's Farewell Address

We pass quickly to our Major Prophecy. We have had many prophets and many prophecies, but I hold that the greatest prophet we ever had—in the true sense of the word prophet (one who is a forthteller—people generally have thought of a prophet as a foreteller, but he is a forthteller, one who speaks forth great truths) was George Washington; and his major prophecy was his Farewell Address.

George Washington becomes our founder more truly than most nations can point to any man as their founder. He was a great man. Certain biographical and historical "debunkers" have tried to bring him down to the common level, but after they have done their worst, George Washington still stands forth as majestic as Mount Hood, his patriotism unassailed, and as yet unapproached. George Washington was endowed by nature and Providence with that something which gave him the dignity, the mental power, and the military sagacity and authority to become the Father of the American nation. . . .

Pillars of Support

Of all the dispositions and habits which lead to political prosperity, religion and morality are indispensable supports.

Washington's Farewell Address, September 17, 1796.

This great man with limbs of oak, this great man with the mountain mind, and the crystal soul, serves one term and is reelected for another term. He could have been unanimously elected for the third term, but he chose not to stand for third term. Then, deciding he should not stand for the third term, he thought that he ought to tell his fellow Americans why, so he issued his Farewell Address. . . .

He said, for instance, that a nation ought to preserve its credit,

22

and that it ought never in times of peace to incur national debt. A nation ought to pay its way as it goes in times of peace, so that in an emergency of war, it will be able to finance itself. He also said that we should not stir up disunion. He pled against the deep damnation of disunion—arraying one class against another. He pled for education. He knew that whenever a people undertook to do their own dictatorship, they assumed the obligations, as well as the privilege of the function, and they could not govern themselves unless education were widely diffused, and the electorate were intelligent. He said many things in that speech which ought to be read today. The Farewell Address is our Major Prophecy.

Psalms: The Star Spangled Banner

We come quickly to the Psalm of Americanism. . .the Star Spangled Banner.

Francis Scott Key, in that song, is not narrowly nationalistic at all, simply fervently patriotic. He does not glorify war. He uses the imagery of battle, but uses it only to glorify the flag. It is the flag, not the war, that is glorified.

There is a philosophy of colors: White stands for the blending of all the virtues; blue, because it is the color of the heavens, stands for honesty, truth, and purity. The stars represent ideals, as well as the states; and red is the sign of courage.

May I say to you that, aesthetically considered, without any reference at all to the things for which it stands, the aesthetic arrangement of the length in proportion to the width, the arrangement of the little square heaven of blue and the stars in it, and the stripes—that flag is the most beautiful flag which floats anywhere under the whole canopy of Heaven.

But we honor it not for its aesthetic value, and the song glorifies it not for its aesthetic beauty, but because of that for which it stands—a pledge that liberty shall prevail, that righteousness shall be done, that justice shall be meted out wherever the flag floats. Its stars laughing down their delightful light by day and night, and its stripes stroked in ripples of white and of red, are the symbol of our Government, and that is why we honor it. That is the Psalm of Americanism.

Gospel: Lincoln's Second Inaugural Address

I move quickly and briefly to the Gospel of Americanism. This would have to come out of the heart of the savior of the American Union—and who is the savior of the American Union? Only one person can qualify for that position—Abraham Lincoln. . . .

I hold that the second inaugural address of Abraham Lincoln is the greatest literary production that has ever come from an American hand. You have to get the condition of the times in mind to appreciate it at its real worth. The Civil War has been wallowing its bloody way across the heart of the Nation for four years. The end is near at hand. Lincoln's own party in the North is demanding revenge. Everywhere, lust, hate, and spite—an eye for an eye, a tooth for a tooth; everywhere recriminations and calling of names. Here comes this man whose whole history has been one of freedom from bigotry and intolerance. Lincoln would not be caught up in hysteria that would prompt him to burn a flag of a nation with which we technically are not at war, or call everybody with whom he did not agree a Fifth Columnist, a Nazi, or anything else. Lincoln was broad-minded and great-hearted.

He now is ready to deliver his second inaugural address. All that morning, that 4th of March 1865, it has been drizzling rain. The crowd is out there in front of the Capitol in Washington. Lincoln comes onto the east portico of the Capitol. He is tall, gaunt, his shoulders stooped as though the burden of his country's woes were heavier than he could bear; his eyes sunken as though the knuckles of sorrow had pushed them back into their sockets.

As he begins to speak, voice high with emotion, there is a rift in the cloud, and a sun-beam falls straight upon Lincoln. The clouds gradually roll back until the whole crowd is flooded with light. Lincoln delivers his short inaugural. It is like a page torn out of the prophecy of Isaiah, freighted with moral intensity, talking about God, then he comes to that last great sentence—I think the greatest in American literature—"With malice toward none; with charity for all; with firmness in the right, as God gives us to see the right, let us strive on to finish the work we are in; to bind up the nation's wounds; to care for him who shall have borne the battle, and for his widow and his orphans—to do all which may achieve and cherish a just and lasting peace among ourselves and with all nations." That is the Gospel of Americanism.

Epistle: Wilson's "The Road Away from Revolution"

I have but one more. It is the Epistle to the Americans. Many things clamored for inclusion in "The American Canon;" but, as I went on sifting, it seemed to be that there was one and only one, and that was the last article Woodrow Wilson ever wrote, his article entitled "The Road Away from Revolution.". . .

Woodrow Wilson, trained in the South and North, historian, college professor, university president, Governor of a state, President of the United States, increasing in strength with each new responsibility and never losing the ideals that he inherited from his Presbyterian preacher father,—Woodrow Wilson carried the nation through the First World War. War over—he retired, a broken man.

In 1923, the Spring of the year, Wilson seems to have had a

24

premonition of the trouble which came on the country in 1929 and following, and he expressed a wish to write an article to save his country, if he could, from what he saw ahead. . . .

Keep in mind that Wilson was a capitalist and believed in the capitalistic system. He was afraid of what he saw ahead and was trying to forewarn his fellow Americans so that this system under which America had prospered and become great, might remain unimpaired. He pled, therefore, that capitalists should use their capital in the service of others. Service—that was the great plea of Wilson. He said that we must introduce the spirit of Jesus and Christianity into our business life, into our commercial and industrial affairs. His article I call an Epistle to the Americans.

Thus I have given you in brief outline what I call "The American Canon," the canonical scriptures of true Americanism.

"The American experience is unique, and this dooms to failure any attempt to sum up our way of life in slogans and dogmas."

America's Values Are Found in an Unspoken Faith

Daniel J. Boorstin

Daniel J. Boorstin is one of America's leading historians. A former Librarian of Congress, Mr. Boorstin is also a Rhodes Scholar and a worldwide educator. He has authored numerous books and was awarded the Pulitzer Prize in 1974 for his trilogy *The Americans*. In the following viewpoint, Mr. Boorstin describes America's unspoken faith, namely, a continued belief in the value system that has been part of American society since its founding. He claims Americans, though they believe their political life is based on an almost perfect theory, accept it as a given and have felt no need to articulate it in a professed theory. This "givenness," in his opinion, is peculiar to America and flows from unique geographical and historical facts.

As you read, consider the following questions:

1. What basic paradox does Mr. Boorstin see in American political thinking?
2. What American characteristic does the author refer to in his use of the term "givenness"?

Daniel J. Boorstin, "Our Unspoken National Faith," *Commentary*, June 12, 1953, pp. 327-37. Reprinted from *Commentary* by permission. Copyright © 1953 by the American Jewish Committee.

The marvelous success and vitality of American institutions is equaled by the amazing poverty and inarticulateness of our theorizing about politics. No nation has ever believed more firmly that its political life was based on a perfect theory—and yet no nation has ever been less interested in political philosophy, or produced less in the way of a theory. To explain this paradox is to find a key to much that is characteristic—and much that is good—in our way of life. . . .

The essential fact is that we have always been more interested in *how our society works* than we have in its theoretical foundations. . . .

The tendency to abstract the principles of political life may sharpen issues for the political philosopher. It becomes idolatry when it provides statesmen or a people with a blueprint for remaking their society. Especially in our own age (and at least since the French Revolution of 1789), more and more of the world has sought in social theory no mere rationale for institutions, but just a blueprint. The characteristic tyrannies of our age—Nazism, Fascism, and Communism—have expressed precisely this idolatry. They justify their outrages because their "philosophies" require them. Recent European politics shows us men of all complexions seeking explicit ideological systems for society. . . .

Givenness and American Values

The American experience is unique, and this dooms to failure any attempt to sum up our way of life in slogans and dogmas. This is why we have nothing in the line of a theory that can be exported to other peoples of the world.

At the heart of the matter lies a characteristically American belief for which I have invented the name "givenness." It is our way of taking for granted that an explicit political theory is superfluous for us precisely because we already somehow possess a satisfactory equivalent. "Givenness" is the belief that values in America are in some way or other automatically defined: *given* by certain facts of geography or history peculiar to us.

This conviction has three faces: first, we believe that we have received our values as a gift from the *past*; that the earliest settlers or Founding Fathers equipped our nation at its birth with a perfect and complete political theory adequate to all our future needs.

The second is the notion that in America we receive values as a gift from the *present*; that our theory is always implicit in our institutions. This is the idea that the American Way of Life harbors an American Way of Thought, which can do us for a political theory, even if we never make it explicit, or never are in a position to confront ourselves with it.

27

The third part of "givenness" is a belief which links these first two. It is a belief in the *continuity* or homogeneity of our history. We see our national past as an uninterrupted continuum of similar events, so that our past merges indistinguishably into our present. This makes it easy for us to believe, at the same time, in the idea of a pre-formed original theory given to us by the Founding Fathers, and the idea of an implicit theory always offered us by our present experience. Our feeling of continuity in our history makes it easy for us to see the Founding Fathers as our contemporaries. It induces us to draw heavily on the materials of our history, but always in a distinctly non-historical frame of mind.

American Values as a Gift from the Past

The dominating idea that our values are a gift from our past may be likened to the obsolete biological notion of "preformation." That is the idea that all parts of an organism pre-exist in perfect miniature in the seed. Biologists used to believe that if you could look at the seed of an apple under a strong enough microscope you would see in it a minute apple tree. Similarly, we seem to believe that if we could understand the ideas of the earliest settlers—the Pilgrim Fathers or Founding Fathers—we would find in them no mere 17th or 18th century philosophy of government, but the perfect embryo of the theory by which we now live. We believe, then, that the mature political ideals of the nation existed clearly conceived in the minds of our patriarchs. . . .

Our belief in a perfectly pre-formed theory helps us understand many things about ourselves. In particular, it helps us to see how it has been that, while we in the United States have been unfertile in political theories we have possessed an overweening sense of political orthodoxy. But in building an orthodoxy from what are in fact quite scanty early materials, we have of necessity left the penumbra of heresy vague. The inarticulate character of American political theory has thus actually facilitated heresy hunts and tended to make them indiscriminate. The heresy hunts which come at periods of national fear—the Alien and Sedition Acts of the age of the French Revolution, the Palmer Raids of the age of the Russian Revolution, and similar activities of more recent times—are directed not so much against acts of espionage, as against acts of irreverence toward that orthodox American creed supposed to have been born with the nation itself. . . .

It is commonplace that no fundamental theoretical difference separates our American political parties. What need has either party for an explicit political theory where both must be spokesmen of the *original* American doctrine on which the nation was founded?. . .

American Political Values

Out of the heritage from England, the experience with government in the colonies, the struggle for independence, the weakness of the Confederation, the creation of the Federal Republic, and the experience of more than a century and a half of independence, including four years of civil war (1861-1865), have come American values in the area of politics:

1. The concept of the state as a utilitarian device created to provide for the common defense and to further the general welfare.

2. Freedom and responsibility of the individual adult citizen to have a voice in the government under which he lives, as exemplified in the right and responsibility to vote.

3. Freedom of access to knowledge of all kinds save only when disclosure of particular information would endanger the whole community. This access is achieved through a system of public education, the practice of academic freedom, and the existence of a free press.

4. Freedom to express orally or in writing opinions honestly held concerning economic, religious, political, or social matters. In the case of political opinions, this freedom is limited by the requirements that actions to carry opinions into effect must conform to the procedures for changing the policies or structure of the state as set forth in the Constitution of the United States. A further general limitation is that expression of opinion must not be so inciting as to create a clear and present danger of panic or disorder.

5. The protection of the free citizen against unreasonable invasions of privacy by officers of government.

6. The right of free citizens to assemble peaceably.

7. The supremacy of civil authority over the military in conformity with the principle that the civil authority is the decision-making power and the military is the instrument, when needed, to carry decisions into effect.

8. The concept of the American Federation as a "permanent union of permanent states," firmly established after the Civil War, maintained by judicial enforcement of the Constitution and forbidding nullification or secession on the part of the states.

Ralph H. Gabriel, *American Values: Continuity and Change* (Westport, Connecticut: Greenwood Press, 1974), pp. 161-62. Reprinted by permission of the publishers, Greenwood Press, a division of Williamhouse-Regency Inc., 51, Riverside Avenue, Westport, Connecticut, 06880, and the author Ralph H. Gabriel from his *American Values: Continuity and Change*, first published in 1974.

The mystic rigidity of our "pre-formation" theory has not, however, militated against great flexibility in dealing with practical problems. Confident that the wisdom of the Founding Fathers somehow made provision for all future emergencies, we have not felt bound to limit our experiments to those which we could justify with theories in advance. In the last century or so, whenever the citizens of continental Western Europe have found themselves in desperate circumstances, they have had to choose among political parties each of which was committed to a particular theoretical foundation for its whole program—"monarchist"—"liberal"—"Catholic"—"socialist"—"fascist"—or "Communist." This has not been the case in the United States. Not even during the Civil War: historians still argue over what, if any, political theory Lincoln represented. In the crisis which followed the Great Depression, when Franklin D. Roosevelt announced his program for saving the American economy, he did not promise to implement a theory. Rather he declared frankly that he would try one thing after another and would keep trying until a cure was found. . . .

American Values as a Gift from the Present

We have been told again and again, with the metaphorical precision of poetry, that the United States is the *land* of the free. Independence, equality, and liberty, we like to believe, are breathed in with our very air. No nation has been readier to identify its values with the peculiar conditions of its landscape: we believe in *American* equality, *American* liberty, *American* democracy, or, in sum, the *American* way of life.

Our belief in the mystical power of our land in this roundabout way has nourished a naturalistic point of view; and a naturalistic approach to values has thus, in the United States, been bound up with patriotism itself. What the Europeans have seen as the gift of the past, Americans have seen as the gift of the present. What the European thinks he must learn from books, museums, and churches, from his culture and its monuments, the American thinks he can get from contemporary life, from seizing peculiarly American opportunities. . . .

The character of our national heroes bears witness to our belief in "givenness," our preference for the man who seizes his God-given opportunities over him who pursues a great private vision. Perhaps never before has there been such a thorough identification of normality and virtue. A "red-blooded" American must be a virtuous American; and nearly all our national heroes have been red-blooded, outdoor types who might have made the varsity team. . . . Our national heroes have not been erratic geniuses like Michelangelo or Cromwell or Napoleon but rather men like Washington and Jackson and Lincoln, who possessed the commonplace virtues to an extraordinary degree.

The Continuity of American Values

The third aspect of the idea of "givenness" helps us understand how we can at once appeal to the past and the present, and find no contradiction in doing so.

By this I mean the remarkable continuity or homogeneity of

American history. To grasp it, we must at the outset discard a European cliche about us, namely that ours is a land without continuity or tradition, while in Europe man feels close to his ancestors. The truth of the matter is that anyone who goes to Europe nowadays cannot fail to be impressed with the amazing, the unique continuity of American history, and, in contrast, the *dis*continuity of European history. . . .

Let me explain. I have recently been abroad, where I spent the better part of a year in Italy. My impressions there sharpened that contrast which I have been describing between the American and the European image of the past. The first church I visited was the Capella Palatina in Palermo, where Christian mosaics of the 12th century are surmounted by a ceiling of Moslem craftsmanship. Throughout Sicily one comes upon pagan temples on the foundations of which rose churches which in the Middle Ages were transformed into mosques, and which later again were used as Christian chapels. . . .

In Europe one need not be an archaeologist or a philosopher to see that over the centuries many different kinds of life are possible in the same place and for the same people. Who can decide which, if any of these, is "normal" for Italy? It is hardly surprising, then, that the people of Europe have not found it easy to believe that their values are given by their landscape. They look to ideology to help them choose among alternatives.

In the United States, of course, we see no Colosseum, no Capella Palatina, no ancient roads. The effect of this simple fact on our aesthetic sense, though much talked of, is probably less significant than on our sense of history and our approach to values. We see very few monuments to the uncertainties, the motley possibilities of history, or for that matter to the rise and fall of grand theories of society. Our main public buildings were erected for much the same purpose for which they are now being used. The Congress of the United States is still housed in the first building expressly constructed for that purpose. Although the White House, like the Capitol, was gutted by fire during the War of 1812, it, too, was soon rebuilt on the same spot; in 1952 another restoration was completed. Our rural landscape, with a few scattered exceptions—the decayed plantation mansions of the South, the manor houses of upstate New York, and the missions of Florida and California—teaches us very little of the fortunes of history. . . .

The impression which the American has as he looks about him is thus one of the inevitability of the particular institutions, the particular kind of society in which he lives.

"Many of us are now looking to government for security. Many of us are no longer willing to accept individual responsibility for our own welfare."

Traditional Values Are Being Eroded by Indifference

Dean Russell

Dean Russell is a former staff member of the Foundation for Economic Education (FEE). FEE was founded in 1946 to provide for the study, exploration, and promotion of private ownership, free exchange, open competition, and limited government. The following viewpoint is taken from a pamphlet Mr. Russell wrote for FEE. He claims the values championed by America's founders, particularly individual liberty and individual responsibility, are being eroded by a citizenry more concerned with government guaranteed security. In his opinion, America's heritage is being lost more through weakness than through deliberate design.

As you read, consider the following questions:

1. Why did America's founding fathers distrust government?
2. What new idea did the founders introduce?
3. In the author's opinion, how are individual freedom and responsibility related?

Dean Russell, "The Bill of Rights," an undated pamphlet distributed by the Foundation for Economic Education. Reprinted by permission from the Foundation for Economic Education.

What was the reason—the real reason—that caused those early American patriots to distrust a federal government which they were about to bring into existence? Why did the individual citizens within the various sovereign states demand a bill of rights before ratifying the Constitution? Why did statesmen of the caliber of Washington, Jefferson, Adams, and Franklin wish to severely restrict the authority of the central government and to strictly limit the power of its leaders?

There was a reason, a vital reason—a reason that many present-day Americans have forgotten. A reason that, unless we relearn it, will surely mean the loss of personal freedom and individual liberty for all mankind.

Here is the reason: The power of government is *always* a dangerous weapon in *any* hands.

The founders of our government were students of history as well as statesmen. They knew that, without exception, every government in recorded history had at one time or another turned its power—its police force—against its own citizens, confiscated their property, imprisoned them, enslaved them, and made a mockery of personal dignity.

That was true of every *type* of government known to mankind. That was true regardless of how the government leaders came to power. It was true—then as now—that government leaders *elected by the people* frequently turn out to be the worst enemies of the people who elect them. Hitler was a recent example. He was not the first; he is not likely to be the last.

A New Idea

It was for this reason that the founders of the American republic introduced into that government a completely new idea.

What was this new idea? Was it the regular election of government leaders by the people? As wise a decision as that was, it was not new. The Greeks, among others, had used it.

Was it the wide dispersal of the powers of government among federal, state, and local units? An excellent system, but not new. It had already proved of practical value in France and other countries.

Was the American method of governmental "checks and balances" a new idea? It was a well-conceived plan, but it was not completely original with us. The British system of King, House of Lords, and House of Commons once embodied the same principle.

Here is the new idea: For the first time in known history, a written constitution specified that certain institutions and human relations were to be *outside* the authority of government. The government was specifically forbidden to infringe them or to violate them.

The Reason for Government

This was a revolutionary concept of government! The idea of inalienable rights and individual freedom had never before been incorporated into a national constitution. Never before in history had the people said to the government: "Thou shalt not."

American Character Has Softened

The dateline is London, March 22, 1775. The occasion: Edmund Burke's speech on conciliation with the American colonies. . . .

Burke was 46 that spring. He had been re-elected to Commons a few months earlier. As an acknowledged leader of the opposition, he was just growing into those significant powers of thought and speech that would serve him to his death in 1797. It is Burke to whom American conservatives look today as the fountainhead of their philosophy. His insights, like good wine, grow better with the years. . . .

Burke pleaded with the king's ministers to consider both the advantages of peaceful trade and the uncertainties of distant war. But there was a third consideration as to America: "I mean its temper and character."

"In this character of the Americans a love of freedom is the predominating feature which marks and distinguishes the whole. . . . This fierce spirit of liberty is stronger in the English colonies, probably, than in any other people of the earth." . . .

What has become of that "love of freedom that 200 years ago marked the American character? Is it still strong, still lively? Does our temper still embrace "a fierce spirit of liberty"? The melancholy answer is no. As a people we are less independent, less self-reliant, less passionately dedicated to personal responsibility than we were two centuries ago. . . .

The American character has softened, weakened, grown feeble with age.

James J. Kilpatrick, "In 200 Years America Has Lost Something," *Minneapolis Star*, March 24, 1975. "Copyright Washington Star Syndicate 1975".

Always the government had been able to say to the people: "You may, or you must." Heretofore, government had *granted* certain freedoms and privileges to the people. But the Bill of Rights said, in effect: "We the people are endowed by our Creator with natural rights and freedoms. The *only* reason for our having a government is to protect and defend these rights and freedoms that we already have as individuals. It is sheer folly to believe that government can give us something that already belongs to us."

These free people then listed in their Constitution those specific functions that they wanted government to handle. Then they forbade the government officials to do anything not commanded of them in the Constitution.

But even so, the people were afraid that the elected leaders of the new government might misunderstand the ideals of human dignity, of individual freedom, of the proper functions of government. So, as specific examples of what they meant, the American people added the Bill of Rights to the Constitution. It might better be called a *Bill of Prohibitions* against government. It is filled with such phrases as: "Congress shall make no law. . .," ". . .the right of the people. . .shall not be infringed. . .," "The right of the people. . .shall not be violated. . . ."

These personal and individual rights include freedom of worship, free speech and a free press, the right to assemble together, the sanctity of person and home, trial by jury, the right to life, liberty, and the private ownership of property.

Finally, to make absolutely sure that no government official could possibly misinterpret his position as servant rather than master, the people added two more blanket restrictions against the federal government. The Bill of Rights specifies that: "The enumeration. . .of certain rights shall not be construed to deny. . .others retained by the people." And: "The powers not delegated to the United States by the Constitution. . .are reserved to the States. . .or to the people."

Individual Freedom

It was this philosophy of individual freedom and individual responsibility—reflected in the Bill of Rights—that attracted to this country millions of persons from the government-oppressed peoples of Europe. They came here from every country in the world. They represented every color, every race, and every creed. They were in search of *personal freedom*, not government-guaranteed "security." And as a direct result of the individual freedom specified by the Constitution and the Bill of Rights, they earned the greatest degree of security ever enjoyed by any people anywhere.

Those new Americans swelled the tide of immigrants by writing the praise of freedom in their letters to relatives and friends who still lived in the countries with *strong* governments, with *one-man* rule, with *government ownership* of the means of production, with *government-guaranteed* "security," with *government* housing, and *state-controlled* education.

Equal Rights

Their letter read, in effect: "Here the government guarantees you nothing except life, liberty, and the right to own whatever you have honestly acquired. Here you have the personal respon-

'Eternal vigilance is the price of liberty'
Wendell Phillips—attributed to Thomas
Jefferson

LePelley in *The Christian Science Monitor* © 1974 TCSPS

sibility that goes with individual freedom. There is no law or custom that prevents you from rising as high as you are able. You can associate with anyone who wishes to associate with you. Here in America you can do as you please as long as you do not violate the rights of other persons to do as they please. These rights are recorded in the American Constitution and the Bill of Rights. The same documents specify that three-fourths of the states must be in agreement before these rights can be taken away. And, of course, it is foolish to imagine that people will ever voluntarily give up their freedom."

Such letters would not be completely true today, because that freedom is gradually being lost. But the "progressive" laws and "popular" court decisions of recent years are not primarily responsible for it. Freedom is seldom lost by a direct vote on the subject. In our case, it just seems to be *seeping away*. The Bill of Rights still exists on paper, but the *spirit* that caused it to be written is disappearing. When that spirit is completely gone, the written words will mean nothing.

Thus it behooves us to inquire why that spirit is now weak, and how it can be revived.

Who Is To Blame?

No one person is responsible for sapping that spirit of individualism. No one political party is to blame. The people are as responsible as the elected and appointed leaders. It is we the people who seem to have forgotten that freedom and responsibility are inseparable. It is we the people who are discarding the concept of government that brought forth the Declaration of Independence, the Constitution, and the Bill of Rights.

In short, few of us seem to want to keep government out of our personal affairs and responsibilities. Many of us seem to favor various types of government-guaranteed and compulsory "security." We *say* that we want personal freedom, but we *demand* government housing, government price controls, government-guaranteed jobs and wages. We *boast* that we are responsible persons, but we *vote* for candidates who promise us special privileges, government pensions, government subsidies, and government electricity.

Such schemes are directly contrary to the spirit of the Bill of Rights. Our heritage is being lost more through weakness than through deliberate design. The Bill of Rights still shines in all its splendor, but many of us are looking in another direction. Many of us are drifting back to that old concept of government that our forefathers feared and rejected. Many of us are now looking to government for security. Many of us are no longer willing to accept individual responsibility for our own welfare. Yet personal freedom cannot exist without individual responsibility.

Thus the American people are on the verge of a final decision. We must choose between the destruction caused by government paternalism, and the security insured by individual freedom with individual responsiblity as expressed in the Bill of Rights. There is no other choice.

"The values of freedom, liberty, and equality of opportunity are dominant themes in U.S. history."

Traditional Values Are Still Operative

John Kenneth White

John Kenneth White is an associate professor of political science at Potsdam College of the State University of New York. He is also the executive director of the Committee for Party Renewal and general editor of the series *The Presidency: Contemporary Issues.* In his most recent book, from which the following viewpoint is taken, Professor White describes how Ronald Reagan's successful presidential politics were based on espousing traditional values. In explaining how Reagan related to the American people and the values they cherish, he identifies the basic political values Americans have held since the country's founding. He claims the "American dream" has changed little since colonial times, and then as now, it is based on the values of liberty, freedom, and equal opportunity.

As you read, consider the following questions:

1. In the author's opinion, what is America's most cherished political value?
2. How does this value relate to equality of opportunity and tolerance of the opinions and lifestyles of others?

Reprinted from *The New Politics of Old Values,* by John Kenneth White, by permission of the University Press of New England. Copyright 1988 by University Press of New England.

"I want a house!" Those were the last words Andre Sakharov's wife, Yelena Bonner, spoke upon leaving the United States in 1986 to return to the Soviet Union. Her dream was the quintessential American dream: to be oneself in one's private dwelling place. "A house," said Bonner, "is a symbol of independence, spiritual and physical." At age sixty-three the Soviet dissident mourned, "I've never had a house . . . [not even] a corner I could call my own." She sadly concluded, "My dream, my own house, is unattainable for my husband and myself, as unattainable as heaven on earth."

Yelena Bonner's "dream" is not so much about home ownership per se as it is a longing for freedom. Observers of that peculiar species called Americans have often described their values by employing metaphorical devices. "The Star Spangled Banner" proclaims the United States to be the *"land* of the free" and the *"home* of the brave." Most countries, including ours, pour considerable quantities of mortar and brick into mausoleums that immortalize national heroes. But the United States has devoted a nearly equal amount of building materials to erect monuments to and representations of an idea: on Ellis Island, the Statue of Liberty; in Philadelphia, the Liberty Bell and Independence Hall; in Boston, the Freedom Trail. These symbols are not mere icons passed from generation to generation but meaningful symbols of our values. A second-generation citizen told of his immigrant forebears' reverence for the Statue of Liberty: "She was America to my parents. They talked about her like she was alive. To them, I guess, she was."

The Value of Freedom

As these symbols demonstrate, the American polity is not a structure of government, but a contract between the government and its people whose clauses contain shared values. Among the most cherished is freedom. A blue-collar worker in the early 1960s said:

> My God, I work where I want to work. I spend my money where I want to spend it. I buy what I want to buy. I go where I want to go. I read what I want to read. My kids go to the school that they want to go to, or where I want to send them. We bring them up in the religion we want to bring them up in. What else— what else could you have?

A 1986 poll found little change in the sentiments expressed by that worker: 88 percent believed that "freedom and liberty were two ideas that make America great."

The value of freedom arrived with the first settlers. From afar William Pitt captured this aspect of the colonists when he told the British House of Lords in 1770: "I love Americans because they love liberty." Six years later Thomas Jefferson elaborated on this theme in the Declaration of Independence: "We hold these truths to be self-evident, that all men are created equal, that they are endowed by their Creator with certain unalienable rights, that among these are Life, Liberty and the pursuit of Happiness."

Capitalism and Democracy Are Still America's Dominant Values

Two major traditions of belief, capitalism and democracy, have dominated the life of the American nation from its inception. Whether these beliefs are described as the *American creed*, the *Lockean settlement*, the *American consensus*, or, as we prefer, the *American ethos*, it is clear that capitalist and democratic values have strongly influenced the course and character of American development, and that they continue to serve as the authoritative values of the nation's political culture.

Herbert McClosky & John Zaller, *The American Ethos*, 1984.

As the years passed, an ideology that was uniquely American took hold. Gilbert K. Chesterton, after visiting the United States in the 1920s, concluded, "America is the only nation in the world that is founded on a creed." In fact, Chesterton discovered the "Rosetta stone" of our society: the core of the American creed is a belief in the malleability of the future by the individual. At the conclusion of their daily "PTL" television show Jim and Tammy Bakker would remind their viewers: "You *can* make it!" The sentence became the couple's signature. Most often, however, the phrase "American dream" is the expression commonly used.

The American Dream

The American dream is as old, and as young, as the United States itself. Regarding the presidency of John Quincy Adams, historian James Truslow Adams wrote that Adams believed his country stood for opportunity, "the chance to grow into something bigger and finer, as bigger and finer appealed to him." More than 150 years later, little has changed. Like the sixth president, people everywhere continue to hope that their lives and their children's lives will be better. But, unlike the United States, few countries express themselves in terms of a national dream. Indeed, the parlance among Western nations is devoid of references to a French, German, or British dream. The term "American dream" has come to stand for the ability of the individual to get ahead. At a 1983 news conference, Ronald Reagan put it this way: "What I want to see above all is that this country remains a country where someone can always get rich. That's the thing that we have and that must be preserved."

Today, Americans of every political stripe extol the American dream. Accepting the Republican presidential nomination in 1960, Richard Nixon told the delegates: "I believe in the American dream because I have seen it come true in my own life." Mario Cuomo echoed Nixon when he chronicled the struggles of his immigrant parents:

> Poppa came in 1926 without a penny. Half a century later the family he and Momma started here are enjoying the milk and honey of the greatest and most abundantly blessed nation in the world. Just the idea that I am considered a possible choice for governor is a dramatic illustration of what this country means. It is the definition of the word "opportunity."

A steelworker interviewed by Studs Terkel captured the sentiments expressed by Nixon and Cuomo more forcefully: "If my kid wants to work in a factory, I'm gonna kick the hell out of him. I want my kid to be an effete snot. I want him to be able to quote Walt Whitman, to be proud of it. If you can't improve yourself, you improve your posterity. Otherwise life isn't worth nothing."

When asked by the Roper Organization in 1986 what the American dream meant to them, most spoke in terms of education and property. Eighty-four percent said the American dream symbolized a high school education; 80 percent said freedom of choice was part of the dream; 70 percent said it was owning a home; 77 percent thought it was their children's receiving a college diploma and 68 percent said it was getting a college education for themselves; 64 percent said financial security was part of the dream; 61 percent said it was realized in "doing better than my parents"; 58 percent said it was owning a business; 52 percent said it meant progressing "from worker to company president."

Equality of Opportunity

The freedom to excel is an important component of the American dream. But another value is also inherent in the concept: equality of opportunity. Americans have been nearly fanatical in their devotion to this particular value. Max Berger wrote that the most indelible impression nineteenth-century British travelers had of their former colonies was "the aggressive equalitarianism of the people." In the film *Knute Rockne—All American*, Rockne's father claimed that only in America could his Norwegian son start on an "equal basis with all other children." This is followed by an on-screen commentary: "Among millions like themselves, simple hard-working people from the old countries following the new road of equality and opportunity which led to America, the Rockne family settled in Chicago." As background, the orchestra plays "God Bless America." . . .

Glorification of the work ethic has endured. In the 1940 film

41

about his life, the pre-Notre Dame Knute Rockne is described this way: "In the great melting-pot of Chicago the Viking boy added a rich sense of humor to his lust for life, and a sturdy body to a level head. But ten years of hard work and sacrifice only strengthened the one dream in his heart." As this narration appeared on theater screens, the orchestra played "America the Beautiful."

The American Dream Lives

Too many people are willing to capitalize on the negatives. . . .

We forget too easily all that we have in this country—our resources and our people, as well as a political tradition that has nurtured personal freedom and prosperity on a scale never equaled in world history. I think we have to remember how far we've progressed in terms of the rights of individuals. I think we have to remember and be grateful for the religious freedoms we enjoy in this country. . . .

I believe we must remind people that this country is still the place of the great American Dream. I'm just one example. I'm a first-generation son of Italian immigrants, heading one of the largest corporations in the world. This happened because no barrier was set that could not be overcome by working hard to achieve what I thought was possible—my own personal dream. . . .

Where else can the sons and daughters of immigrants become vice presidential candidates, governors, heads of industry, or whatever it is they want to be? I believe this truth needs to be told and retold. The American Dream lives. It's as strong today as it ever was.

Vincent A. Sarni, board chairman and CEO of PPG Industries, in *USA Today*, May 1985.

More than forty years later most Americans still believe the dream rests on their individual efforts. A 1984 National Opinion Research Center poll found 84 percent agreeing with the following statement: "America has an open society. Whatever one achieves in life no longer depends on one's family background, but on the abilities one has and the education one acquires." A 1987 study conducted by the same firm shows 66 percent saying that "hard work" is the most important factor in getting ahead; just 15 percent think "luck" is crucial. . . .

Tolerance

Americans are also aggressively equalitarian when it comes to making individual choices. A 1981 Decision/Making/Information study asked respondents to choose between a "Mr. Smith" and a "Mr. Jones." "Mr. Smith believes that consenting adults ought to be able to do whatever they want in private." Mr. Jones, on the other hand, says, "There ought to be laws against certain kinds of behavior since many private actions have social consequences." Despite concerns about pornography and lack of moral standards, 66 percent said they agreed "strongly" or "somewhat" with Smith; just 32 percent agreed with Jones. Pollster Daniel Yankelovich says Americans want to act as they choose, and people should be able to conduct themselves according to their own lights.

This predilection for pluralism extends to highly unpopular views and unconventional lifestyles. National Opinion Research Center studies show considerable public tolerance of persons who are against churches and religion, admitted communists, racists, homosexuals, or who are antidemocratic. In each case, solid majorities believe they should be allowed to speak freely and have books that advocate such beliefs on the shelves of the community library.

Opportunity Without Constraints

The values of freedom, liberty, and equality of opportunity are dominant themes in U.S. history. They explain, for example, why so many Americans admire successful entrepreneurs. In the nineteenth century, Horatio Alger created a role model for many. By the late twentieth century, Chrysler Board Chairman Lee Iacocca had become a folk hero.

Business people are celebrated principally because they embody the American dream. Not surprisingly, then, Americans are obsessed with property (and property rights), largely because they are the tangible products of a triumphant political creed. . . .

The reverence for property is especially strong, even if not everyone has much to show off. In 1972 Democratic presidential candidate George McGovern made what he thought would be a surefire, popular promise to blue-collar rubber factory workers: as president he would seek to increase inheritance taxes so that the rich could bequeath less to their families and more to the government. To McGovern's amazement, he was roundly booed. . . .

Any attempt to limit the American dream meets with considerable resistance. Opportunity without constraints has been a recurrent pattern in our political thought. A 1940 *Fortune* poll found 74 percent rejected the idea that there "should be a law limiting the amount of money an individual is allowed to earn in a year." Forty-one years later, the consensus held: 79 percent did not think that "there should be a top limit on incomes so that no one can earn more than $100,000 a year." Even those who earned less than $5,000 held that opinion. A 1984 National Opinion Research Center survey found 71 percent believed that differences in social standing were acceptable because they resulted from "what people made out of the opportunities they had.". . .

After traveling what was then the breadth of the United States in 1831 and 1832, and after having spoken to notables and ordinary citizens, the Frenchman Alexis de Tocqueville remarked, "All the domestic controversies of the Americans at first appear to a stranger to be incomprehensible or puerile, and he is at a loss whether to pity a people who take such arrant trifles in good earnest or to envy that happiness which enables a community to discuss them." Tocqueville's observation was undoubtedly inspired by the relative ideological homogeneity in the United States—especially when compared to his native land. No wonder that he found the young nation's political disputes almost quaint, even charming. . . .

Henry Steele Commager believes that since the nation's founding, the character of the American people has not changed greatly nor has the "nature of the principles of conduct, public and private, to which they subscribe." Our values may be constant, but the circumstances in which they are applied are not. The whiff of civil war, the onset of a depression, or the ravages of inflation inevitably cause Americans to take stock of the situation, their expectations of government, and settle upon a course of action in a manner consistent with the American creed.

"We have slowly imbibed the values of the authoritarian way of life, to the point where few of us question it."

Democratic Values Are Being Usurped by a National Security State

Sidney Lens

Sidney Len's [1912-1986] many books include *The Crisis of American Labor, Radicalism in America,* and *Poverty: America's Enduring Paradox.* He was senior editor of *The Progressive,* contributing editor to *Dissent* and *New Politics,* and co-editor of *Liberation,* before his death in 1986. The following viewpoint was taken from his book, *Permanent War: The Militarization of America,* which he completed shortly before he died. Mr. Lens argues that two Americas exist: one legal and democratic, the other illegal, secretive, and authoritarian. Since 1945, the second government, constructed around the National Security Council and an imperial presidency, has removed itself from the control of Congress and the American people.

As you read, consider the following questions:

1. What point does the author make in claiming that the United States is engaged in permanent war?
2. What democratic values are endangered by the National Security State he describes?

Since 1945 the United States has been engaged in a permanent war. It is not permanent in the sense that it will never end, for all things must eventually end but, rather, permanent in the sense that it is fought every day on every continent and there is no single day when either side can claim definitive victory. This permanent war is unique because it takes two forms: one is the kind of war we have known throughout history, with armies, navies, and air forces confronting each other in open battle; the other is a new type of war fought by subversion, dirty tricks, secret manipulation, coups d'état, even assassinations. Korea and Vietnam are examples of the first form, with the United States directly engaged against two Soviet proxies. The 1973 overthrow of the Allende government in Chile by an American-supported group is an example of the second. . . .

The Impact of Permanent War

Like all wars the permanent war has restructured the institutional life of the nations involved, in particular the United States. War, after all, is the worst emergency a nation-state ever confronts, and special measures and institutions are required to meet the emergency. In World War II, for instance, the government exacted a no-strike pledge from the labor movement so that war production might proceed with little interruption. To deny war material to the men at the front while workers and employers in the rear resolve their differences in work stoppages would be intolerable—a major battle could be lost, even the war itself, because of supply shortages. As a corollary to the no-strike pledge, the Roosevelt administration had to create a number of institutions to avoid economic hazards such as uncontrolled inflation. If workers could not strike they at least needed some mechanism to adjudicate contractual disputes and grievances; hence a War Labor Board was established with powers to resolve such differences. A lid also had to be placed on prices; hence an Office of Price Administration was created to pass on price increases. There was also a rationing board to see to it that scarce items—gasoline, meat, cigarettes—were distributed equitably and a Selective Service system and draft board were needed to see to it that men were enrolled in the military on an orderly basis. A host of new bodies were fashioned: the Office of Production Management, the War Production Board, the Office of Strategic Supply, the Supply, Priorities, and Allocation Board, the Office of Technical Development, and the Office of Emergency Management. A censorship office was created to guard against publication of "sensitive" material, and the Office of Strategic Services was charged with espionage and subversion behind enemy lines. Not only were new agencies added, but the structure and size of government changed decisively. Richard Barnet tells us that "in 1939 the federal government had about eight hundred thousand civilian employees, about 10 percent of whom worked for national security agencies. At the end of the war the figure approached four million, of which more than 75 percent were in national security activities.

Changes of this magnitude were made in order to deal with a relatively short war—four years. The permanent war under way since 1945-47 has already lasted ten times as long. Inevitably, it was bound not only to rearrange the old institutional patterns, but to modify attitudes toward law and order, alter traditional beliefs, refashion the economy and above all, sire a new form of government—a twin government. . . .

The National Security State

What is the National Security State? Well, it began, officially, with the National Security Act of 1947; it was then implemented in January 1950 when the National Security Council provided a blueprint for a new kind of country, unlike anything that the United States had ever known before. This document, known as NSC-68 for short, declassified only in 1975, committed—and still, fitfully, commits—us to the following program. First, never negotiate, ever, with Russia. This could not last forever; but the obligatory bad faith of U.S.-Soviet meetings still serves the continuing plan. Second, develop the hydrogen bomb so that when the Russians finally develop an atomic bomb, we will still not have to deal with that enemy without which the National Security State cannot exist. Third, rapidly build up conventional forces. Fourth, put through a large increase in taxes to pay for all of this. Fifth, mobilize the entire American society to fight this terrible specter of Communism. Sixth, set up a strong alliance system, directed by the United States (this became NATO). Seventh, make the people of Russia our allies, through propaganda and C.I.A. derring-do, in this holy adventure— hence the justification for all sorts of secret services that are in no way responsible to the Congress that funds them, and so are in viola- tion of the old Constitution.

Gore Vidal, *The Nation*, June 4, 1988.

We still have one president and one Congress in the United States but, in effect, we now have two governments. One govern- ment remains open, formally democratic; the other operates in the shadows, secretive and authoritarian. The open government is not untainted, but at least in the formal sense it tolerates the freedoms we have become accustomed to: free speech, free press, and the rest. The average American, then, believes we are still a "free people," living in a true democracy.

The government that counts, nevertheless, is the second one con- structed around the National Security Council (NSC) and an imperial presidency, which makes secret, far-reaching decisions about war, foreign policy, and, indirectly, the economy, without consulting either the Congress or the American people. This National Security State is an authoritarian state which has removed itself from most popular controls to avoid punishment for violations of American and international law and the central principle of the American way of life, "government by consent of the governed." It doesn't act this way as a lark or to enjoy the perquisites of power, but because there is no other way to carry out the day-to-day activities dictated by the existence of the permanent war. To function as a democracy would make it impossible to continue the war.

The best known transgressions of legality by the National Security State are those which have been directed against foreigners and foreign governments. The attempts (sometimes with the aid of the Mafia) to assassinate Fidel Castro, the financing of counter-revolutionary forces against the governments of Jacobo Arbenz Guzmán in Guatemala, Mohammed Mossadegh in Iran, the Sandinistas in Nicaragua are a few examples of covert foreign activity. But the true measure of the National Security State includes what it has done to shred democratic rights and values at home. If none of this seems immediately apparent it is because the subversion has taken place over a period of four decades, step by step, and we have slowly imbibed the values of the authoritarian way of life, to the point where few of us question it.

The Erosion of Democratic Values

For example, in 1956 the Federal Bureau of Investigation (FBI) established the Counterintelligence Program (COINTELPRO) to ferret out alleged radicals, disrupt their organizations, and discredit them personally. This was the same kind of tactic that the Soviet KGB had been criticized for carrying out in its sphere of influence. The FBI committed 239 actual break-ins and burglaries against fifteen organizations—more than 90 against the Socialist Workers Party alone. None of these activities was conducted with legal search warrants; all were patent violations of American law. Yet, apart from a small number of leftist and liberal publications there was no public outcry for an investigation. Then FBI chief, J. Edgar Hoover was never indicted for having ordered these criminal acts, even though he had taken an oath to uphold the law without fear or bias when he was installed in office. None of the attorneys general or the presidents whom they served while these illegal acts were taking place was impeached or even reprimanded, even though they too had taken an oath to uphold the law.

Americans generally have a decent respect for the law, but the permanent war has eroded their values. . . .

After four decades of permanent war Americans have adjusted

to a political regimen in which government officials can do almost anything under the cover of such code words as *national security* or *executive privilege*, without being held legally accountable. Even in the rare instances where they are brought to trial and convicted, they are judged and treated by a different standard. . . .

Militarism Threatens American Values

Militarism is on the rise in the United States. While a strong military posture is essential, overemphasis on military power within the government and American society undermines our strength as a nation and jeopardizes the democratic process in the United States. Huge and increasing amounts of money support military programs while civilian programs are underfunded or eliminated altogether. This diversion of resources to the military threatens the American values our military is supposed to defend. Military concerns dominate America's foreign and domestic policies and its economy. Americans are persuaded to accept and support military actions instead of pursuing more constructive methods to promote U.S. interests through diplomatic, economic, scientific, and cultural means.

Center for Defense Information, *The Defense Monitor*, vol. XV, #3, 1986.

Early in the permanent war many liberals demanded that the CIA either be dissolved or at least divested of its covert action assignments. Such proposals are no longer heard. Complaints are voiced over this or that excess committed by the CIA and on two or three occasions there have been official investigations of those excesses, but the need for an agency that regularly engages in unlawful activity both at home and abroad is seldom contested. Nor has there been any recent demand that the 1949 law which gave the Agency the right to keep secret what it spends—in direct contravention of the Constitution which demands that spending by all agencies be a matter of public record—be rescinded. The public has been conditioned to accept the principle that the government has a right to commit such illegal acts as arming foreigners to invade a sovereign country, the commissioning of perjury and burglaries, on the theory that there is a superior law to the one we have been living under for two centuries—the law of national security.

The corrosion of legal and moral values during the period of permanent war has been accompanied by a corrosion of basic tradition. The most compelling impact on the American way of life since World War II has been the reversal of the two-century-old traditions against imperialism and militarism. . . .

At the end of the Revolutionary War, Washington dissolved the national army and sent it home, leaving defense entirely to the ragged and inept state militia. Less than six months after he resigned his commission and returned to Mount Vernon, the Continental Congress stated the nation's views on militarism in plain terms: "Standing armies in time of peace are inconsistent with the principles of republican governments, dangerous to the liberties of a free people, and generally converted into destructive engines for establishing despotism."

Years later when President Washington asked Congress to establish a regular army consisting of four regiments of infantry and one of artillery—a total of 2,631 men—"to awe the Indians, protect our trade, prevent encroachments," he conceded that "a *large* standing army in time of peace hath ever been considered dangerous to the liberties of the country." His only justification was that a "few troops" would be "safe." Congress, however, did not agree. Admittedly the Constitution did authorize a standing army, but James Madison, in defending the provision, subsequently made the same sort of apology as Washington. An army on a small scale, he said, "had its inconveniences," but on "an intensive scale its consequences may be fatal." Clearly for most of the founders of the country military preparedness was a dangerous drug to be taken in small doses at best. That tradition was little challenged until after World War II. Prior to each war military forces were relatively small, and though they were substantially enlarged during hostilities, they always contracted when the fighting had ended. As of 1845, just before the Mexican War, the military contingent stood at a meager 9,000 officers and men; as late as 1904 at a relatively small 53,000; and in 1939, as World War II was about to begin in Europe, 185,000—less than a tenth of its present size. . . .

Elections Are of Minor Importance

The continued, even escalating, power of the military in American life wrecked the antimilitarist tradition and paved the way for a reoriented and remodeled America. One of the grievances that had been levied against King George III by the authors of the Declaration of Independence was that "he has affected to render the military independent of and superior to the civil power." Woodrow Wilson made a similar observation about militarism a century and a quarter later: "So long as you have a military class, it does not make any difference what your form of government is; if you are determined to be armed to the teeth, you must obey the only men who can control the great machinery of war. Elections are of minor importance." . . .

Conclusion

The primary cost that the United States has paid for its imperial policy has been the permanent war, with all its associated surcharges. That includes more than 100,000 battlefield deaths in

Korea and Vietnam (not to mention a couple of million Koreans and Vietnamese), $3 trillion in arms expenditures, and a sextupling of the national debt. But most of all, it includes the establishment of a National Security State and the unyielding trend toward totalitarianism. . . .

The Military Is Number One

Generally speaking, in what American institution do you have the most confidence?

Until 1986, if you were a typical American asked that question by Gallup pollsters, you would have responded "church or organized religion." Moreover, the clergy had been in first place for many years.

No more. The 1986 Gallup data shows a major drop in confidence in the church, from 66 percent in 1985 down to 57 percent in 1986.

And who would you think is in first place now? The Supreme Court? Congress? Newspapers? Television? Banks?

None of the above. According to Gallup, the most popular institution in America is—get this—the military! The Harris Poll and the Gallup Poll don't always agree, but on this one the 1986 year-end Harris data concurs: Americans, says Harris, have the most confidence in "the leaders of the military"—more than leaders in medicine, universities, the Supreme Court, or organized religion.

Ben Wattenberg, *The Washington Times*, January 8, 1987.

One day in the not-too-distant future the American people will have to make a decision of even greater import than those their forebears made in the 1770s, 1860s, and 1930s. They will have to decide whether to continue as at present, toward a totalitarian society, a possible nuclear war, and economic disintegration; or whether they will end the permanent war, dismantle the National Security State, and find a means other than imperialism to achieve economic abundance.

"The American Government of today operates on new premises. . . . The protection of liberty has been replaced by the granting of privileges."

Democratic Values Are Being Lost to Self-Interest

John A. Howard

John A. Howard is councilor at the Rockford Institute where he served as its president until 1986. The Institute describes its purpose as "seeking to re-establish an ethical consensus in American public life." In the following viewpoint, Mr. Howard asserts that since World War II the US has undergone a fundamental change in the values, attitudes, and priorities of its citizens. He claims that liberty, the original primary concern of American government, has been cast aside in favor of self-interest, with people trying to obtain special privileges for themselves. In Mr. Howard's opinion, the shift has been so dramatic that he describes it as the "Second American Revolution."

As you read, consider the following questions:

1. What is the "Second American Revolution" that the author identifies?
2. What does the author claim are six disastrous consequences of welfare state government in America?
3. Do you agree or disagree with the author's analysis? After reading this viewpoint, what future do you predict for America?

John A. Howard, speech delivered to the American Farm Bureau Tax and Spending Limitation Conference, Chicago IL, September 18, 1978.

The problem to be confronted is initially one of economics. . . .

As the quick-witted Clare Booth Luce has observed, the Congress is like an economic wino, who knows full well that its continued overspending will put the United States on the economic trash heap of history, but is incapable of resisting its compulsion to spend. . . .

I want to examine with you the conditions which have spawned the taxing and spending syndrome, because they are, I believe, the same conditions which have given rise to increasing corruption and crime, the disintegration of the family, and most of the other serious difficulties inside our nation which dismay every conscientious and thoughtful citizen. The fundamental problem is one of a change in the values, attitudes and priorities of the citizens. Let us consider the changes that have occurred in the political arena.

The Principle of Liberty

First, it must be recognized that in any group situation, there is an ever-present push-pull between what the individual wants to do and what he is supposed to do as a member of the group. This two-way pull operates even in the groups we most enjoy. The regular meeting of a social club may conflict with a daughter's birthday, vacation plans may coincide with major responsibilities you have in your church, or the fatigue of a long day's work may argue against attending a meeting of the Farm Bureau. So, too, with a government. The obligations of the citizen to vote or pay taxes or provide military service may well conflict with powerful personal reasons to the contrary. The point is that in every group situation, there has to be some strong benefit or attraction which group membership offers that has a chance to overcome whatever opposite influences affect the individual, so that the group members will decide for the group often enough that the group purposes will be fulfilled. There has to be a justifying principle which causes the individual to sacrifice his own preferences in order to sustain his membership in the group.

At the time the United States became a nation, the justifying principle was liberty. The hope of freedom from unjust taxes and tyrannous government was what caused the troops to fight the long, arduous revolutionary war and the protection of liberty was the leit motif woven into the Constitution and the explicit objective of the Bill of Rights. As long as the preservation of liberty remained the top priority of our national government, the nation continued to grow stronger subject, of course, to the fluctuations which characterize all human affairs. As long as the protection of liberty remained the top priority of the national government, the people were able to live in reasonable harmony with each other except for the Civil War which was, in fact, a disagreement about the nature of liberty and the individuals to whom the privileges of liberty were available. For a century and a half, the folks in Washington, for the most part, saw their primary role as facilitating the proper activities of the citizens in the pursuit of *their own life* purposes, adjudicating their conflicts and protecting their persons from assault and their property from theft and vandalism.

Five Reasons for America's Success

Today in our affluent society, we are enjoying so much of the fruits of this great system of ours that most of us forget just how and why we have become so prosperous.

How is it that one-seventeenth of the world's population can produce almost one half of the world's wealth? How could the American people, in the short span of five generations, have changed an undeveloped wilderness continent into the tremendously rich and powerful nation that we now take for granted?

Well, first our Founding Fathers wrote the Constitution, the greatest document to govern people that the world has ever seen. Living and working under our Constitution and Bill of Rights, Americans created the most successful major society in all human history—and they did it all without government aid. It was built on these five principles:

1. We had a *belief in God*—and this religious background made us reliable and dependable with one another.

2. We had *limited government*—and this limited our national expenses and gave us surplus capital for tools and a good living standard.

3. We had *individual freedom*—every man could work at what he wanted.

4. We had *incentive*—which was simply the right to keep the fruits of our labor.

5. We had *competition*—the thing that makes businessman and employee alike serve his fellow man well.

From "Will We Keep Our Freedom?" by Walter Knott. A pamphlet published by Americanism Educational League.

Then in the middle third of the twentieth century, there was a second American Revolution which radically changed the nature of government and altered the government's relationship to the people. The American government of today operates on new premises and is structured to serve new purposes with the result that liberty, as it was conceived two centuries ago, has been cast aside as a matter of governmental concern. Since there were no barricades and no bleeding casualties in this Second American Revolution, many citizens suppose they still have the same government that was founded by their forebears, albeit one that has been adapted to meet the proclaimed requirements of the twentieth century. If so, they are greatly mistaken. The protection of liberty has been replaced by the granting of privileges, benefits and services. That is the new justifying principle, not liberty, but the distribution of gifts and favors.

This change of governmental purpose was welcomed by many citizens. The hardships imposed by the Great Depression seemed to justify the use of the vast powers and resources of the central government to assist the people in their time of need. A compassionate citizenry eventually became accustomed to having the Congress authorize help for an endless list of folks who asked for help. Unfortunately, the open-hearted voters who supported this change in the role of government did not understand the dynamics of governmental paternalism; they did not foresee the cancerous interplay between the power of those in office to grant favors and the eagerness of the citizens to receive favors.

The *dream* of a more humane society has turned into a *nightmare* of governmental extravagance and corruption, of unfulfilled promises on a gigantic scale, of foolish, useless, counterproductive and expensive programs, and a populace increasingly divided into militant groups competing fiercely against each other for the favors dispensed by the government. We are fast moving into the proverbial war of all against all, everyone trying to obtain special privileges for himself.

The disastrous consequences of the welfare state government as opposed to the government of liberty are apparent on all sides, but let us register on several of those consequences which have denatured specific aspects of our government and devastated its relationships with the people.

Six Consequences of Welfare State Government

1. The Congress, as you know, is charged with enacting the laws which govern all the citizens of the nation. Since those laws apply to everyone, it is fitting that they should be discussed and voted upon by delegates elected from across the country. If bad laws are enacted, each citizen has his own Congressmen and Senators whom he can hold accountable for the vote, and to whom he may turn for redress if a law unjustly injures him. That, at least, is the theory.

However, once the Congress opened the floodgates to the tide of laws providing special benefits for particular groups, it became utterly impossible for our elected representatives to give proper attention to the enormous volume of legislation proposed and passed. It is bad enough that legislators are voting into law many bills the consequences of which they cannot begin to foresee, but an even more grievous phenomenon has occurred. In some instances, the actual lawmaking function has simply been delegated to unelected functionaries in the executive branch of government. In a speech before a group of college presidents, the Director of the Office of Civil Rights in HEW reported on several major civil rights laws which had been phrased only in general terms by the Congress, leaving the actual provisions of the law to be written by the staff of the Civil Rights office. The Constitution of the United States was not designed to serve a welfare state, and the Congress, now hopelessly snowed under by the welfare state activities it has generated, is evading, at least in part, its primary Constitutional function.

Government Is the Problem

It is a typical illusion to believe that our people do not trust the government because of lack of ethics. . . . Were the ethics of officials never so high, people would still be angry. Why? Because we are surrounded by government. We swim in government. Too much familiarity does not breed respect. . . .

People sense the state's looseness and corruption, when checks arrive a few dollars higher than they should. Sometimes, a friend urges a working wife to "go on unemployment," something she would never have thought of a decade ago—and it soon becomes a cyclical way of life: work a little, collect a little.

Millions have discovered that an unemployment check, at a middle income level, is worth more than a wage. No taxes are withheld. No expenses for transportation, lunch or clothing. Sure beats working.

Larger and larger segments of the population are busy learning "angles," searching legitimate ways to rip off the government—honestly, according to the rules, but in a way that cheapens all who take part.

The problem in the United States is not a system of corrupt officials in a corrupt bureaucracy. The problem is a system that is corrupting the population.

Michael Novak, "A People of, by and for the Government," *Minneapolis Star and Tribune*, April 13, 1977. Reprinted with author's permission.

---

2. The advent of the welfare state has also fundamentally skewed the basis on which the voters judge who is the best candidate for national office. To an increasing extent, honesty, breadth of knowledge, good judgment and the other sound and honorable qualities which one would hope to find in candidates for high office are being subordinated to a very different set of characteristics.

In the new order, when voters are concerned about what benefits the elected officer will provide for them, promises, hypocrisy, deceit, log-rolling and clout are fast becoming the characteristics of electability. As Harold Blake Walker noted, of twenty-one Congressmen linked in one way or another with political wrongdoing or personal scandal prior to the 1976 election, nineteen were re-elected. Criminal activity and flagrant immorality have become insignificant in the view of the ever-greedier voters of the welfare state. . . .

The Purpose of Taxation

3. Another massive and destructive consequence of the Second Revolution is the change in the purpose of taxation. When liberty was the by-word, taxes were collected only to pay to operate the government. Now a large and rapidly growing portion of the taxes is collected for the express purpose of redistributing the wealth. This concept denies the meaning of private property. Once redistribution is accepted as a proper function of government there is, of course, no logical point at which to stop short of the total equalization of whatever wealth still exists. This confiscation of assets discourages productive people from working hard, and encourages lazy people to loaf. It is the kiss of death to an economy and it is inherently and eternally the enemy of liberty.

4. The new role of government also brings into sharp focus a wasteful self-contradiction of bureaucracy. If people are employed to attend to a problem, the last thing they want to do is solve that problem and put themselves out of work. One can only regard with awe and admiration the great skill of the bureaucrats in nourishing a problem into something of gigantic proportions, generating research, undertaking surveys, holding conferences, traveling to the far corners of the earth to learn if the residents of Oz and Shangri-La have the same problem, preparing reports, holding press conferences, appointing committees, expanding the staff, opening regional offices, hiring consultants, publishing articles, visiting campuses, etc., all intently focused upon the problem often without any measurable effect in reducing it. . . .

The bureaucracy has a fairly consistent record of not solving the problems it tackles, thus assuring that the jobs of the problem-solvers will be safeguarded and multiplied.

5. The welfare state, in its fervor to bring about utopia, is engaged in a whole network of programs, operating with the heavy hand of the tyrant to enforce what the government, in its limited wisdom, has proclaimed to be the principles of justice. Some time ago a young man stopped by to see me. He works as a field agent for a national church group, calling upon student organizations affiliated with his church that operate on both public and private campuses. It seems that some of the civil rights legislation has

Schools Must Teach Democratic Values

We call for a special effort to raise the level of education for democratic citizenship. . . . We fear that many young Americans are growing up without the education needed to develop a solid commitment to those "notions and sentiments" essential to a democratic form of government. Although all the institutions that shape our private and public lives—family, church, school, government, media—share the responsibility for encouraging democratic values in our children, our focus here is on the nation's schools and their teaching of the social studies and humanities. . . .

Our call for schools to purposely impart to their students the learning necessary for an informed, reasoned allegiance to the ideals of a free society rests on three convictions:

First, that democracy is the worthiest form of human governance ever conceived.

Second, that we cannot take its survival or its spread—or its perfection in practice—for granted. . . .

Third, we are convinced that democracy's survival depends upon our transmitting to each new generation the political vision of liberty and equality that unites us as Americans—and a deep loyalty to the political institutions our founders put together to fulfill that vision. As Jack Beatty reminded us in a *New Republic* article one Fourth of July, ours is a patriotism "not of blood and soil but of values, and those values are liberal and humane."

Such values are neither revealed truths nor natural habits. There is no evidence that we are born with them. Devotion to human dignity and freedom, to equal rights, to social and economic justice, to the rule of law, to civility and truth, to tolerance of diversity, to mutual assistance, to personal and civic responsibility, to self-restraint and self-respect—all these must be taught and learned and practiced. They cannot be taken for granted or regarded as merely one set of options against which any other may be accepted as equally worthy.

American Federation of Teachers, *Education for Democracy*, 1987.

---

been interpreted to require every campus organization to file an affidavit that its membership is open to all students. The student organization served by my visitor is only open to members of his church and has as its purpose, to help its members grow in their knowledge and commitment to their faith. Since these groups could not sign the affidavit of open membership, the field representative had called on presidents, deans and ombudspersons on the various campuses, to seek advice on what to do about this dilemma. The answer he received was virtually the same on all campuses; Tell your student group to lie about it. Have them sign the affidavit, not intending to abide by it. Here is bureaucracy gone berserk, forcing dishonesty upon the officers of the institutions whose purpose it is to train our youth, and teaching deceit to the students. The welfare state by nature is a tyranny which in order to carry out its judgments must impose its will on the people, trampling on the most sacred tenets of liberty.

6. Another aspect of the damage wrought in the governmental transition from the guardian of liberty to the dispenser of privileges is manifest in the enactment of the minimum wage. This is some of the cruelest legislation ever devised. The only leverage which the under-qualified worker has available to him in obtaining a job is a willingness to work for less than the going wage. This opportunity is now blocked by law. It has become illegal to pay him at a rate appropriate to what he can actually produce. When the minimum wage was first enacted, it put thousands of black youth out of work, and every time the minimum wage has been raised, thousands more have been added to the rolls of the unemployed. Far kinder, and far more intelligent to let the under-qualified and the handicapped earn at the level of their capacities trying to prove by their performance that they qualify for higher wages, and when necessary, to supplement their earnings with charity. . . .

Well, these six points—the partial transfer of legislative power by the Congress to bureaucrats in the executive branch, the acceptance by the voters of dishonesty and moral turpitude in candidates for high office if they can only deliver enough favors to their constituents, the collection of taxes for the express purpose of redistributing the wealth, the inherent difficulty of bureaucrats' not wanting to solve problems when such resolution would put them out of work, the denaturing of religious and other institutions by imposing a rigid and unworkable interpretation of justice, and the cruel and inflationary impact of the minimum wage— these are just a small sampling of the kinds of destructive consequences resulting from the revolutionary change in the purpose of government. . . .

The Antidote

The antidote to the economically ruinous welfare-state philosophy of government is, I believe, the reestablishment as priorities in the minds and hearts of our citizens, those principles of responsible liberty to which the Founding Fathers of our country were dedicated and which made possible the development of the most humane and productive society the world has ever known. Among those principles, I would cite as priorities

1. Reverence for God
2. Personal integrity
3. Lawfulness
4. A commitment to the sanctity of the family

5. Economic self-reliance

6. A decent regard for one's neighbor

There are, I believe, ways in which these values can be reestablished in our society, and one of the principal endeavors of our Institute focuses on how that might be accomplished, but that is another speech.

Let me conclude with a quotation and a response to it. The quotation comes from Andrew Hacker's book, *The End of the American Era*, published in 1968. He asserts:

> Only a few decades remain to complete the era America will have known as a nation. For the United States has embarked on its decline since the closing days of the Second World War. . . . It is too late in our history to restore order or reestablish authority: The American temperament has passed the point where self-interest can subordinate itself to citizenship.

Mr. Hacker has brutally identified the basic question. Has the American temperament reached the point where self-interest cannot subordinate itself to the unselfish principles of liberty?

If the voters should be successful in putting limits on governmental spending and taxing only for the purpose of trying to salvage their savings and ease their household budgets, then Mr. Hacker's prediction will, I fear, prove accurate. If, however, such action is perceived as a first step in reestablishing the integrity of government with balanced budgets and with the eventual elimination of governmental programs which by their nature corrupt the citizens, then we will be on our way to disproving Mr. Hacker's grim prophecy.

Ranking American Values

This activity will give you an opportunity to discuss with classmates the values you and your classmates consider important and the values you believe are considered most important by the majority of Americans.

© King Features Syndicate 1975

Part 1

Step 1. The class should break into groups of four to six students and discuss the meaning of the Hagar cartoon.

Step 2. Working individually within each group, each student should rank their values listed below, assigning the number 1 to the value he or she personally considers most important, the number 2 to the second most important value, and so on, until all the values have been ranked.

Step 3. Students should compare their rankings with others in the group, giving the reasons for their rankings.

_____ financial security
_____ freedom of speech
_____ equality of opportunity
_____ self-reliance
_____ loyalty to country
_____ tolerance of others
_____ freedom of religion
_____ individual initiative
_____ right to private property
_____ government by law and not people
_____ concern for the underdog
_____ fair play
_____ justice
_____ order in society

Part 2

Step 1. Working in groups of four to six students, each group should rank the values listed in what the group considers the order of importance to the majority of Americans. Assign the number 1 to the value the group believes is most important to the majority of Americans, the number 2 to the second most important value, and so on until all the values have been ranked.

Step 2. Each group should compare its ranking with others in a classwide discussion.

Step 3. The entire class should discuss the following questions.

1. What noticeable differences do you see between the personal rankings in part 1 and the perceived ranking of the majority of Americans in part 2?

2. How would you explain these differences?

3. What conclusions would you draw about America's future in light of your rankings in parts 1 and 2?

Periodical Bibliography

The following articles have been selected to supplement the diverse views presented in this chapter.

David W. Brown
"Civic Virtue in America," *Kettering Review*, Spring 1986.

Henry Steele Commager
"The Revolution as a World Ideal," *Saturday Review*, December 13, 1975.

Robert A. Goldwin
"Of Men and Angels," *Vital Speeches of the Day*, June 1, 1976.

Max Gordon
"Reclaiming the American Ideal," *The Nation*, April 5, 1975.

Meg Greenfield
"Deep in the Ethics Bog," *Newsweek*, February 6, 1989.

William Johnson Jr.
"Lincoln and Watergate: The American Past Speaks to the American Future," *The Christian Century*, June 25, 1973.

Irving Kristol
"Republican Virtue," *Kettering Review*, Fall 1988.

Peter McGrath
"In Order To Form a More Perfect Union," *Newsweek*, May 25, 1987.

George W. Maxey
"The Qualities of the Early Americans," *Vital Speeches of the Day*, January 1, 1944.

M. Scott Peck
"A New American Revolution," *New Age*, May/June 1987.

Lawrence W. Reed
"The Fall of Rome and Modern Parallels," *Vital Speeches of the Day*, August 1, 1979.

Jeffrey St. John
"Reviving America's Revolutionary Principles of Liberty," *Vital Speeches of the Day*, October 1, 1976.

James L. Sundquist
"Improving the Capacity To Govern," *The Brookings Bulletin*, Fall 1980.

Time
"To Revive Responsibility," February 23, 1981.

Gore Vidal
"How To Take Back the Country," *The Nation*, June 4, 1988.

What Are America's Social Values?

**AMERICAN
V·A·L·U·E·S**

Chapter Preface

The social values of contemporary Americans differ greatly from those of a generation or two ago. Talking and chewing gum, for example, were the major offenses in America's classrooms in the 1940s. Today, drug abuse, gang violence, and assault are the problems that plague our schools.

Are America's new social values responsible for these horrors? How can the situation be improved? Daniel Yankelovich, in the chapter's last viewpoint, claims American society is struggling to find a new middle ground between an old ethic of sacrifice for others and a new ethic more concerned with self-fulfillment. Other viewpoints in this chapter claim that Americans have become so obsessed with themselves that their sense of community has suffered.

"Our values have not changed. . . . these values are ingrained in our character."

America's Basic Values Have Not Changed

Harry J. Gray

Harry J. Gray was the chairman and chief executive officer of United Technologies Corporation until 1987. From 1979 until 1986, his company ran a series of full page messages in the *Wall Street Journal* about basic American values. In the following viewpoint, taken from a 1984 speech, Mr. Gray describes what he believes to be America's basic values. He feels these values are part of the American character, and although many changes have occurred in American society, he argues that traditional values have endured.

As you read, consider the following questions:

1. What are the traditional American values the author identifies?
2. What advantages does he think Americans possess over foreign competitors?
3. Do you agree with the author's conclusions? Why or why not?

From a speech by Harry J. Gray, delivered at the College of Commerce and Business Administration at the University of Illinois on May 3, 1984.

A lot of things have changed since those days of the Great Depression and the Second World War. It's not just that the price of bread costs more than 9 cents a loaf! Our country and the rest of the world have changed dramatically and in fundamental ways. We have just to look around us. The world is completely different.

Developments in technology have been a catalyst for progress and have made life better for people on a scale never before recorded in history.

The revolution in medical science has given people the genuine prospect of a lengthy and healthy life.

The widespread availability of the arts and humanities has given to nearly all of us the opportunity to be exposed to, and to challenge, philosophies and ideas previously available only to the elite of society.

And we have seen an upheaval in national frontiers and political relationships that no one at the time could possibly have imagined.

In the past four decades we have experienced revolutions in science, in technology, in culture, in world politics and in many other fields.

They were revolutions unparalleled in their scope and impact.

They were revolutions with as profound an effect on the way people live as in any other time in history. They have changed the world. And, in many ways, they have changed *us*, too.

America's Values Remain Unchanged

Yet, if we look beyond the externals to the essentials, I think we find that the really important things have *not* changed. I refer to the traditional values—the simple, basic truths—all of us believe in and try to live by. These are the essential American virtues that have made our country and our institutions great. Other things may change, but our national virtues remain constant.

Sometimes we forget them. Some of us may try to live without them. But they are part of our culture. They are national characteristics that distinguish us as a people. They are our heritage from the past and our legacy to the future. They are the same virtues I learned to respect and practice while growing up in this area, when I was a student at the University of Illinois, during my service in the 5th infantry division, and throughout my business life.

I know the importance all kinds of people place on these things from the tremendous response we at United Technologies have received from a national advertising program we began in 1979.

For corporate advertising, this program was most *un*traditional in its approach, its style, and particularly its content. Beginning in February 1979—and every month since then—we have been running a series of full page messages in the *Wall Street Journal*.

Our messages address human concerns, and they speak to people as people. *Not* as a business to customers. *Not* as a corporation to investors. *Not* as educators to students. But as people to people. And we speak to them *not* about our products or our company. We speak to them about life in general, everyday experiences, and concerns common to us all, whatever our callings. We speak about the things that the *Wall Street Journal*, in referring to our messages, calls "the enduring truths."

America's Dominant Values

In an exploration of the dominant personal and social values of American society, two sociologists, James Christianson and Choon Yang, rank-ordered American values based on people's expressed preferences. This is how Americans ranked American values:

1. Moral integrity (honesty)
2. Personal freedom
3. Patriotism
4. Work (your job)
5. Being practical and efficient
6. Political democracy
7. Helping others
8. Achievement (getting ahead)
9. National progress
10. Material comfort
11. Leisure (recreation)
12. Equality (racial)
13. Individualism (nonconformity)
14. Equality (sexual).

Other scholars concur, suggesting that most major dilemmas in our society center on values, whether we are talking about the views of Robert Bork or the character of Gary Hart, Joseph Biden, Pat Robertson or Jesse Jackson. Always, we come back to activism and hard work, achievement, efficiency, materialism, progress, freedom, individualism, quality, morality, humanitarianism and conformity as central values.

Everette E. Dennis, *Vital Speeches of the Day*, March 15, 1988.

In our messages we talk about the importance of learning . . . the dignity of hard work . . . the meaning of patriotism . . . the need to take the initiative . . . the good that comes from helping others. We talk about ambition . . . perseverance . . . respect. We speak to the head and to the heart.

The simple yet powerful theme that unites all our messages is that the way we perform as individuals will determine how we perform as a nation.

These messages break entirely new ground in corporate advertising. For one thing, they're not even signed. There's just a small note at the bottom telling readers where to write if they'd like reprints.

And people have written. We have received over half a million letters in response to these ads and we have distributed three million reprints. Our corporation has won all sorts of acclaim because of them. And they have had an impact far beyond the readership of the *Wall Street Journal*.

They've been reprinted in the *Congressional Record*, on menus, and napkins. Johnny Carson read one of our messages on his show. Ann Landers has reprinted eight of them. School boards in several cities have made copies by the tens of thousands for distribution to students. Military leaders have told me our messages are used by the services as motivational tools. Five of our messages were judged to be among the 10 best-read ads to appear in the *Wall Street Journal* in the past decade. . . .

I suppose there are many reasons why these messages have found such responsiveness from the public. If I wanted to pick one reason, however, I guess I would use those words of an Illinois political leader of three decades ago and say—we talk sense to the American people.

The Value of Learning

For instance, we talk about the importance of learning. Our country always has placed a high value on education. It was Thomas Jefferson who said two centuries ago, "If a nation expects to be ignorant and free, it expects what never was and never will be."

A battle for the future constantly is being waged in the classrooms of the world. There is an old saying which goes as follows: "If you want one year's prosperity, grow grain. If you want ten year's prosperity, grow men and women." Through quality education we can fortify our national resolve, renew confidence in our national purpose, and enrich the spirit of our times.

The Value of Hard Work

Because of the importance we place on learning, it's only natural that we also place a value on hard work. Work gives flavor to life. Contrary to popular belief, adversity is not why people develop. A lot of people have had adversity and have done nothing. It's because people work hard that they accomplish something. It's not so much the heroics of a few but the constant workings of the many which have lasting impact.

Our value to society comes when someone says, "Let me see your work." The glib tongue may open a door or two. But the real test of people's worth can be measured by the care they give to the job in front of them. We celebrate the dignity of work because hard work is another basic truth we have learned to value.

Patriotism is more than waving the flag. It goes beyond expressing love of country and adherence to American values and institutions. In its best sense, patriotism involves commitment and action. It means participating and building. It has to do with living our lives in ways that fortify our strengths as a society and acknowledge and remedy our weaknesses.

Patriots are doers. They are serving on school boards, working with the disadvantaged, developing products, ringing doorbells for candidates, removing discriminatory barriers, and doing all the other things that need to be done to make our country better and to enhance the American character.

The Value of Initiative and Ambition

Initiative and ambition are also distinctive American attributes. If you wait for other people to make things happen for you, the real world will pass you by. I am reminded of a cartoon where two vultures are sitting on a telephone wire. Nothing happens for a long time. Finally, one says to the other: "I'm tired of waiting. Let's go out and kill something!" A healthy, aggressive attitude is a good thing. We need more people who are willing and able to take the initiative. Ambition is the spur to action. It makes purpose great and achievement greater. Ambition is a vice only if you have more of it than you have of ability.

Ambition for ourselves also means having ambition for other people and helping them out. Professors Sandy Sandage, Fred A. Russell, and Fred Seibert were great influences on my life when I was at the University. They developed my interests and encouraged me. America is filled with perceptive teachers, stern drill sergeants, demanding employers, and caring parents who had the kindness and foresight to go the extra mile and help out other people.

Other Values

We're a nation that respects the individual, believes in liberty rather than authority, admires perseverance in the face of adversity, and values that rare quality known as leadership. It's easy to follow public opinion. It's difficult to mold it. It's easy to have a good idea—if someone else thinks of it. It's easy to move, if you are pushed. Genuine leaders know where they are going, and how to get there. Like a good pathfinder, they stay in front to clear the way, to anticipate dangers, to work around obstacles, or to remove them. In the words of a Spanish philosopher, "Mountains culminate in peaks and nations in men."

These are some of the values we hold as Americans. They are some of the enduring truths we at United Technologies have talked about in our *Wall Street Journal* messages. They are values that we respect and try to live by. Change is a constant in our society. But our values have not changed. They were important to us forty years ago, when I was a young man in Illinois. They are important today. They will be just as valid, just as true, forty years from now, and years to come after that.

The American Advantage

Our country has succeeded because these values are ingrained in our character. They are part of what it means to be an American. Our country has succeeded because how we perform as individuals has determined how we perform as a nation. . . .

We live in a country where people have the fullest possible freedom to praise, to criticize, or discuss and debate as we see fit. On that premise our country was created. On that premise it has grown to greatness. We live in an open society. Throughout our history we always have shown a willingness to entertain new ideas, a tolerance for experimentation, an eagerness to try something different.

Our society was built on freedom of religion, freedom of the press, freedom of speech, trial by jury. These freedoms have allowed our imaginations to flourish.

On the back of the one dollar bill is a Latin inscription: *annuit coeptis*. It means: be favorable to bold enterprise. Benjamin Franklin chose this motto because he believed imagination was the singular characteristic of the people he helped forge into a new nation.

To see the imaginative individual at work is to see the uncommon marvel of daring and deliberation working together, each carried to its highest level. The result sometimes may puzzle us, oftentimes stir us. But it will always rivet our attention.

Our capacity for imagination has led us to expand the American frontiers across the continent.

Our capacity for imagination has brought about technological achievements which have changed our lives dramatically, irreversibly, and for the better.

Our capacity for imagination has given America its competitive edge.

I hope we never lose this capacity.

Let me close with another one of our *Wall Street Journal* messages—one of my favorites. It's called "You're The Finest."

> In just 200 years, your country through freedom and hard work, has changed the world. In agriculture, industry, education, medicine, law, transportation, and on and on. No country can match America's record in religious freedom, civil freedom, human rights, the importance and dignity of the individual. We do have our differences. But when we join together in times of crisis, our strength is awesome. Among all the world's nations, America still stands out front. You're an American. You're the finest ever—and don't you ever, ever forget it.

"Everybody is feverishly intent on making money."

Money Has Become America's Basic Value

Robert Nisbet

Robert Nisbet, the author of more than a dozen books, is a historian, sociologist, and former Albert Schweitzer professor of humanities at Columbia University. The following viewpoint is taken from Mr. Nisbet's most recent book, *The Present Age*. In it he claims the Framers of the Constitution would be struck by three basic changes in modern America: the prominence of war in American life since 1911, the Leviathan-like presence of national government, and the number of Americans who are only loosely attached to groups and traditional values and are so plainly governed by a cash nexus.

As you read, consider the following questions:

1. How does the author define the "loose individual?"
2. To what does the term "evaporated property" refer, and how has it given rise to a society motivated by a cash nexus?
3. Do you think his examples of the importance of cash in various areas of American life are exaggerations or typical representations?

Repeatedly in history the combination of war and political centralization leads to a fraying effect upon the social fabric. Threads are loosened by the tightening of power at the center. Dr. Johnson once told Boswell of a man in London he knew who "hung loose upon society." Loose in the sense of the loose cannon, the ship that slips its hawser, the dog its leash, the individual his accustomed moral restraints.

The Loose Individual

Without doubt there are a great many loose individuals in American society at the present time: loose from marriage and the family, from the school, the church, the nation, job, and moral responsibility. What sociologists are prone to call social disintegration is really nothing more than the spectacle of a rising number of individuals playing fast and loose with other individuals in relationships of trust and responsibility. . . .

The chief aspect of the society around him was, for Tocqueville, the eroding away of traditional associations like family, social class, and "craft fraternities" of economic life. With the disappearance of such associations the individual is left freer and freer of the restraints which normally establish checks upon behavior. The government, Tocqueville argues, far from trying to impede this erosion of limits, encourages it in the interest of its own power.

Money becomes the common denominator of human life. It acquires an "extreme mobility" and "everybody is feverishly intent on making money. . . . Love of gain, a fondness for business careers, the desire to get rich at all costs . . . quickly become ruling passions under a despotic government." Government is the primary force in it all; such government weakens where it strengthens: weakens normal social authority as it strengthens itself through laws, prohibitions, and taxes. As the blood rushes to the head of society, it leaves anemic the local and regional extremities. . . .

Two Kinds of Societies

Two ideal types come to mind which give emphasis as well as perspective to the kind of society that Carlyle and Marx sought to limn. In the first, possibly the kind that Marx called primitive communism, all relationships in a community are formed solely of the trust, allegiance, fealty, and responsibility which emanate from the kinship roles of the members of the community. No monetary or other denominator exists to dilute the directness of the social bond.

In the second ideal type, there are no such personal, role-determined relationships at all in society. Every act of service, responsibility, protection, and aid to others is an act presupposing or calling for monetary exchange, for cash payment. What individuals do for their spouses, for their children and kinsmen, for neighbors and all other common partners in the business of maintaining family, job, citizenship, and even personal identity itself, rests upon the cash nexus and nothing else.

Most Americans, if asked which of the two ideal types just described most resembles American society at the present time, would doubtless choose the second, and who is to say they are wrong? It is evident that while ancient personal values of trust, loyalty, and selfless service to others have by no means disappeared, they do not count as much in the marketplace as they once did. And "marketplace" as a setting has come to include more and more relationships once declared utterly alien to it. When Balzac said that "the power of a five-franc note has become sovereign," he was referring to the France of the post-Napoleonic age. The power of the five-dollar bill, sufficently exerted, is enough to open all doors in America today. . . .

The Only Common Value Is Currency

People are concerned with marginal tax rates and whether their mortgage interest is going to be a write-off. So many other values have diminished: patriotism, religion, family. All that is really left is money. It is the way you keep score. It's one of the few values that still survives.

The teacher or the minister, who didn't make a lot of money but was respected in the community, is less and less a factor. Now everybody's getting their M.B.A. because that's the game these days.

The only value is common currency. A woman who is a good mother at a cocktail party, with all the other people doing all these other things, is almost embarrassed. There are a lot of people doing a good job taking care of kids, but in terms of what's hip, it's Bill Cosby's wife, the lawyer. Not Bill Cosby's wife who stays home and is a mother. That's where the action is, where the media buzz is.

Bruce Bendinger in Studs Terkel, ed., *The Great Divide*, 1988.

Almost half a century ago, the distinguished Harvard economist Joseph Schumpeter, in his *Capitalism, Socialism and Democracy*, laid out clearly the essential processes leading to the business and financial scene of the present. Schumpeter referred to an "evaporation" of property; more particularly, an "Evaporation of Industrial Property" and an "Evaporation of Consumer Property," both reflecting a historical trend of tidal proportions that had been going on in the West and especially in America over the past century. The effect of Schumpeter's evaporation of industrial property—looking at the matter solely from the property-holder's viewpoint—was the substitution of the "soft" property of shares of stock and bonds for the "hard" property of land, buildings, and machines that the property-holder had once managed as well as owned in the passive sense and had been very much a part of in its operation. Independently of volition such a property-holder had a distinct stake in society, a role of social responsibility based upon day-to-day mingling with managers, workers, and consumers.

Very different is the "evaporated" property owner, typically possessing shares of stock existing in their own seemingly detached, stock market world, independent of their owner's will beyond the buying and selling of the shares. There is far less stake in society in this kind of property. After all, a single safe-deposit box can hold many millions of dollars of property, the whole requiring little of the attention and responsibility that are mandatory when property exists in the forms of land, buildings, and machinery. An atmosphere of not only impersonality but irresponsibility is created by evaporated property. . . .

Morality Becomes Expendable

Morals inevitably suffer, meaning particularly the morals of honesty and loyalty to others. Morals are no emanations from heaven; everywhere, from the beginning of conscience in the human race, from the time when the human mind first made the astounding leap from "is" to "ought," what we call morals are firmly set in what the Romans called the mores, customs and habits of age and sanctity. As a result of the disappearance or sharp reduction of the disciplines upon the self which went inescapably with older kinds of property, and of the rise of the present widely spread monetary unit of property—that is, of liquidity, of cash nexus—morality becomes expendable. Who needs it? . . .

Cash Is the Thing

If cash is the real thing instead of land development, factories, manufacturing, and the creation of products and services important to society, then certain other things will automatically assume importance too: frenzied buying and selling in the multitude of markets available in this country and throughout the world, a pronounced turning from product creation to simple ordinary money creation, and, as the record makes plain, leveraged buy-outs, networks of mergers, takeovers, insider tradings legal and illegal, poison pills, golden parachutes, and much else.

In such circumstances the loose individual flourishes. For in an epoch of high liquidity, incessant turnover of shares, and fast-moving takeovers, mobility on the part of the operator is imperative. Those who are mired in tradition, in ancient concepts of trust, honor, and loyalty to house will be losers. Looseness of economic muscle is indispensable. "Conservative" was once an accolade to a bank or brokerage house. Today it is anathema. . . .

The cash nexus is the thing! Why build an industry when you can, if you are slick and agile enough, take one over—with junk bonds, if necessary—and then sell it off at the very second the value of the shares reaches a proper point on the market. Such slick agility doesn't help posterity but, as the congressman once asked, what has posterity done for me? What is astounding is the relative ease of the operation. If there is resolute opposition on the part of the management of the corporation being raided, it will almost certainly pay greenmail to the raider, thus ending the threat of takeover and paying off with profits even more easily accumulated than the raider had thought. At all times, of course, looseness is vital to survival. . . .

The Money Society

Money, money, money is the incantation of today. Bewitched by an epidemic of money enchantment, Americans in the Eighties wriggle in a St. Vitus's dance of materialism unseen since the Gilded Age or the Roaring Twenties. Under the blazing sun of money, all other values shine palely. And the M&A decade acclaims but one breed of hero: He's the honcho with the condo and the limo and the Miró and lots and lots of dough. . . .

An overwhelming 93% of surveyed teenage girls deemed shopping their favorite pastime, way ahead of sixth-rated dating. Back in 1967, around 40% of U.S. college freshmen told pollsters that it was important to them to be very well off financially, as against around 80% who listed developing a meaningful philosophy of life as an important objective. But by 1986 the numbers had reversed, with almost 80% aspiring plutocrats as against 40% philosophers. . . .

The money society has expanded to fill the vacuum left after the institutions that embodied and nourished those values—community, religion, school, university, and especially family—sagged or collapsed or sometimes even self-destructed.

Now we live in a world where all values are relative, equal, and therefore without authority, truly matters of mere style. Says Dee Hock, former chief of the Visa bank-card operation: "It's not that people value money more but that they value everything else so much less—not that they are more greedy but that they have no other values to keep greed in check. They don't know what else to value." Or as University of Pennsylvania sociologist E. Digby Baltzell puts it: "When there are no values, money counts."

Myron Magnet, *Fortune*, July 6, 1987.

Everyone wants to be rich but, equally important, loose in his relationship to anything—equities, family, church, lodge, whatever. In such a scene even the rich don't feel rich. Money becomes its own end, thus leading to a kind of contempt that lies uneasily inside the narcotic-like fascination of money. . . .

One more note on loose individuals and the cash nexus. Even treason has lately moved from ideology to cash. Recall that when the physicist Klaus Fuchs stole almost the entirety of the atom bomb secrets from Britain and America, he did so for love of Communism and the Soviet Union alone. Today, as the recent Walker case demonstrates, treason and treachery are strictly cash on the barrelhead. How loose can you get?

Cash in the Universities

The loose individual prowls the halls of academe as well as Wall Street these days. What is wrong with the contemporary university will not be made right by encounter sessions on Aristotle and Rousseau under the banner of Great Books; nor will it be improved by general smatterings courses aiming to produce the well-informed mind. . . .

Within months of Pearl Harbor campuses rang to the sound of uniformed recruits hup-hupping their marched and ordered way from class to class, building to building. Dormitories overnight became military barracks.

More significant by far was the militarization of research in the universities. This could involve structural change in the university. For centuries research was individual, self-chosen, and responsible only to the audience for which it was done. But of a sudden in early World War II the Project came into being, to transform university research forever. The Project was financed by the government, labeled and code-numbered by the government, and usually declared secret by the government. The Manhattan Project, which yielded up the atom bomb, is perhaps the most celebrated, but there were—and are to this day—thousands of others. Today they are typically known as institutes, bureaus, and centers. They net lots of dollars. . . .

Once the big money, in the form of project and institute research, invaded the campus, two nations tended to form in every faculty: the first, institute- and project-linked, arrogant in its possession of money that required no sense of obligation to the academic community; and the second, older nation, still committed to the ideal of *teaching* as well as research and to the hoary concept of *service*. The new nation easily subjugated the old everywhere. . . .

Cash in Sports

The cash nexus and loose individual have many haunts beyond Wall Street and the Multiversity. It is not easy to think of a major pursuit in America in which monetary units have not yet triumphed over the motivations and discipline of old. Three, eminently diverse, areas come to mind: sports, religion, and government service.

In sports a significant evolution of power has taken place since World War I: We have seen the original amateur—once a term of honor in our society—succeeded by the professional, the respectable professional, it should be said; then by the agent, ever solicitous of his client's income and investments and, of course, his own percentage. Sports have become as conspicuous and flagrant an example of the profit motive and the bottom line as any commercial operation known. But sports are something else: a secular religion in America, one that ranks only just behind education, which is by now a civil religion. . . .

The cash nexus threatens to outstrip anything found in corporate America and on Wall Street. We honor the free agent who, having had the chains of serfdom struck off, is now at liberty to run from one team to another as fancy and financial reward determine. We are glad to see him reach the position of hanging loosely on the sport. But fans identify powerfully with *teams*, and the greatest of individual heroes from Babe Ruth and Ty Cobb down to Walter Payton and Lawrence Taylor are linked with given teams as closely as with their own names. We all know that money is important in the form of salaries, bonuses, and other forms of remuneration, but we also know that, just as it is impossible to glean genuine heroes from the ranks of stockbrokers, bankers, salesmen, and vice-presidents for production, it becomes more and more difficult to keep one's mind on the performance of a Dave Winfield on the baseball diamond when rivaling it are the lush details of his latest contract—in the millions naturally, and made a little more interesting perhaps by the division into present income, deferred income, options, a special trust, and even, so help us, a foundation in his name. What confounds some of us is that all this is printed on the once-sacrosanct sports page, not the financial. . . .

Cash in Religion

Turning to religion, more particularly to the large and extremely important part of it that exists on the airwaves, radio and television alike, we are also confronted by a passion for gold and a looseness of ethics that have little to do with religion as it was once understood, and is still understood by a large number of Americans. Churches become gaudier; their ancillary activities, ranging from elaborate hostelries for unwed mothers all the way to Disneyland types of entertainment facilities—income tax-exempt, of course—more numerous and generally profit-making; and their campaigns for gifts of money more fevered all the time. When you turn the televangelist on, you find yourself making mental bets as to just how long he will be able to restrain the plea, demand, threat, as the case may be, for money and more money the while he discourses on God and love of fellow man.

Seemingly there is nothing too crass, vulgar, and avaricious for some parts of the Christian ministry today. Anything, *anything*, is allowable if it can be counted on to yield cash and profit: whether an Oral Roberts threatening his television audience with his own death for want of eight million dollars—which, for good or ill, he got in time—or Jim and Tammy Bakker lolling in the luxury of the garden of one of their several homes, now preaching but only a little, now weeping just a little, now kissing a little, all the while beseeching their television congregation to send more money in—to add yet another thrill to their Heritage USA Theme Park in North Carolina, which is something less than Disneyland but something a great deal more than your garden-variety carnival. . . .

Cash in Government Service

It was once thought that government service as a career, whether military or nonmilitary, was its own reward: in stability, security, and ultimate pension. One did not go into government service if his life's aim was that of making money. That too was once thought—but no longer. True, it is still impossible to earn or otherwise make sizable sums of money while actually in service, but for almost any admiral or general or civilian equivalent in the nonmilitary areas of government, there is a great deal of money to be had by cannily biding one's time. To see the government career not as a service or calling but rather as a necessary preface to the real career in business, books, lectures, articles, etc., with very high rewards almost guaranteed, *that* is the way to have one's cake and eat it too. . . .

The revolving door between government and corporate America works overtime in the present age, in this late part of the age. Occasionally, greed becomes so imperious that a decent wait of a year or so between status of secretary or White House aide and that of entrepreneur becomes mentally and physically impossible to endure. Then, with a mighty huffing and puffing, the wheels of justice begin turning; special prosecutors may be appointed, subcommittees of Congress set up, and so forth. Rarely, though, is anyone seriously impeded as he rushes through the revolving door. The word *unethical* has become, in our loose society, quite possibly the single most difficult word to define in the American language. . . .

Our society and culture today are manifestly closer to the complete cash nexus, the total monetary regime, than they were at the beginning of the century. Sharp, unethical, self-serving practices are, or so the vast bulk of ongoing journalism and social criticism tells us, no longer limited to the ranks of those living on the margins of society. Such once-common and respected exclamations as "You have my word on it," "It's a matter of honor for me," "No contract is needed between friends" would today invite derision for the most part.

"Much of what passes for high-visibility heroism today is morally neutral. Society can no longer distinguish between right and wrong."

America Must Rediscover Heroism

Dick Keyes

Dick Keyes, the director of L'Abri Fellowship in Southborough, Massachusetts, is the author of *Beyond Identity* and is currently working on a book about heroism. In the following viewpoint, he claims heroes provide meaning for society by identifying and personifying important values and character traits. Today's heroes, in his opinion, are not really symbols that embody important meaning for society. They are only celebrities who are morally neutral. Aside from their fame, they represent little in the way of traditional values worthy of emulation.

As you read, consider the following questions:

1. Why does the author claim Americans' lost belief in an "invisible world" has destroyed their ability to establish heroes?
2. What point does he make when stating that America now reveres celebrities rather than heroes?
3. Why does he think heroes are necessary?

Dick Keyes, "Lite Champions," *Christianity Today*, May 13, 1988. Reprinted with permission.

Nowadays heroes come and go with alarming frequency. Oliver North is a goat one day, a hero the next. And so it is with Gary Hart, Jim and Tammy Bakker, and hordes of other politicians, Christian figures, athletes, and entertainers. Have we reached Andy Warhol's society of the future when everyone will be famous—but only for 15 minutes?

Heroes Identify Society's Values

Americans have always taken heroes seriously, and rightly so. Heroes, whether we are aware of it or not, focus the human imagination and thereby shape the lives and personalities of their admirers. Public heroes also provide coherence at a deep level to the society of which they are a part. This is what makes our present confusion about heroes particularly troubling. How can they exert this influence if they rise and fall, inflate and deflate like soap bubbles on the wind? It is no small thing when the heroes of a society are in disarray, because heroism touches the human spirit deeply at so many levels—the psychological, the sociological, and the theological.

You can see the psychological importance of heroism early in a child's life. Think of the hats a child puts on—those of the nurse, the fire chief, the soldier. Long before a child is aware of abstract moral rules, he or she has a fertile imagination and wants to be like certain kinds of people and unlike others.

Even as we grow older, we are motivated not just by rules and laws, but by stories, by images of flesh-and-blood people who have lived in a way we find admirable and attractive.

On a social level, we do not need to look far to see the significance that people like Elizabeth I, Washington, Lincoln, Churchill, and Gandhi had for their respective countries. (Of course, on the dark side of heroism, there was Hitler, who was probably the most skilled architect of a hero system in our century.) . . .

Heroism is not dead in our society, but it has been besieged by two powerful forces: cynicism and trivialization. Together they bring about a crisis of the imagination that has deeply affected our society.

Cynicism Undermines Heroism

We are living at a time when the very word *hero* has come to carry cynical connotations. Many loud and learned voices are claiming there is no such thing as human greatness at all, and there never was. There has been a widespread loss of confidence that meaning for human life can ever be expressed in words. This is obviously devastating, because heroes must be heroic in terms of meanings, values, or standards—without which their heroism would be indistinguishable from villainy or random behavior. If the foundation for meaning is cut away, the human need for heroism will shrivel up in boredom and alienation. Or it will hang in mid-air, waiting to attach itself to the fragmented, arbitrary, and sometimes fanatical meanings that either individuals will create for themselves, or charismatic leaders will prefabricate for them.

The existentialist Ernest Becker has given an incisive thumbnail sketch of the history of meaning. He points out that for all of known civilization, people have believed in two worlds: one that you could see, and one that was invisible. They lived in the visible world, but they believed in the unseen world, in which lived spirits, hobgoblins, gods, goddesses, and God. The invisible world provided the basis for meaning and value, and hence, for what was heroic. It was the source of cohesion for their society. However, about the middle of the last century, people began to be told that there was no invisible world. It did not exist and never had. They were living a lie.

Becker then looks at what happened to heroism as a result. Once the door to the invisible world was closed and barred, we had to derive a sense of the heroic from the visible, tangible, material world.

Why We Need Heroes

The hero overcomes the ordinary and attains greatness by serving some great good. His example very nearly rebukes us; telling us that we fail, not by aiming too high in life, but by aiming far too low. Moreover, it tells us we are mistaken in supposing that happiness is a right or an end in itself. The hero seeks not happiness but goodness and his fulfillment lies in achieving it. . . .

This is why we need heroes so desperately. By deed and symbol, they replenish our spiritual strength: They are tangible proof that man does not live by reason alone—that he has a moral conscience which is divinely inspired, that he may freely choose virtue over sin, heroism over cowardice or resignation.

George Roche, *Imprimis*, August 1986.

He writes in *The Birth and Death of Meaning*: "People no longer drew their power from the invisible dimension, but from intensive manipulation of very visible Ferraris and other material gadgets. They try to find their whole fulfillment in a sex partner or an endless succession of partners, or in their children."

Suddenly the theater of heroism has shrunk. There is nothing beyond ourselves to which we correspond except the vast impersonal. Lost is God and the moral and heroic absolutes that made sense under his reign, and with it the idea of distinctive human dignity. The British philosopher C.E.M. Joad put it well: "Although

83

there was scientific basis for saying that man was the highest primate, there was none for placing him outside the animal kingdom in the matter of unique rights; he was only the star performer in the zoo. Suppose, then, someone put him in a cage or made a slave of him; was there any biological or sociological law which said this could not be done?"

Admittedly, we do different tricks than the other animals in the zoo. But unless there is a God in whose image we are made, all our higher ideals for justice, goodness, and beauty are just pretensions, mirages in the consciousness of the human animal. At the philosophical level, there is therefore little confidence in human distinctiveness, let alone heroism.

The Sciences Contribute to Cynicism

The human sciences have also made a major contribution to cynicism about human greatness, especially as they treat the subjects of motivation and freedom. We are told that human choice is not what it appears to be. If we accept the sophistications of some views of psychology, we know that what appears to be heroic—for example, a man or woman's act of courage in saving another's life—is, in fact, a desperate attempt to win the approval of a long-dead parent who had withheld love in the childhood years. What, then, has become of the hero? He or she is transformed in our minds into a neurotic, and with a slight turn of the mind, admiration is changed to pity and condescension.

Psychoanalysis has always been a great equalizer of people. This, of course, puts it at loggerheads with heroism, which by definition gives attention to what is extraordinary. The influence of Freud, although great in psychology and psychiatry, may have been even more pervasive in literature, history, and the arts in general. He set a pattern in his early study of Leonardo da Vinci when he explained that da Vinci's extraordinary creativity could be accounted for by his repressed homosexual desires. As an "in-closet" homosexual, such psychic energy was built up inside him that it was sublimated into his artistic and engineering accomplishments.

By this psychoanalytic method, any heroic act can be seen to have self-serving, even sordid roots. We are left with our attention fixed on the internal crippling of a person, and we are thoroughly uninspired by that person's genius.

Space does not allow a survey of the debunking strands in psychology, sociology, history, anthropology, sociobiology, and economics. Despite the many helpful contributions these fields have made, there has been a tendency to see individuals as only products of intrapsychic, socioeconomic, or biological forces beyond their control. These factors eclipse the drama of life—stories with unfolding narratives of agonizing choice and action.

In the name of science and under the aura of its authority and sophistication, some of the work in these disciplines simply obscures those things most important and most admirable in human existence.

The Trivialization of Heroes

The second great force besieging heroism today is trivialization. While the acid of cynicism dissolves the very idea of the heroic, the force of trivialization at first seems to be blowing the horn for the heroic. On closer observation, however, we discover trivialization dilutes heroism. It contributes just as much as cynicism to the loss of the heroic. The media are prime culprits. In his landmark work, *The Image*, Daniel Boorstin complains that we have exchanged heroes for celebrities. While a hero is someone who has done something great or honorable and therefore commands respect, a celebrity is "known for his well-knownness" and is envied for it. He is the "human pseudo-event."

Trivialization takes two forms. First, true heroes are trivialized. Second, trivial people are inflated to heroic status.

Charles Lindbergh was one of the first heroes to be trivialized by the news media's power. His flight was extraordinary, but relatively uncomplicated—insufficient to satisfy the public's hunger for information about him. Therefore, his rise to fame itself became the focus of the news, with all the complications and tragedy that it brought to his life. What the press had made of him was more newsworthy than what he actually did, and hero became celebrity.

More recently, Lenny Skutnik, the man who rescued a woman from the icy Potomac River after the Air Florida plane crash, observed the same thing. After he had appeared on television beside Nancy Reagan at the State of the Union address, he reported that when people would come to him they no longer asked, "Hey, aren't you the guy who jumped in the river and saved the lady?" but instead, "Hey, aren't you the guy who was on the State of the Union?"

Today's Heroes Are Only Famous People

The second form of trivialization—inflating superficial people to heroic status—is more destructive. It provides us with a new cast of fascinating people each week, and with fame as the central virtue. *The National Enquirer* is always ready to feed our inquiring minds, and *People Weekly* magazine to keep us abreast of the most recent divorces and indictments among celebrities. In a recent study of the top ten American heroes, seven were in show business, and most were considered not so much for who they were but for their stage or celluloid images. Much of what is admired actually does not exist except in the form of image. Like the dehydrated desert wanderer, we are navigating by mirages.

This is very serious. Today's heroism is one of style, not of character, where the important points are driving a Mercedes or BMW, and wearing Calvin Klein or Ralph Lauren fashions. Even in the "serious" world of politics, what seems to matter is physical appearance, an attractive family, and a quotable quip on every current issue. (Of course, for someone who wants to be a celebrity badly enough, that is always possible. All one needs to do is to shoot a famous person.)

Not only are certain individuals trivialized, but heroism itself has become superficial. As long ago as 1959, Earl Blackwell and Cleveland Amory compiled the voluminous *Celebrity Register*. In it the television comedienne Dagmar was listed beside the Dalai Lama, Anita Ekberg beside Dwight Eisenhower, and Jane Russell beside Bertrand Russell.

As long as fame is the highest value, we cannot make important distinctions between celebrities and true heroes. Could it be that some of our televangelists have pulled God himself into the triviality of America's consumer culture, where faith is a commodity and theology is lite—all for your entertainment pleasure?

Today's Heroes Are Morally Neutral

Although the forces of cynicism and trivialization seem to start off in opposite directions, they in fact feed each other. The more cynical one is, the more life seems to be trivial. The more life seems trivial, the more cynicism is justified. There is a symbiotic relationship between the two, the result of which makes it very difficult to develop a healthy sense of heroism.

The heroism that survives the acid of cynicism and the inflation-deflation cycles of trivialization is apt to be a heroism out of reach of the vast majority of people. This is because there is no modern transcendent source of meaning. As long as heroism is linked to moral character, it can provide a focus of aspiration for common people, for the possibility of moral choice is available to any of us. But much of what passes for high-visibility heroism today is morally neutral. Society can no longer distinguish between right and wrong. . . .

If we follow the heroics of Clint Eastwood or James Bond, we will end up dead or in jail. What if (like the vast majority of us) our physical endowments are such that the heroism of beauty or professional sports is simply not an option? Or how many of us can be rock music stars? Wealth and its accouterments may be a little more accessible, but they are still unavailable to most people.

What we have is a heroism that has a different function than it used to have. The hero was once a focal point for aspiration, but this is no longer realistically the case. After initial short-lived aspiration, the modern hero is apt to produce two responses—

daydreaming and self-hatred. We daydream about what life would be like if we walked in the shoes of the hero, but we detest ourselves for falling so far short. . . .

Admiration without aspiration ends ultimately in frustration. My life seems so dull compared to Clint Eastwood's roles. This turns easily to compensatory heroism: using a hero not to aspire to, but, by a vicarious voyage of identity, to silence the need for aspiration. The compensatory hero does not fire our ideals; he compensates for our lack of ideals. He or she reduces us to obedient little people, because we are without any imaginative moral vision that could call us to break with conformity. This, not true religion, is the opiate of the masses, leaving us easy victims to the seductions of the consumer culture.

As columnist Russell Baker said of *Raiders of the Lost Ark*, "you want to make sure nobody in the audience thinks you're an outdated sap who really believes in swashbuckling. So you keep winking at the audience by making the whole thing so preposterous that they'll know you're only kidding." Heroes like Indiana Jones are often held up as proof that true heroism remains. In fact, they are only attempts to have one's cake and eat it too— to get an imaginative charge out of a story, but still preserve a basic cynicism.

Conclusion

True heroes challenge the excuse-laden mediocrity of our lives and open us to new possibilities of what we might be. As such, they are uncomfortable to live with and are often unwanted. If we can debunk or trivialize them, we give ourselves a reprieve from their challenge and from the shame of our shortfall. This reprieve is one of the payoffs of the cynic or, in biblical language, the scoffer. However, there are great losses involved that we are only now beginning to see. C.S. Lewis wrote that "in trying to extirpate shame we have broken down one of the ramparts of the human spirit, madly exulting in the work as the Trojans exulted when they broke their walls and pulled the horse into Troy."

In a world without heroes, there is no shame, but neither is there glory and honor or a positive moral imagination. Time will tell whether the Trojan horse is already in the city or not. The 1987 Fourth of July edition of *Newsweek* celebrated everyday heroes from each of the 50 states. It was moving in that they were selected because they were unknown, and they cared in imaginative and costly ways—usually about other people less fortunate than themselves. It is gratifying that these are *Newsweek*'s heroes, but it is less encouraging when we realize that there are other "heroic virtues" that have left larger footprints on the American imagination. The advertisements within that same magazine predictably show that it is in fact beauty, talent, money, and power that are considered to be the real motivating levers to human action.

87

Ranking American Heroes

This activity will give you an opportunity to see what values you and your classmates consider important by ranking the American heroes listed below. A person's choice of heroes and the reasons for his or her choice should give some insight into what is considered personally important.

© King Features Syndicate 1975

Part 1

Step 1.   The class should break into groups of four to six students.

Step 2.   Working individually within each group, each student should rank the Americans listed below, assigning the number 1 to the person whose lifestyle is most admired, the number 2 to the next most admired, and so on, until all Americans have been ranked.

Step 3.   Each student should compare his or her ranking with others in the group, giving the reasons for their ranking.

Step 4.   The class as a whole should rank the American heroes, using the same procedure as in step 2.

American Heroes

_____ Tom Cruise (movie star)
_____ Jane Fonda (actress and political activist)
_____ Ronald Reagan (former president of the United States)
_____ Ralph Nader (spokesperson for the American consumer)
_____ Jesse Jackson (political activist)
_____ Sandra Day O'Connor (first female supreme court justice)
_____ Lee Iacocca (president of Chrysler Corporation)
_____ Eddie Murphy (comic and entertainer)
_____ Phyllis Schlafly (social and political activist)
_____ Alice Walker (poet, author of _The Color Purple_)
_____ William Buckley (publisher of _National Review_)
_____ Edward Kennedy (US senator from Massachusetts)
others _____
       _____
       _____

Part 2

Working in either small groups of four to six students, or all together, the class should discuss the Beetle Bailey cartoon.

1. What commentary is it making about television heroes?
2. Do you agree with the cartoon's message?
3. Are television heroes true examples of people most Americans admire?
4. How do Americans determine their heroes?

"My proposal is for the revival or reassertion of personal responsibility in all human acts, good and bad."

America Must Rediscover Sin

Karl Menninger

Karl Menninger, psychiatrist, teacher, philosopher, and crusader for penal reform, is cofounder of the Menninger Clinic and Menninger Foundation in Topeka, Kansas. He is also the author of several influential books, including *The Human Mind, The Crime of Punishment,* and *Whatever Became of Sin?* In the following viewpoint written almost two decades ago, Dr. Menninger delivers a message that is still as relevant as today's newspaper. Dr. Menninger contends that many of society's ills can be traced to an excessive concern with the self and the disappearance of the concept of sin. He states that a refusal to accept responsibility for individual human acts has contributed to the moral dilemmas facing American society.

As you read, consider the following questions:

1. What does Dr. Menninger mean when he claims sin has disappeared in American society?
2. What does he refer to when he uses the term sin?
3. What does he propose?

Karl Menninger, *Whatever Became of Sin* (New York: Hawthorn Books, Inc., 1973), pp. 8-17, 46, 178. Reprinted by permission of Hawthorn Books, Inc. from *Whatever Became of Sin?* by Karl Menninger, M.D. Copyright © 1973 by Karl Menninger, M.D. All rights reserved.

91

''**W**hat ails the American spirit?'' an editor asked of some of our seers. ''It is the age of rubbish,'' answered one. ''Religion just doesn't play the role it used to play. . . .Few other things. . . can hold the culture together. . . . Young people don't have anything that they want to do. . . .they haven't decided what they want their lives to say.''

''The malaise of the American spirit,'' declared a professor of government, ''cannot be blamed on wrong-headed policies, inept administrations, or even an inability to understand the dimensions of our current discontents. The reasons are more fundamental. . .arising from the kind of people we have become. . . .We cannot bring ourselves to make the personal sacrifices required to sustain domestic order or international authority.''. . .

Daniel J. Boorstin, director of the National Museum of Science and Technology at the Smithsonian Institution, puts our current situation this way: ''. . .we have lost our sense of history. . . .lost our traditional respect for the wisdom of ancestors and the culture of kindred nations. . . . Flooded by screaming headlines and hourly televised 'news' melodramas of dissent and 'revolution,' we haunt ourselves with the illusory ideal of some 'whole nation' which had a deep and outspoken 'faith' in its 'values.' ''. . .

Well, that's what some of our prophets are saying today. The reporters wrote it down for all to read. Many others have spoken and written similarly. . . .

The Disappearance of Sin

In all of the laments and reproaches made by our seers and prophets, one misses any mention of ''sin,'' a word which used to be a veritable watchword of prophets. It was a word once in everyone's mind, but now rarely if ever heard. Does that mean that no sin is involved in all our troubles—sin with an ''I'' in the middle? Is no one any longer guilty of anything? Guilty perhaps of a sin that could be repented and repaired or atoned for? Is it only that someone may be stupid or sick or criminal—or asleep? Wrong things are being done, we know; tares are being sown in the wheat field at night. But is no one responsible, no one answerable for these acts? Anxiety and depression we all acknowledge, and even vague guilt feelings; but has no one committed any sins?

Where, indeed, did sin go? What became of it?

Lt. William Calley was portrayed to the world as a bloody villain, in both the English and American senses of that adjective. He slaughtered helpless women and babies with the hypocritical justification that they might be carrying concealed explosives. He was formally accused and tried for military disobedience as well as murder before a jury of peers who had been engaged in the same business of military destruction, and

92

The Sin of Affluence

"It is preoccupation with possession," said Bertrand Russell "more than anything else that prevents men from living freely and nobly."

This was a profound conclusion by a very wise man; does it receive any serious consideration?. . .

Greed, with other symptoms, is frequently seen—not treated! The sense of helplessness which this propensity in a patient choked by his great possessions can arouse in a therapist is great. Two of my former patients come to mind. One, whose annual income was over a million dollars, was brought by relatives for treatment after he had made an attempt at suicide. Life, he said, no longer held anything of interest for him. "And I haven't the slightest idea," he said, "what to do with all my money. I don't need it, but I can't bear to give any away."

"So you decide to kill yourself," I asked, "in order to get away from it?"

"Well, what else can I do?" he replied weakly.

"Could you establish a memorial to your beloved father, endowing certain art forms in the smaller cities over the country, all named for him?"

"Oh," he said, brightening, "that would be wonderful! He would have loved that. Sure, I could do it, easily. I would enjoy it. It would honor him, well, both of us, forever. Let me think about it. I might just do that."

But he didn't. He didn't do anything. He existed for a few more years, then died, prematurely, to the satisfaction of his heirs and business associates who were not yet in his predicament, although they suffered from the same "disease."

I remember another patient who would become very angry when approached by anyone for a contribution to a cause.

"Why should I give what I have to others?" he demanded. "It's mine. I'm no socialist. I earned this—some of it—and I'm keeping it, not sharing it. It is mine, I tell you."

"But," I reminded him, "you are very unhappy with it. And you are very lonely. You have no heirs. You could make many people happier, including yourself, by disbursing some of it. Why be Mr. Scrooge?"

But he, too, went away sorrowing, for he, too, had great possessions. That was twenty years ago. He is still an unhappy Scrooge, still "in treatment" with one of my colleagues for the relief of all sorts of symptoms other than greed.

Karl Menninger, *Whatever Became of Sin?*

he was found guilty.

But a great cry went up from the people. Many sectors of the general public angrily disputed the possibility that what Calley did could be properly labeled a crime. Indeed, many would not concede that he even committed a sin or made a mistake. He had obeyed orders (they said); he had done what everyone wanted done or was doing, and it was for the sake of a great righteousness. Some might (and did) find him technically guilty of a crime, but what he did was right; it was no sin. It was a glorious, patriotic deed.

The Sixth Commandment, "Thou shalt not kill," obviously made a tacit exception of bullocks, lambs, Indians, Philistines, and Viet Cong. Every slayer can find reasons for making his particular violation an exception, a non-crime if not a non-sin. Hitler had his reasons for killing the Jews. Custer had his reasons for killing the Sioux. Our military men had reasons for killing Viet Cong soldiers, and the Viet Cong had their reasons for killing ours. Under certain circumstances purposive killing is frequently declared, by one side or another, to be a non-crime. But is it ever a non-sin? Or, is nothing now a sin?

Avoidance of the Word

The very word "sin," which seems to have disappeared, was a proud word. It was once a strong word, an ominous and serious word. It described a central point in every civilized human being's life plan and life style. But the word went away. It has almost disappeared—the word, along with the notion. Why? Doesn't anyone sin anymore? Doesn't anyone believe in sin?. . .

What Do You Mean by "Sin"?

"Now, Dr. Karl. You ought to define that word. What do you mean by 'sin'?" All kinds of things have been called sin in times past. It has been used as a scarehead for controlling the ignorant for centuries. But just what have you in mind? What kind of sin do you mean? Carnal sin? Mortal sin? Venial sin? Original sin? Existential sin?"

I could counter with, "What *was* the sin that no longer exists?" I mean any kind of wrongdoing that we used to call sin. I have in mind behavior that violates the moral code or the individual conscience or both; behavior which pains or harms or destroys my neighbor—or me, myself. You know, and *Time* knows—what wrongdoing is, and if a better word than sin is available, use it. . . .

I believe there is "sin" which is expressed in ways which cannot be subsumed under verbal artifacts such as "crime," "disease," "delinquency," "deviancy." There *is* immorality; there *is* unethical behavior; there *is* wrongdoing. And I hope to show that there is usefulness in retaining the concept, and in-

94

deed the word, SIN, which now shows some signs of returning to public acceptance. I would like to help this trend along. . . .

My proposal is for the revival or reassertion of personal responsibility in all human acts, good and bad. Not total responsibility, but not zero either. I believe that all evildoing in which we become involved to any degree tends to evoke guilt feelings and depression. These may or may not be clearly perceived, but they affect us. They may be reacted to and covered up by all kinds of escapism, rationalization, and reaction or symptom formation. To revive the half-submerged idea of personal responsibility and to seek appropriate measures of reparation might turn the tide of our aggressions and of the moral struggle in which much of the world population is engaged.

We will see our world dilemmas more and more as expressing *internal* personal moral problems instead of seeing them only as *external*, social, legal, or environmental complexities.

> *"We have committed what to the republican founders of our nation was the cardinal sin: we have put our own good . . . ahead of the common good."*

America Must Rediscover Its Traditions

Robert N. Bellah, et al.

The following viewpoint is taken from the book *Habits of the Heart*, coauthored by Robert N. Bellah and a team of scholars from a variety of disciplines. The authors interviewed over two hundred individuals in an attempt to determine how Americans make sense of their lives and how they think of themselves and their society. In this study of American values, goals, purposes, and attitudes, the authors conclude that the country's historical preoccupation with individualism has had a cancerous effect on the common good. They call for a revitalization of the Biblical and republican roots that form the foundation of American culture. Unless Americans reawaken their traditional communal memories, the authors warn, unchecked individualism could lead to a loss of freedom.

As you read, consider the following questions:

1. In the authors' opinion, how has individualism weakened American culture?
2. To what do the authors refer when using the phrase the litmus test of Biblical and republican traditions?

Robert N. Bellah, et al., *Habits of the Heart*. Berkeley, CA: The University of California Press, 1985. © 1985 The Regents of the University of California.

How ought we to live? How do we think about how to live? Who are we, as Americans? What is our character? These are questions we have asked our fellow citizens in many parts of the country. We engaged them in conversations about their lives and about what matters most to them, talked about their families and communities, their doubts and uncertainties, and their hopes and fears with respect to the larger society. . . .

The fundamental question we posed, and that was repeatedly posed to us, was how to preserve or create a morally coherent life. But the kind of life we want depends on the kind of people we are—on our character. Our inquiry can thus be located in a longstanding discussion of the relationship between character and society. In the eighth book of the *Republic*, Plato sketched a theory of the relationship between the moral character of a people and the nature of its political community, the way it organizes and governs itself. The founders of the American republic at the time of the Revolution adopted a much later version of the same theory. Since for them, as for the Americans with whom we talked, freedom was perhaps the most important value, they were particularly concerned with the qualities of character necessary for the creation of a free republic.

Habits of the Heart

In the 1830s, the French social philosopher Alexis de Tocqueville offered the most comprehensive and penetrating analysis of the relationship between character and society in America that has ever been written. In his book *Democracy in America*, based on acute observation and wide conversation with Americans, Tocqueville described the mores—which he on occasion called "habits of the heart"—of the American people and showed how they helped to form American character. He singled out family life, our religious traditions, and our participation in local politics as helping to create the kind of person who could sustain a connection to a wider political community and thus ultimately support the maintenance of free institutions. He also warned that some aspects of our character—what he was one of the first to call "individualism"—might eventually isolate Americans one from another and thereby undermine the conditions of freedom.

The central problem of our book concerns the American individualism that Tocqueville described with a mixture of admiration and anxiety. It seems to us that it is individualism, and not equality, as Tocqueville thought, that has marched inexorably through our history. We are concerned that this individualism may have grown cancerous—that it may be destroying those social integuments that Tocqueville saw as moderating its more destructive potentialities, that it may be threatening the survival of freedom itself. . . .

Much of the thinking about our society and where it should be going is rather narrowly focussed on our political economy. This focus makes sense in that government and the corporations are the most powerful structures in our society and affect everything else, including our culture and our character. But as an exclusive concern, such a focus is severely limited. . . .

America was colonized by those who had come loose from the older European structures, and so from the beginning we had a head start in the process of modernization. Yet the colonists brought with them ideas of social obligation and group formation that disposed them to recreate in America structures of family, church, and polity that would continue, if in modified form, the texture of older European society. Only gradually did it become clear that every social obligation was vulnerable, every tie between individuals fragile. Only gradually did what we have called onto-logical individualism, the idea that the individual is the only firm reality, become widespread. Even in our day, when separation and individuation have reached a kind of culmination, their triumph is far from complete. The battles of modernity are still being fought.

An Agenda for America

As an agenda for reconstituting the American experiment and for salvaging an economic system bogged down in a deadly cultural swamp, three propositions seem self-evident:

1. An ethic of self-denial, with historic religious roots, is the only cultural foundation upon which the American economy can rebuild.

2. Patriotic sentiment, or a sense of common identity and involve-ment in a common enterprise, necessitates a significant degree of value agreement.

3. The ancient "republican virtues" as adapted by the modern middle class—self-sacrifice for family and community, the exercise of civic duty, the love of social equity and human dignity, and a preference for the public interest to one's own—remain the indis-pensable bulwark of a free and prosperous people.

Alan C. Carlson, *Persuasion at Work*, December 1982.

But today the battles have become half-hearted. There was a time when, under the battle cry of "freedom," separation and in-dividuation were embraced as the key to a marvelous future of unlimited possibility. . . .

There is a widespread feeling that the promise of the modern era is slipping away from us. A movement of enlightenment and liberation that was to have freed us from superstition and tyranny has led in the twentieth century to a world in which ideological fanaticism and political oppression have reached extremes unknown in previous history. Science, which was to have unlocked the bounties of nature, has given us the power to destroy all life on the earth. Progress, modernity's master idea, seems less compelling when it appears that it may be progress into the abyss. And the globe today is divided between a liberal world so incoherent that it seems to be losing the significance of its own ideals, an oppressive and archaic communist statism, and a poor, and often tyrannical, Third World reaching for the very first rungs of modernity. In the liberal world, the state, which was supposed to be a neutral nightwatchman that would maintain order while individuals pursued their various interests, has become so overgrown and militarized that it threatens to become a universal policeman. . . .

America's Biblical and Republican Traditions

If we are not entirely a mass of interchangeable fragments within an aggregate, if we are in part qualitatively distinct members of a whole, it is because there are still operating among us, with whatever difficulties, traditions that tell us about the nature of the world, about the nature of society, and about who we are as people. Primarily biblical and republican, these traditions are, as we have seen, important for many Americans and significant to some degree for almost all. Somehow families, churches, a variety of cultural associations, and, even if only in the interstices, schools and universities, do manage to communicate a form of life, a *paideia*, in the sense of growing up in a morally and intellectually intelligible world.

The communities of memory . . . are concerned in a variety of ways to give a qualitative meaning to the living of life, to time and space, to persons and groups. Religious communities, for example, do not experience time in the way the mass media present it—as a continuous flow of qualitatively meaningless sensations. The day, the week, the season, the year are punctuated by an alternation of the sacred and the profane. Prayer breaks into our daily life at the beginning of a meal, at the end of the day, at common worship, reminding us that our utilitarian pursuits are not the whole of life, that a fulfilled life is one in which God and neighbor are remembered first. Many of our religious traditions recognize the significance of silence as a way of breaking the incessant flow of sensations and opening our hearts to the wholeness of being. And our republican tradition, too, has ways of giving form to time, reminding us on particular dates of the great events of our past or of the heroes who helped to teach us what we are as a free people. Even our private family life takes on a shared rhythm with a Thanksgiving dinner or a Fourth of July picnic.

In short, we have never been, and still are not, a collection of private individuals who, except for a conscious contract to create a minimal government, have nothing in common. Our lives make sense in a thousand ways, most of which we are unaware of, because of traditions that are centuries, if not millennia, old. It is these traditions that help us to know that it does make a difference who we are and how we treat one another. Even the mass media, with their tendency to homogenize feelings and sensations, cannot entirely avoid transmitting such qualitative distinctions, in however muted a form.

The Good Old Days

Leading school discipline problems:

1940	Today
Talking	Drug abuse
Chewing gum	Alcohol abuse
Making noise	Pregnancy
Running in the hallways	Suicide
	Rape
Getting out of place in line	Robbery
	Assault
Wearing improper clothing	Burglary
Not putting paper in wastebaskets	Arson
	Bombings

This comparison is the result of a study conducted by the Fullerton, California police department and the California Department of Education.

But if we owe the meaning of our lives to biblical and republican traditions of which we seldom consciously think, is there not the danger that the erosion of these traditions may eventually deprive us of that meaning altogether? Are we not caught between the upper millstone of a fragmented intellectual culture and the nether millstone of a fragmented popular culture? The erosion of meaning and coherence in our lives is not something Americans desire. Indeed, the profound yearning for the idealized small town that we found among most of the people we talked to is a yearning for just such meaning and coherence. But although the yearning for the small town is nostalgia for the irretrievably lost, it is worth considering whether the biblical and republican traditions that small town once embodied can be reappropriated in ways that respond to our present need. Indeed, we would argue that if we are ever to enter that new world that so far has been powerless to be born, it will be through reversing modernity's tendency to obliterate all previous culture. We need to learn again from the cultural riches of the human species and to reappropriate and revitalize those riches so that they can speak to our condition today. . . .

Our Cardinal Sin

For several centuries, we have been embarked on a great effort to increase our freedom, wealth, and power. For over a hundred years, a large part of the American people, the middle class, has imagined that the virtual meaning of life lies in the acquisition of ever-increasing status, income, and authority, from which genuine freedom is supposed to come. Our achievements have been enormous. They permit us the aspiration to become a genuinely humane society in a genuinely decent world, and provide many of the means to attain that aspiration. Yet we seem to be hovering on the very brink of disaster, not only from international conflict but from the internal incoherence of our own society. What has gone wrong? How can we reverse the slide toward the abyss?

In thinking about what has gone wrong, we need to see what we can learn from our traditions, as well as from the best currently available knowledge. What has failed at every level—from the society of nations to the national society to the local community to the family—is integration: we have failed to remember "our community as members of the same body," as John Winthrop put it. We have committed what to the republican founders of our nation was the cardinal sin: we have put our own good, as individuals, as groups, as a nation, ahead of the common good.

The Litmus Test of Our Traditions

The litmus test that both the biblical and republican traditions give us for assaying the health of a society is how it deals with the problem of wealth and poverty. The Hebrew prophets took their stand by the 'anawim, the poor and oppressed, and condemned the rich and powerful who exploited them. The New Testament shows us a Jesus who lived among the 'anawim of his day and who recognized the difficulty the rich would have in responding to his call. Both testaments make it clear that societies sharply divided between rich and poor are not in accord with the will of God. Classic republican theory from Aristotle to the American founders rested on the assumption that free institutions could survive in a society only if there were a rough equality of condition, that extremes of wealth and poverty are incompatible with a republic. Jefferson was appalled at the enormous wealth and miserable poverty that he found in France and was sanguine about our future as a free people only because we lacked such extremes. Contemporary social science has documented the consequences of poverty and discrimination, so that most educated Americans know that much of what makes our world and our neighborhoods unsafe arises from economic and racial inequality. Certainly most of the people to whom we talked would rather live in a safe, neighborly world instead of the one we have.

The Problem of Our Ambivalence

But the solution to our problems remains opaque because of our profound ambivalence. When times are prosperous, we do not mind a modest increase in "welfare." When times are not so prosperous, we think that at least our own successful careers will save us and our families from failure and despair. We are attracted, against our skepticism, to the idea that poverty will be alleviated by the crumbs that fall from the rich man's table, as the Neocapitalist ideology tells us. Some of us often feel, and most of us sometimes feel, that we are only someone if we have "made it" and can look down on those who have not. The American dream is often a very private dream of being the star, the uniquely successful and admirable one, the one who stands out from the crowd of ordinary folk who don't know how. And since we have believed in that dream for a long time and worked very hard to make it come true, it is hard for us to give it up, even though it contradicts another dream that we have—that of living in a society that would really be worth living in.

What we fear above all, and what keeps the new world powerless to be born, is that if we give up our dream of private success for a more genuinely integrated societal community, we will be abandoning our separation and individuation, collapsing into dependence and tyranny. What we find hard to see is that it is the extreme fragmentation of the modern world that really threatens our individuation; that what is best in our separation and individuation, our sense of dignity and autonomy as persons, requires a new integration if it is to be sustained. . . .

On the basis of our interviews, and from what we can observe more generally in our society today, it is not clear that many Americans are prepared to consider a significant change in the way we have been living. The allure of the packaged good life is still strong, though dissatisfaction is widespread. Americans are fairly ingenious in finding temporary ways to counteract the harsher consequences of our damaged social ecology. Livy's words about ancient Rome also apply to us: "We have reached the point where we cannot bear either our vices or their cure." But, as some of the more perceptive of the people to whom we talked believe, the time may be approaching when we will either reform our republic or fall into the hands of despotism, as many republics have done before us.

Our Problems Are Moral Not Political

We still have the capacity to reconsider the course upon which we are embarked. The morally concerned social movement, informed by republican and biblical sentiments, has stood us in good

102

stead in the past and may still do so again. But we have never before faced a situation that called our deepest assumptions so radically into question. Our problems today are not just political. They are moral and have to do with the meaning of life. We have assumed that as long as economic growth continued, we could leave all else to the private sphere. Now that economic growth is faltering and the moral ecology on which we have tacitly depended is in disarray, we are beginning to understand that our common life requires more than an exclusive concern for material accumulation.

Perhaps life is not a race whose only goal is being foremost. Perhaps true felicity does not lie in continually outgoing the next before. Perhaps the truth lies in what most of the world outside the modern West has always believed, namely that there are practices of life, good in themselves, that are inherently fulfilling. Perhaps work that is intrinsically rewarding is better for human beings than work that is only extrinsically rewarded. Perhaps enduring commitment to those we love and civic friendship toward our fellow citizens are preferable to restless competition and anxious self-defense. Perhaps common worship, in which we express our gratitude and wonder in the face of the mystery of being itself, is the most important thing of all. If so, we will have to change our lives and begin to remember what we have been happier to forget.

We will need to remember that we did not create ourselves, that we owe what we are to the communities that formed us, and to what Paul Tillich called "the structure of grace in history" that made such communities possible. We will need to see the story of our life on this earth not as an unbroken success but as a history of suffering as well as joy. We will need to remember the millions of suffering people in the world today and the millions whose suffering in the past made our present affluence possible.

Above all, we will need to remember our poverty. We have been called a people of plenty, and though our per capita GNP has been surpassed by several other nations, we are still enormously affluent. Yet the truth of our condition is our poverty. We are finally defenseless on this earth. Our material belongings have not brought us happiness. Our military defenses will not avert nuclear destruction. Nor is there any increase in productivity or any new weapons system that will change the truth of our condition.

We have imagined ourselves a special creation, set apart from other humans. In the late twentieth century, we see that our poverty is as absolute as that of the poorest of nations. We have attempted to deny the human condition in our quest for power after power. It would be well for us to rejoin the human race, to accept our essential poverty as a gift, and to share our material wealth with those in need.

"We must go back to some of the old ways if we are ever going to truly save our Mother Earth."

America Can Learn from Indian Values

Ed McGaa

Ed McGaa, an Oglala Sioux, lawyer, author, teacher, and former Marine fighter pilot, presents a perspective on American Indian values in this viewpoint. In describing the values of Indian culture, he attacks the stereotype of Indians as pagans, savages, and heathens. Although recognizing the positive contributions made by white culture, he is critical of the greed and destructiveness of white America. He suggests white America could learn much from Indian values.

As you read, consider the following questions:

1. What is the dilemma of the non-Indian world in the author's opinion?
2. Why does Mr. McGaa claim white people migrated to America?
3. What do the four sacred colors of the American Indian stand for? How do the values they represent differ from the values represented by those who worship gold or green as their sacred colors?

Ed McGaa, "The Dilemma of the Non-Indian World. . ." *Dimensions*, Summer, 1973, pp. 14-15. Reprinted with permission from the author.

The dilemma of the non-Indian world is that you have lost respect for your mother—Mother Earth—from whom and where we have all come from.

We all start out in this world as tiny seeds—no different from the trees, the flowers, the winged people, or our animal brothers, the deer, the bear or Tatanka—the buffalo. Every particle of our bodies here today comes from the good things that Mother Earth has put forth.

Mother Earth

This morning at breakfast we took from Mother Earth to live as we have done every day of our lives. But did we thank our Mother Earth for giving us the means to live? The old Indian did. When he drove his horse in near to a buffalo running at full speed across the prairie, he drew his bow string back and as he did so, he said, "Forgive me brother, but my people must live." After he butchered the buffalo, he would take the skull and face it to the setting sun as a thanksgiving and an acknowledgment that all things come from Mother Earth.

The Indian never took more than he needed. Today the buffalo is gone. It is very late, but there is still time to revive and rediscover the old American Indian value of respect for Mother Earth.

You say Ecology. We think the word Mother Earth has a deeper meaning. If we wish to survive, we must respect her. She is very beautiful and already she is showing us signs that she may punish us for not respecting her. Also, we must remember she has been placed in this universe by the one who is all-powerful, the Great Spirit above or Wakontankan—God.

A few hundred years ago, there lived in this land of Minneota—much water—a people, the American Indian, who well knew a respect and value system that enabled him to live here without having to migrate away from his Mother Earth in contrast to the white brother who migrated by the thousands from his Mother Earth because he had developed a different value system from the American Indian.

Carbon dating techniques say we were here for 30,000 to 80,000 years and that if we did migrate, it was because of a natural phenomenon—a glacier—and not because of a social system that had a few rich controlling many, many poor, causing them to migrate as happened in Europe from 1500 to the present. We Indian people say we were always here.

We, the American Indian, had a way of living that enabled us to live within the great complete beauty that only the natural environment can provide. The Indian tribes had a common value system and a commonality of religion without religious animosity that preserved that great beauty that man definitely needs. Our four commandments from the Great Spirit are *Respect for*

Mother Earth, Respect for the Great Spirit, Respect for Fellow Man (we are and will continue to be a nonprejudiced people) and *Respect for Individual Freedom*, provided that individual freedom does not threaten the people, the tribe, or Mother Earth.

Our Sacred Colors

Our four sacred colors are red, yellow, black, and white. They stand for the four directions—red for the east, yellow for the south, black for the west, and white for the north. From the east comes the rising sun and new knowledge from a new day. From the south will come the warming southwinds that will cause our mother to bring forth the good foods and grasses so that we may live. To the west where the sun goes down, the day will end and we will sleep and we will also hold our spirit ceremonies at night, from where we will communicate with the spirit world beyond. From the north will come the white winter snow that will cleanse Mother Earth and put her to sleep so that she may rest and store up energy to provide the beauty and bounty of springtime. We will also create through our arts and crafts during the long winter season.

All good things come from these sacred directions. These sacred directions or four sacred colors also stand for the four races of man—red, white, black, and yellow men. We cannot be a prejudiced people because all men are brothers, because all men have the same mother. You are my white sister and you are my white brother and you are my black brother and my black sister because we have the same mother—Mother Earth. He who is prejudiced and hates another because of his color hates what the Great Spirit has put here. He hates that which is holy and he will be punished even during this lifetime as man will be punished for violating Mother Earth. This is what we Indian people truly believe.

The Great Spirit

We, the Indian people, also believe that the red man was placed in America by the Great Spirit, the white man in Europe, the black man in Africa, and the yellow man in Asia. What about the brown man? The brown man evolved from the sacred colors coming together. Look at our Mother Earth. She, too, is brown because the four directions have come together. After the Great Spirit, Wakontankan, placed them in their respective areas, he appeared to them in a different manner and taught them ways so that they might live in harmony and true beauty. Some men, some tribes, some nations have still retained the teachings of the Great Spirit. Others have not. (This no doubt shocks some of you Christians who have the stereotype that we Indian people are pagans, savages or heathens, but we do not believe that you control the way to the spirit world that lies beyond.) We believe that the Great Spirit loves all his children equally, although he must be disturbed at times with those of his children who have raped and pillaged Mother Earth because they worshipped gold or green as their sacred colors and placed materialistic acquisition as their god even to the point of enslaving their fellow man so that they may own and possess more material goods.

Brothers and sisters, we must go back to some of the old ways if we are ever going to truly save our Mother Earth and bring back the natural beauty that every man seriously needs, especially in this day of drugs, tranquilizers, insane asylums, ulcers, extreme poor, extreme rich who share nothing, prisons, jails, rigid boundaries, germ warfare, and complete annihilation weapons.

Indian and White Ways

A great Hunkpapa Sioux chief, Sitting Bull, said to the Indian people, "Take the best of the white man's road, pick it up and

take it with you. That which is bad, leave it alone, cast it away. Take the best of the old Indian ways—always keep them. They have been proven for thousands of years. Do not let them die.''

My friends, I will never cease being an Indian. I will never cease respecting the old Indian values, especially our four cardinal commandments and the values of generosity and sharing. I believe that the white man became so greedy that he destroyed many things. I also believe that the white man has done a great deal of good in this world. He has good ways and he has bad ways. The good way of the white man's road I am going to keep. The very fact that we can all speak freely, the very fact none of us here are hungry, the very fact that we talk a common language and many of us have come from a great distance and can still exchange knowledge, the fact that we can exchange knowledge immediately over a wire to another country, shows the wisdom of my white brothers. These ways I will always keep and cherish, but my white brothers, I say you must give up this materialism to excess. Keep those material goods that you need to exist. Be more of a sharing and a generous person. Have more respect for the aged and family tradition. Have more respect for family that extends not only from mother and father to son and daughter but goes on to grandmothers and grandfathers and aunts and uncles, goes out to the animal world as your brother, to Mother Earth and Father Sky and then to Tankashilah, the Grandfather.

Tankashilah means Grandfather. Wakontankan means the Great Spirit. They are both the same. When we pray directly to God, we say Tankashilah because we are so family-minded that we think of Him as our Grandfather and we are His grandchildren. And, of course, Mother Earth is our mother because Grandfather intended it so. This is a part of the great deep feeling and psychology that we have as Indian people. It is why we

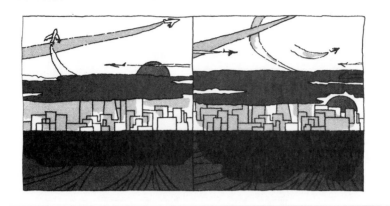

preserved and respected our environment for such a long period.

Remember that Mother Earth is truly a holy being and that all things in this world are holy and must not be violated and that we must share and be generous with one another. You may call it in your fancy words psychology, theology, sociology, or philosophy. Call it whatever you wish, but think of Mother Earth as a living being. Think of your fellow man as a holy person who was put here by the Great Spirit Being, of the four sacred colors. And think of brown also as a sacred color. You will be far more successful as a nation.

Only with the thought that Mother Earth is truly a holy being, and that all things in this world are holy and must not be violated and that we must share and be generous with one another—only with this thought—you must think of Mother Earth as a living being. Think of your fellow man as a holy person who was put here by the Great Spirit Being and think of the four sacred colors. With this philosophy in mind you will be far more successful to truly understand the Indian's respect for Mother Earth.

"Society is struggling to find the middle ground between the old ethic of sacrifice for others and the new ethic of looking to one's own inner needs."

America's Values
Are Changing

Daniel Yankelovich interviewed by Robert C. Nelson

Daniel Yankelovich is the founder and chairman of the opinion research organization The Yankelovich Group, and co-founder and president of The Public Agenda Foundation. In 1981, his book *New Rules: Searching for Self-Fulfillment in a World Turned Upside Down,* described how Americans were casting off traditional social values and developing a new social ethic which was not yet clearly defined. In the following viewpoint, taken from an interview with Robert C. Nelson for *The Kettering Review,* he elaborates on this continuing cultural shift. He claims America is engaged in an agonizing search, trying to honor traditional forms of commitment, while at the same time attempting to find new forms of self-expression.

As you read, consider the following questions:

1. What basic values does Yankelovich claim form America's cultural bonds?
2. How does the author think the nature of commitment is changing?
3. Does the author think the country's cultural diversity will help or hinder the search for a new social ethic?

Robert C. Nelson, "An Interview with Daniel Yankelovich," *Kettering Review,* Fall 1988. Reprinted with permission.

Nelson: Five years ago there was polarity in values. Left and right were really taking the opposite positions. This could be seen even in values in the classroom. Now, surprisingly, a consensus is emerging. Do you see it that way and can you explain it?

Yankelovich: Well, there is a struggle now for the center. I think the country is coming out of a very long period of partisanship, of swinging from one extreme to the other, and it is looking for a central position. That is in the political domain. I see that happening also in the domain of social and personal values.

Nelson: Really? These are not just attitudes you are talking about, but really deep values.

Yankelovich: The really deep values. In the 1960s, young people in college leapt to an extreme of the social spectrum. In every society you need to balance individualism with social conformity and the social bonds that keep people together—the need to sacrifice for one another. And economic realities give a frame and a constraint within which that struggle takes place. What happened in the sixties happened because young people in college didn't have experience of the world. They were making the assumption that somehow there was enough affluence for everybody, that the time had come to repair all social problems, and that we had the resources to do it. With that presumption of infinite affluence, they leapt to the extreme of individualism, rejecting the ethic of self-sacrifice for others, the ethic of self-denial and replacing it with a focus on self—"the me generation."

Nelson: Indulgence?

Yankelovich: Indulgence! That was an extreme view. What is interesting is that it didn't fade away. It wasn't a flash in the pan. It wasn't like SDS (Students for a Democratic Society) that came up in the Vietnam War and then was gone with the war. It found a profound reverberation in the society at large, but it was too extreme.

What I see happening today, in the same way, parallel to the political scene, is that the society is struggling to find the middle ground between the old ethic of sacrifice for others and the new ethic of looking to one's own inner needs and potential and self-expressive desires.

Learning To Give

It is evolutionary. In the 30 years that I have been studying social change, it is very clear that change doesn't work in a straightforward linear way. It works through such pendulum swings. You go from one extreme to the other; and then you spend most of the years sorting it out. We're in a sorting-out period. It is not another pendulum swing but rather an effort to redress that assumption of the sixties that there was infinite affluence. That bumped up against reality in the seventies and eighties—scarcity,

111

limitation of resources, recognition that we can't do everything, budget deficits, people struggling to make a living, a decline in the standard of living, and the need to put on another earner in every family just in order to make ends meet. This kind of external reality has brought people to the realization that it isn't possible to live a life where you can focus exclusively on your own needs.

Nelson: How does a society discover its capacity for generosity? Do you mandate it, or do you beckon it forth somehow?

Yankelovich: That capacity has to preexist. You find it in family values. It is the way people are brought up. It is an atmosphere of stability, of acceptance, of love, of faith, that creates it. Now if you have that, you can evoke either selfishness or generosity. That's partly a function of leadership.

Changing Beliefs

Throughout most of this century, Americans believed that self-denial made sense, sacrifice made sense, obeying the rules made sense, subordinating the self to the institution made sense. But doubts have now set in, and Americans now believe that the old giving/getting compact needlessly restricts the individual while advancing the power of large institutions—government and business particularly—who use the power to enhance their own interests at the expense of the public.

Daniel Yankelovich, *New Rules: Searching for Self-Fulfillment in a World Turned Upside Down,* 1981.

Our national leadership has emphasized a certain kind of selfishness, a self-seeking, social Darwinism. But that goes against the grain, against the innate generosity and innate sense of fairness that Americans have imbibed as part of their upbringing and culture. You can evoke generosity, self-sacrifice, or you can discourage it.

Nelson: Does education have any special role to play in this change?

Yankelovich: Well, I think so. It seems to me that the concept of education without values and without a value context is an empty abstraction. There is no choice. You cannot say that we can have either a value-free education or one with values. You either have one with *explicit* values or one where the values are hidden. I think it is better to have them explicit. For America is held together by a handful of core values.

Nelson: Check them off. What kinds of things are the bonds?

Yankelovich: The bonds—the common values in this incredibly diverse society—include, first and foremost, the belief in freedom, political freedom, individual freedom. They include an emphasis on equality of opportunity: not equality in the abstract; not the concept that everybody is equal; but the concept that everybody should have an equal crack. They include a belief in education as the way in which acceptable inequality is equalized, where people are enabled to achieve. They include an emphasis on hard work and effort. Ours is not an elitist society: we don't believe that the people who make it to the top make it because they are brighter. We believe they make it because they try harder. If they've gotten an education, it isn't because they are brighter, but because anybody who wants an education should be entitled to get one. That's an aspect of equality of opportunity. Interestingly, the core values of America include a little bit of emphasis on luck. One of the reasons we don't want to tax away all the riches of the richest people is—who knows, the wheel of fortune might spin in my direction!

Values of that sort are fundamental to the American experience, fundamental to the American dream. It would seem to me that whether you are teaching American history or social values, you have to convey to people that this is the essence of the American experience and that it is what holds us together as a people—not language, not the kind of homogeneity that a society like Sweden or Japan has. We have incredible diversity, but in the midst of it we have this core of shared values that is the very essence of American life.

Nelson: You see this not just in attitudes, but as behavior as well.

Yankelovich: I see it as a behavior and a struggle. It's a struggle. I have written about the search for an ethic of commitment. I think that lies at the heart of the struggle in this sense: the struggle focuses on how much freedom the individual can have. There is a consensus in the country that political freedom is institutionalized and extreme and embodied in the Bill of Rights: it's built in. But there is no such consensus on social freedom and individual expressiveness. In fact, the emphasis has generally been on sacrifice for others. In my generation, when I was growing up, maybe you wanted to be an architect or a musician, but you settled for being a builder or something else because you couldn't put your own self-expressive needs first. You had to support a family.

Nelson: This was virtuous, too.

Old Ethics and New

Yankelovich: Virtue, that's what I mean by a social ethic. My definition of virtue is sacrificing your own needs for others. When the social revolution of the sixties came, the reason there was such responsiveness among college youth was that Americans were beginning to think, "Well, why can't we have a little more

113

freedom? Why do we have to have a life that is stifled and restricted and conformist?" The search began to find an expanded sphere of individual freedom and to find a kind of a balance. That's where the struggle is.

Now, as we look at behavior, take, for example, the work place. The old ethic was that you worked to make a living, and you had no right to demand that the job be satisfying as well. Money was important. But, if the employer satisfied your demands in that area, you were loyal. You made a total commitment. The opposite extreme is one where you change jobs whenever you feel like it and loyalty doesn't mean anything.

Changing Values

Traditional Values	New Values
Self-denial ethic	Self-fulfillment ethic
Higher standard of living	Better quality of life
Traditional sex roles	Blurring of sex roles
Accepted definition of success	Individualized definition of success
Traditional family life	Alternative families
Faith in industry, institutions	Self-reliance
Live to work	Work to live
Hero worship	Love of ideas
Expansionism	Pluralism
Patriotism	Less nationalistic
Unparalleled growth	Growing sense of limits
Industrial growth	Information/service growth
Receptivity to technology	Technology orientation

Joseph T. Plummer, *The Futurist*, January/February, 1989. This chart shows the shift Joseph Plummer sees occurring as developed Western societies gradually move away from traditional values and toward emerging new values.

Now, the question is whether there is some room for loyalty, but also room for some kind of satisfaction for myself. How do I find the balance? It is even more striking in the domain of family and marriage. The old commitment in marriage was the marriage vow, "in sickness and in health, till death do us part." In certain religious views, like the Catholic view that divorce is sinful and unthinkable, that marriage is a total commitment. But the opposite extreme leads to: "I don't feel like you're meeting my needs today, so good-bye. I'm off." No commitment!

Where, in terms of behavior, do you now find the place to make a commitment? It will not be the old commitment of yesteryear, unqualified loyalty to the employer. It will no longer be the lifelong marriage vow. You find that kind of commitment in certain groups in the population, but if you look at the divorce rate, particularly among younger people with serial marriages, you see that the norm in the society has changed and the nature of commitment is changing. It is an agonizing search to try to honor both extremes—to honor the extreme of the social bond and commitment, yet also to honor the new ethic, to find some form of expressiveness for the self.

Nelson: I still have the same kind of yearning for my youngsters for example; but the realities that they are up against are different. I have bridged this. How do I reconcile *my* expectations and hopes for *them* with their rather hardheaded sense of, "this is just the way it is now and we're making our adjustment to it."

Emergence of Ideals

Yankelovich: The way one defines reality is subjective. In the 1930s the reaction to scarcity, to the Great Depression, was one of helping each other. It was a period in our society which people look back to with nostalgia, because we responded, in an era of scarcity, with a certain generosity and a certain helpfulness. Just as now, if there is a crisis, a storm, a hurricane, homelessness, Americans respond. But society at large is responding to the tightness of the economy with an ethic of everybody for themselves, a scramble. That is not a *necessary* response, any more than was cooperation in the 1930s. You don't have to take the attitude that no one is going to look out for me except myself. That's part of this process of sorting out; it's a hangover from the extremism of the sixties.

Nelson: You study communities, what makes them vigorous and where their flaws are. Do you come across anything that has to do with how you educate our citizens, how you help young people in particular to develop a sense of how they fit into this society, what it expects of them, what they can bring to it that is special, out of their own individuality?

Yankelovich: Young people do have a reservoir of idealism but it is not easy to tap into. It depends on what you feel, too. For example, today people don't feel comfortable with large units, with globalism, or even with the national society. That is somewhat new. It was a struggle in the seventies to find something you could believe in that was larger than the self but not so large that it was abstract and meaningless. So people look at being a couple as something that they can deal with, their own family, and their own community.

What is new, I think, is a renewed interest in the local community, a willingness to be involved and to have idealism evoked in terms of the local community. Then, maybe paradoxically, at the other extreme is an interest in our global fate, because we are tied together by the nuclear threat and by the interdependence of the world—although that is harder to make real and concrete to young people, whereas the local community is something they can see and feel.

I think the idealism of young people can be evoked. Patriotism is very alive. Yearning for a religious meaning is very alive. It is part of that search for something beyond the self to make a commitment to.

Two Kinds of Sacred

Nelson: Is that "the sacred" that you have written about?

Yankelovich: Yes, I refer to sacred, expressive values, and I mean sacred in two senses: one in the religious sense, but then also in the secular sense, the opposite of utilitarian. A lot of the values of the fifties were utilitarian. What can you do for me? What can I buy with it? What good is it? The more recent emphasis on expressiveness has been to find things that are good in and of themselves, sacred in that sense. Friendship, a relationship, a relationship to nature, to beauty—this is the expressive side of life. And it is sacred both in the sense that it has a touch of divinity and also in a sense that it is valued for other than utilitarian reasons.

This is the part of life that the new values have been groping to integrate with the old effort, because that was what was excluded from the old—the ability of an individual to achieve full expression when that expression conflicted with the expectations of society.

Nelson: How do you educate for that community, for being good citizens?

Yankelovich: It's a challenge—education for citizenship—that I don't think our schools have mastered very well, or that anybody has a real handle on. Yet I think the potential for doing it is enormous. There is an untapped idealism. There is an untapped hunger for meaning. There is a basis of patriotism. All the raw material is there. But how to evoke and how to shape it? It seems to me that there are a number of ways of doing it. One is to provide students with a better intellectual understanding of how the society is held together. How do you take such an incredibly diverse society as ours and give it some stability and cohesiveness? There is a wonderful story to be told there. I think that I would emphasize most the desire for participation and the right to participate.

The Need To Participate

I've been talking about new expressive values. One of the strongest of them is the need to participate—the feeling that I, as an individual, should have the right to control the decisions that affect my life. If you say first that decisions made in remote places like Washington affect your life, then also demonstrate—whether it is a tax bill or inflation—the relevance of public decisions to individual lives. That's almost never done. It's not done in the media, and it's not done in the schools.

Once students understand that these decisions affect their lives, the second step is to convey that they themselves have a certain potency; that if they participate, they can have an effect. Most Americans don't think their views count. The second step is to persuade them that their views count. And that means that the third step is to teach students how to participate. Participation is not an easy subject. There are ways to participate that bring everything to a grinding halt and create paralysis. But there are other ways to participate that are important and meaningful. What is the role of the citizen? What is the role of the expert? We are an elite-dominated, expert-ridden society, with too much expertise, not enough citizen participation. We're not going to get back to a good balance unless the schools play their role not only in teaching students of their right to participate, but teaching them how and why. Almost no one understands what participation means and how to do it. I would put a lot of emphasis on unraveling that mystery. It really is a mystery. The fact that we don't understand it is creating a real flaw in the democratic process.

Public Truth

Nelson: Does the fact that the society is so mixed culturally and ethnically, and increasingly so, complicate this kind of process?

Yankelovich: It complicates it, but it doesn't make it impossible. Understand that public truth is different from scientific truth. Scientific truth is a matter of fact and a matter of verification. Public truth is looking at something from a variety of points of view. It comes to important matters of values and judgment. You want to see an issue from many points of view. An affluent, upper middle-class white person is going to have a different point of view from a minority person. Someone in the South is going to have a different point of view from someone in another part of the country. There is a better chance of getting the truth, in this sense, when you have diversity, because you see the same subjects from a variety of points of view. We've got to put a little bit of time and effort into it, but actually, our diversity helps.

Nelson: You make the point that the self, to be individual, to have a sense of fulfillment and commitment, has to be connected to something outside just the little individual life.

Yankelovich: That has grown out of the actual experience of people. As they experimented with new values in the sixties—the focus on the self, on self-indulgence, on duty to self, rather than to others—they expected that search would bring great satisfaction, exultation of spirit. What a terrible disappointment it was when they found themselves lonely and cut off and without meaning, when the very purpose of the search was to find *more* meaning in individual experience. They began to realize that narcissism doesn't work, that isolation doesn't work. A self that is totally separate has no meaning. Meaning comes from relatedness.

Then began effort to reestablish, on a different basis, forms of relatedness. It began, I think, in a very constructive way. If people now made a choice, if they made a commitment to family, it was because *they* were making it, not because it was expected of them. Similarly a commitment to work; similarly to religion; similarly to the community. Today it is harder to get commitment. The commitment is more from the heart. It is more real because it has grown out of experience, out of individual risk-taking, and out of the kind of existential struggle that, it seems to me, life is all about. . . .

The Next Generation

Nelson: Do you see society changing significantly in the next generation?

Yankelovich: I think this process of picking and choosing is at a very early stage. It is going to be fascinating to see when the dust clears what society will look like. I think that the change that we have in front of us is still enormous, because the dust hasn't settled. The patterns are not clear.

You take a fundamental area like family and marriage. The dual-earner family is under all kinds of strains. The families where the kids are hers and theirs and ours, the single-parent family, the older people who don't have a role in life because of families that are broken up and the like—none of this is settled. We haven't discovered what new rules family and marriage should follow in a new era, under a new set of values. I think that you are going to see change, but the nature of the change is not going to be an extreme swing of the pendulum. . . .

Nelson: That is a benevolent and not a destructive change by any means.

Yankelovich: I think it is. I think that there are lots of things that are wrong in the country and lots of things that are right in the country. Some of the things that are wrong with the country have to do with some of the institutions that are flawed. My feeling is that one of the things that is profoundly right in the country is the culture, the quest for the right balance of values; I believe that is constructive, and I believe that the old ethic of self-denial had something mean-spirited about it and diminished the individual.

But the selfishness of the sixties didn't make any sense at all. You can't have a society in which people are out only for themselves. So how do you blend the two? How do you balance the two? That is what the national experiment in social values is about.

118

Determining Sin

*'Miss Dugan, will you send someone in
here who can distinguish right from wrong?'*

Drawing by Dana Fradon; © 1975 The New Yorker Magazine, Inc.

Karl Menninger, in viewpoint four, defined sin in general terms as *behavior that violates the moral code or the individual conscience or both; behavior which pains or harms or destroys my neighbor—or me, myself.*

Using Dr. Menninger's definition, examine the following actions. Consider each action carefully. *Mark VS for actions you feel are very sinful. Mark SF for actions you feel are slightly sinful. Mark NS for actions you feel are not sinful.*

If you are doing this activity as the member of a class or small group discussion, compare your answers with other class or group members. Be able to defend your answers. You may discover that others will come to different conclusions than you. Listening to the rationale others present for their answers may give you valuable insights.

If you are reading this book alone, ask others if they agree with your answers. You too will find this interaction very valuable.

VS = *very sinful*
SF = *slightly sinful*
NS = *not sinful*

119

1. Using violence to achieve valuable goals
2. Obeying a superior's orders to execute unarmed civilians in a war situation
3. Dropping nuclear weapons on enemy cities in a retaliatory attack
4. Getting an abortion
5. Failing to aid an injured pedestrian lying by the side of the road
6. Stealing a small item from a large company
7. Stealing a large item from a large company
8. Sexual relations between consenting homosexuals
9. Collecting unemployment payments when able to work
10. Lying
11. Stealing from a neighbor
12. Living as husband and wife when not married
13. Pretending to love someone to have sexual relations with that person
14. Selling dope to support yourself
15. Using dope
16. Getting drunk frequently
17. Buying something with the intention of not paying the bill

Periodical Bibliography

The following articles have been selected to supplement the diverse views presented in this chapter.

John Alexander	"Once Upon a Time," *The Other Side*, May 1988.
Ezra Bowen	"Looking to Its Roots," *Time*, May 25, 1987.
Christianity Today	"Decadence American Style," April 7, 1987.
Christianity Today	"In Search of Heroes," November 8, 1985.
Norman Corwin	"The 365-Day Fantasy," *National Forum*, Fall 1987.
Dolores Curran	"The Spice of Life," *Salt*, March 1987.
Everette E. Dennis	"American Media and American Values," *Vital Speeches of the Day*, March 15, 1988.
Albert DiIanni	"Morality and the Decline of the United States," *America*, September 10, 1988.
Nicols Fox	"What Are Our Real Values?" *Newsweek*, February 13, 1989.
John Leo	"The Dubious Art of Shifting Blame," *U.S. News & World Report*, October 17, 1988.
Susanna McBee	"The State of American Values," *U.S. News & World Report*, December 9, 1985.
Merrill McLoughlin	"A Nation of Liars," *U.S. News & World Report*, February 23, 1987.
Marian H. Neudel	"Being 'Only Human' vs. Being a Mensch," *Tikkun*, November/December 1988.
Joseph T. Plummer	"Changing Values," *The Futurist*, January/February, 1989.
David Rankin	"A State of Incivility," *Newsweek*, February 8, 1988.
Milton Rokeach, et al.	"The Great American Values Test," *Psychology Today*, November 1984.
Robert J. Samuelson	"The Discovery of Money," *Newsweek*, October 20, 1986.

Eric Sevareid	"The Balance of America," *Philip Morris Magazine*, Summer 1986.
Walter Shapiro	"What's Wrong?" *Time*, May 27, 1987.
David Sheff	"Portrait of a Generation," *Rolling Stone*, May 5, 1988.
U.S. News & World Report	"Morality," December 9, 1985.
Daniel Walden	"Where Have All Our Heroes Gone?" *USA Today*, January 1986.
Steven W. Webb	"Moral Resurgence and Contradictory Currents," *Eternity*, August 1987.
David Wells	"How To Avoid Offensive Language While Saying Absolutely Nothing," *Christianity Today*, January 15, 1988.
Philip Yancy	"Imagine There's No Heaven," *Christianity Today*, December 12, 1986.

3 CHAPTER

What Are America's Economic Values?

AMERICAN
V·A·L·U·E·S

Chapter Preface

America is one of the wealthiest countries in the world. Many people argue that this wealth is no accident. They argue that America's vibrant cultural values are responsible. These values include an admiration and cultivation of entrepreneurship, individual effort, and a strong work ethic, these supporters argue.

Others disagree and argue that America's wealth is evidence of an obsessive emphasis on money, greed, and power. They point to white-collar crime, insider trading, and harmful products like the Dalkon Shield IUD to show that America's business values are corrupt at heart. These incidents and others point up the need to reexamine America's business values. For example, according to a 1987 survey by the Ethics Resource Center, more than 92 percent of the country's graduate business schools include ethics in the curricula, compared with only a handful in 1962.

This chapter presents seven viewpoints that give the reader an opportunity to examine America's economic values.

> *"A lot of our best and brightest young people are being corrupted by the lure of Wall Street fortunes."*

An Easy Money Ethic Is Corrupting American Business

Lee Iacocca

Lee Iacocca, Chrysler Corporation's famous chairman, sold over six million copies of his autobiography, published in 1984. In his new book, from which this viewpoint is taken, he describes some of the ills he sees afflicting American industry. In his opinion, many of today's college graduates have abandoned the traditional values of American business, like making useful products, creating jobs, and strengthening the country's industrial base. Their focus instead is on shuffling paper, deal making, and amassing quick fortunes.

As you read, consider the following questions:

1. Why does the author consider the current practice of corporate raiding detrimental to America's economic health?
2. Why does Iacocca place some blame at the door of college professors for the unethical situation he describes?

One morning as I was reading *The Wall Street Journal*, I came across some startling news. The paper was running two big stories about U.S. Steel and Goodyear being pounced on by a pair of corporate raiders. I said to myself: *Now wait a minute. Those companies are my two biggest suppliers. Without them, I don't make cars.* Yet here were these interlopers coming in and I was nothing but an innocent bystander. That was the moment when this merger mania really hit home to me. Things had gone entirely too far in Wall Street's version of Monopoly®.

Like all my counterparts in the business world, I was aware of the existence of raiders. And I knew they were adding a worrisome new dimension to the job of management. But I hadn't paid much attention to their antics because they were always doing their dirty work out of my sight. Now, for the first time, they had come to my meat house. Mr. Carl Icahn had dropped in. Sir James Goldsmith had stopped by.

Once they hit me where it mattered, I felt that it was time to offer a little perspective on who these guys were. Were they really Robin Hood and his Merry Men, as they claimed? Or were they Genghis Khan and the Mongol hordes?

All I know is what I see—and what I don't.

I see billions of dollars tied up in new corporate debt to keep the raiders at bay while research and development goes begging. I see billions going for greenmail, dollars that ought to be building new high-tech factories. I see confidence in Wall Street's integrity lower than at any time since the crash of '29. I also see a huge share of America's best management talent wasted on takeover games when it should be devoted to strengthening the industrial base of the country.

But I don't see the raiders creating jobs. I don't see them boosting productivity. And worst of all, I don't see them doing a single thing to help America compete in the world. . . .

Corporate Raiders Are Modern Robber Barons

When people in other countries hear about all this nonsense, they must think we're a little crazy. I never read about a merger in Japan. I never hear of any leveraged buyouts there either. The Japanese probably don't even know what the phrase means. Over there, businessmen use wealth to create more productivity and to put more people to work. Here, nobody's building a better mousetrap anymore. They're trying to figure out how to do a leveraged buyout of the mousetrap company.

Along the way to making their killing, these raiders don't care if a company is decimated and people are thrown out of their jobs. Imagine Carl Icahn, up to his ears in TWA, wanting to try to get hold of U.S. Steel. He says the company isn't going to make it anyway, because it isn't modern enough and it's tried to diversify into gas and oil, so how much damage can he do?

Well, I know that type. He would go in there and sell off the steel business, because it's a capital-intensive business, while hanging on to the oil and gas reserves; that's all he's interested in. So the famous U.S. Steel (now USX) would be gone. And Bethelehem Steel would not be far behind. Then LTV, already in bankruptcy, would follow them right down the tubes. It's a helluva way to restructure the country's once-mighty steel industry.

Why should we allow these rugged individualists to rape the whole world? If you look in the history books, you'll see that we had these types before: the Robber Barons and the so-called railroad barons of the nineteenth century, who got this land for nothing and didn't care about anything but making money. But at least they left us some railroads and some prosperous industrial companies. Today's raiders simply shuffle paper. In a small world, in which we've got to compete with potent nations like Germany and Japan, we're going nowhere fast. If we were getting more productive in the process, then I'd say fine. That's what these raiders promise will happen. . . .

Our Dilemma

In a strange way, war and commerce have both become equally depersonalized, carried on by individuals located in windowless rooms, talking into telephones and looking at computer screens, thousands of miles removed from each other. In the case of commerce, they buy and sell. In the case of war, they can incinerate the Earth, without ever seeing another human being.

For the businessmen and the politicians who function in such an environment, virtually the only discipline that can be applied is ethical. Financial scandals are not new, nor is political corruption. However, the potential profits, and the ease with which they can be made from insider trading, market manipulation, conflict-of-interest transactions and many other illegal or unethical activities are too great and too pervasive to be ignored. At the same time, those institutions that historically provided the ethical basis to the society—the family, the church and the primary school—are getting weaker and weaker. Hence, our dilemma.

Felix G. Rohatyn, *Ethics in American Business: A Special Report*, 1988.

I'm particularly troubled by the deeper issue that has brought on this recklessness. And that's the deteriorating values of businessmen today, especially the freshly minted ones. It's time that somebody started to question the system that breeds these kinds of people. Why is it that talented young men and women aren't interested in going into industry but flock to Wall Street? Their only desire is to join some big firm, become a partner, and start doing deals. They're all hoping that by the time they're thirty they'll be making $5 million or $6 million and have their own airplane and even their own airport.

A lot of our best and brightest young people are being corrupted by the lure of Wall Street fortunes. The employment at investment banking firms and arbitrage firms has grown by leaps and bounds in the last few years. Try to get any of those people to come into industry. They laugh in your face. Although October 19, 1987, or Black Monday, may cut down on the laughs.

A worrisome attitude has taken hold among young businessmen. It's called "I want a lot and I want it now." This young breed thinks people like me had our sights set way too low. I wanted to make a million dollars in my lifetime, and I thought that was dreaming big dreams. They want $50 million. And they want it this afternoon.

The conversation I hear in business circles is always about the deal and the play and the chase and the odds. It sounds a lot more exciting than talk about how we're going to compete or change the union work rules or return to common sense. Let's face it, those things aren't fun to read about over coffee in *The Wall Street Journal*.

These kids not only want to make bigger money, they also want to make it the easy way. Their attitude is: "I'm not my brother's keeper. Who said I was born on this earth just to create jobs for other people? I expect somebody to provide me with a job." Well, if everybody had that attitude in the past, there wouldn't be any jobs at all right now. There wouldn't be any companies to put into play either.

The anxiety of these young people to make money has risen to such a fever pitch that it was inevitable corruption would set in. Not only do you have dirty pool being shot, in the form of greenmail and the like, but you've got guys like Ivan Boesky and Dennis Levine surreptitiously moving the cue ball around. I've never seen so many business scandals in the papers as I have in the last few years. It's ridiculous. The financial pages read like the police blotter.

I just knew that once the possible profits reached into the billions this activity was going to get out of hand. I'm reminded of that old advice: "Don't spend time around a gambling casino. It brings in the worst kind of hoods in the world, because there's too much loose cash lying around." Wall Street has been converted into one big parimutuel machine. And it's brought in the seedy element.

The Problem Is Our Permissive Society

I'm going to sound old-fashioned here, but to my mind the core of the problem is our permissive society. That's what makes kids going to college think that there's a difference between blue-collar crime and white-collar crime. They think white-collar crime is only a little bit illegal. Where I come from, a crime is a crime.

I never saw these values in people of my generation. I can't really give you a precise number, but I'm going to pick 98 percent. That's how many business leaders are guys like me who didn't inherit their wealth but worked hard, climbed up the rungs of the ladder, and after thirty years learned how to build a better garden hose or, in my case, how to build a better Mustang or a minivan.

A Lesson in Values

Before the insider-trading scandal broke, Ivan Boesky, the famous arbitrageur, decided he wanted to buy a large national magazine. In this venture, I became an extremely minor partner and an extremely major voyeur.

It was a pretty lousy experience, all in all. We didn't get the magazine—partly because Ivan changed his mind about something at the last second. . . . We lost. Someone else obviously had a more generous banker. But I did get an education—a scary lesson in value, and in values.

I learned that the value of a company was determined by what a man with a lot of nerve and a decent track record (a record, it turned out, built on playing with a stacked deck) could persuade a banker to give him. It was as simple as that. Not only the magazine we were after, but almost every American institution, was up for sale, at a price determined by the eagerness of bankers to put their funds to work.

I also learned that there was a huge gap between the real world of business and the unreal world of finance—or maybe I should say, the world of numerology. It was the manipulation of numbers, often in mystical processes, that enabled people like Boesky to buy—or at least to threaten to buy and, in the process, to transform—actual corporations with living, breathing people inside. . . . The business itself is no longer as important as the process of acquiring it. The money and the thrill are in the transaction, not in the managing or producing.

"I don't do it for the money," writes Trump at the beginning of his repulsive new book, *Trump: The Art of the Deal*. "I've got enough, much more than I'll ever need. I do it to do it." . . . Capitalist morality does not reside in markets driven by greed. It resides in the companies and partnerships and corporations themselves—in the way they treat their employees and their communities, in the goods they produce, in the values they represent.

The values of society's producers, in short, are more important and more lasting than those of its financiers and traders.

James K. Glassman, *Washington Post National Weekly Edition*, January 18-24, 1988.

They put their nose to the grindstone and now they're reaping the benefits of that diligence. With rare exceptions, I find my peers to be good family men who are honest and ethical. Sure, there are some business guys who are dumb, but they usually get found out.

These young hotshots have forgotten how the system is supposed to work. It used to be that the purpose of the financial world was to serve the needs of business. In fact, that was its only reason for being. The financial system was to generate capital so that people could put it to work and create jobs and raise our standard of living. Now everything's reversed. The corporations have become the playthings of the financial market. The system has flip-flopped. . . .

Professors Have Been Teaching the Wrong Stuff

On November 6, 1986, I got two letters in the mail from the presidents of two universities—Lehigh and M.I.T. When I read them, I thought to myself that maybe they'll be historic documents someday, because both presidents had come to an identical conclusion. It had dawned on them that their schools had taught many of this country's professors. M.I.T. alone turns out 11 percent of all the engineering professors in the United States. It's an amazing number. Now these schools suddenly realized that those professors have been teaching students the wrong stuff.

Basically, the message they've given our kids is to go out into the world and make a quick buck for themselves. Nobody was stupid enough to advise a kid to go out and get his hands dirty by making something and helping this country become productive. Only uneducated fools would do that. If you've got the business smarts, they say, go to Wall Street and make a killing; if you're a technical whiz, they send you to a Southern California defense contractor to work on black boxes for the military—neither of which has anything to do with productivity.

They tell me we've got twenty-three thousand of the finest minds in America at Hughes Aircraft working on Star Wars and other classified projects. The Japanese, on the other hand, have an equivalent twenty-three thousand minds working on sharper TV pictures, graphite golf clubs, and electronic instrument panels for cars. They have nothing else to do, since we won't even allow them to work on any sophisticated military gizmos. That's a brain drain that boggles my mind. Our best and brightest put the results of their work into missile silos for storage. The Japanese bring good things to life for the needs and enjoyment of consumers.

Just try to recruit a new graduate from the Harvard Business School or M.I.T. to come work in a car company. He typically tells us: "Go work for Chrysler as a financial analyst? You must be out of your mind. I'm going to Wall Street." And we're not just offering him crumbs. We pay him a cool $50,000 to start.

It's the same story with engineering graduates. "What challenge can there be in trying to build a better car?" they ask. "That's a dying industry. The action is in laser beams."

The real irony to me is that the guys in California getting paid by the Defense Department are the very guys who buy all the Japanese cars on the theory that American cars are not as technically advanced.

In counseling our students, a lot of teachers and advisers have followed the flow of the money. If that approach undercuts the country and causes the industrial base to go to pot, they don't really care. I seriously doubt they've ever given it a second's thought. Their spiel is: "Kid, I've taught you all I know. I want you to be a success. Your becoming an investment banker (or a rocket scientist) will look awfully good in the alumni record." After all, how do we judge success in this country? First and foremost, money.

We Have To Change Our Priorities

To give you a feel for how things have changed, ten years ago Lehigh asked its graduating seniors whom they wanted for a commencement speaker. Their choices were Walter Cronkite, Bill Cosby, and me, in that order. Cronkite and Cosby turned them down, and I accepted. (When I showed up, I said, "Hey, kids, I hear I was your third choice. So what you're going to get is a third-rate speech.") In 1987, when Lehigh asked the seniors whom they wanted, the picks were Clint Eastwood, Steven Spielberg, and Donald Trump: the movies, make-believe, and easy money.

The schools are having the *mea culpa* of their lives. They're finally coming to the realization that they've created a monster. They've figured out that we have our priorities screwed up: We have to train people to do every job, not just the ones in the financial district. The manufacturing process has been sadly neglected in this country, and now's the time to really throw the coals to it.

"The truth is that ethics forms an essential part of our economic system. It is part and parcel of the way we do business."

Ethical Conduct Is the Norm for American Business

M. Euel Wade Jr.

M. Euel Wade Jr., a West Point graduate, is currently senior vice president of Southern Company Services, Inc., where he is in charge of information resources. The following viewpoint is taken from a speech to students at the University of Georgia. In it, Mr. Wade argues that ethical behavior is not only a trait of individuals in America, but also is a value shared by the society as a whole. While he believes many of today's dominant values are more oriented toward money and success, he claims this is not a problem. America's fundamental ethical values, like truthfulness, honesty, and integrity remain undisturbed.

As you read, consider the following questions:

1. What evidence does the author present to prove his claim that American corporations today make a serious commitment to ethics?
2. What comment does Wade make about the shift in goals of college freshmen from "a meaningful life" to "being well-off financially"?

M. Euel Wade Jr., "The Lantern of Ethics," a speech delivered to students at the University of Georgia in Athens, Georgia on November 5, 1987. Copyright 1989 Southern Company Services, Inc. All rights reserved.

More than two thousand years ago, Diogenes walked down a dusty road in ancient Greece. According to legend, as he walked, he carried a lighted lantern in his hand. He carried the lantern because—even in broad daylight—it wasn't easy to find what he was looking for: an honest man.

Today—after all the passing centuries—we read the morning paper or listen to the evening news and wonder if Diogenes would find the search any easier. "Iran-Contra Affair Rocks The Presidency," reads a headline. "Another case of insider trading on Wall Street," begins a newscaster.

In recent years, scandal seems to have become a growth industry. We read about defense contractors who bilk the Pentagon. We hear about banks that launder cash for suspected crooks. And yes, everyone listens when a well-known brokerage firm admits to illegal check-kiting. . . .

Ethics and Capitalism

Scandal has become so much a national preoccupation, there's even a new board game that tests a player's ability to make ethical decisions—it's called *Scruples*.

With so many signs of unethical behavior in society at large, we may wonder if ethics has *any* place in the business world. We may question if "business ethics" hasn't become a contradiction in terms. And we may even ask ourselves if Diogenes would stand a chance if he walked down the country roads, along the city streets, or through the corporate corridors of America today.

To explore some of these issues, I'd like to borrow a couple of concepts from Diogenes' time. The Greeks who lived around that period—philosophers like Plato and Aristotle—spent a lot of their time arguing about ethics and virtue.

In fact, "ethics" comes from the Greek word, "ethos." But when the Greeks talked about "ethos," they saw it as a balance of two concepts: "custom" and "character."

Let's begin, then, by considering ethics as a custom. And when we speak of a custom, we're talking about something people share. Ethics, in other words, isn't just a practice of *individuals*. It's a value shared by society *as a whole*.

Think of the tremendous importance we place on ethics in our *political* system. Fair, honest elections are so much a part of our form of government, we're outraged if someone tries to *steal* an election.

It *makes* the news when they stuff a ballot box in Cook County, Illinois, or when residents of cemeteries vote in Boston. But it makes the news *because* it makes us angry. And we become angry because *un*ethical conduct in politics or government violates a basic custom of our society.

So ethics is the custom that underpins our *political* system. But do we share this passion for ethics in our *economic* system? Some critics of capitalism charge that this system encourages *un*ethical behavior—that it rewards selfishness, dishonesty, and greed. They even cast Adam Smith—the founder of capitalism—as a ruthless man, obsessed with self-interest.

Five Steps To Making Ethical Business Decisions

First, is it legal? Breaking the law is seldom part of the formula for ethical behavior. By ruling out illegal activity, we usually resolve the question at once.

Second, is it an accepted custom? We can choose—or exclude—some forms of conduct on the basis of our knowledge about norms and practices. For example, I know that accepting a dinner invitation from a vendor is permissible in my industry. This custom is seen as a legitimate way of maintaining good working relations.

But I also know that I may *not* accept gifts that would place me or my company under an obligation. That is *not* an accepted custom.

Third, what values are involved? In making difficult decisions, we may find our values in conflict. And the tension may be compounded by the *shifting* values of young people entering the work force today.

According to a recent survey of college students, today's students are far more money and success oriented than students ten or twenty years ago. This shift in values isn't *necessarily* bad.

Money and success are important. But they cannot replace more fundamental ethical values—values like truthfulness, honesty, and integrity. When we find ourselves pulled in two directions, we need to look at where the ethical values point—and walk in that direction.

Fourth, how would I feel if an account of my actions were published in my hometown newspaper? Another question we may ask in the same vein: how would my parents react to such an account? If the answer to either question evokes shame or embarrassment, we should probably rule out that course of action.

Finally, does my decision "feel" right inside? Does it appeal to my highest standards? Is it worthy of all I believe in and value?

M. Euel Wade Jr., *The Lantern of Ethics*, 1989. Copyright 1989 Southern Services, Inc. All rights reserved.

It's true, Smith *did* write about self-interest in his famous book, *The Wealth of Nations*. But his idea—*rational* self-interest as he called it—did not praise or promote being ruthless or selfish. Smith simply showed that—as individuals pursue their own self-interest—they create wealth—more wealth than they would in a society that *forces* them to pursue *its* interest.

Adam Smith's critics also forget that he wrote *another* book—*The Theory of Moral Sentiments*. In that book, he compares capitalism to a race and tells us to run as hard as we can—but not to jostle. He advises us to compete fairly and warns against any violation of "fair play."

Adam Smith—a ruthless, selfish man? Far from it. Capitalism—a system that encourages *un*ethical conduct? Not at all.

Ethics Forms an Essential Part of Our Economic System

The truth is that ethics forms an essential part of our *economic* system, too. It is part and parcel of the way we do business. But not all countries view the custom of business ethics the way we do.

Just as some countries don't enjoy open, free elections—some countries also don't enjoy an economic system that allows open, honest competition. In some countries, you have to pay someone before you can conduct business. They call it "baksheesh"—which means "a gift of money as a favor or reward"—and this payment is an accepted custom.

In our society, we view such payments as unethical conduct because we believe that paying to do business corrupts honest competition. In fact, a few years ago, we heard a *clamor* in this country when several American companies admitted to paying bribes abroad. The companies claimed that these payments were so much a way of life in some countries, they couldn't compete unless they went along.

But time proved they were wrong. Gulf Oil—to cite one example—changed its policy—imposed strict rules against the payments—and found that it *could* compete successfully. And Gulf found that—in some countries—refusing to pay forced local officials to reform the practice.

So, we see that ethics forms the foundation of both our economic and our political system. But, if this is true—why do we read so many headlines about corruption in business?

Let's begin by admitting a truism. We are not a *perfect* society. But that doesn't mean our society *values* unethical conduct.

We should also remember *why* most headlines are written. Headlines are written to *grab attention*—often by shocking us. If practices like insider trading or money laundering were *accepted* in our society, they wouldn't *be* news.

Consider, for example, this headline: "XYZ Corp. Wins Contract through Honesty and Hard Work." Does *that* grab your attention? And yet, it tells how we conduct *most* business in this country.

Is Ethics Less of a Norm Today?

Ethical conduct, then, is the norm—the custom. But still, we may ask—is ethics less of a norm *today* than it once was? To answer that question, let's glance backward a few decades.

Beginning in the '60s, our society swept into a period of

turbulence—a time when we questioned many of our accepted notions and customs. The civil rights movement made us reconsider the way we treat minorities in our society. And the Vietnam conflict raised issues about the way we handle our commitments abroad.

This questioning grew more intense in the '70s when Watergate put the spotlight on *government* ethics. Adding to the chaos of the '70s, a whole catalogue of lesser movements—from the sexual revolution to environmentalism—caused us to reexamine many of the ethical customs our society had accepted for decades.

In recent years, much of that turbulence has subsided. And— as a result of the turmoil we've gone through—we've sharpened our awareness of ethical conflicts. Twenty-five years ago, we didn't hear much about affirmative action, environmental concerns, sexual harassment, and a whole range of issues that we recognize and deal with today.

Still, some people view today's interest in ethics—particularly business ethics—as just a fad. They agree with the point of view expressed in a Jeff Danziger cartoon. The cartoon shows a company president announcing to his staff, "Gentlemen, this year the *trick* is honesty." From one side of the conference table, a vice president gasps, "Brilliant." Across the table, another VP mutters, "But so risky!"

Fortunately, real life corporations show a more *serious* commitment to ethics. One sign of this interest is the number of companies that now issue a corporate code of ethics to employees. My own company does this. And a recent survey found that better than 90 percent of Fortune 500 companies require employees to subscribe to a code of ethics.

These codes map out general principles and philosophy. But they also deal in specifics. For example, when the Pentagon charged General Dynamics with fraudulent billing, the company added this statement to its code: "Shifting of costs to inappropriate contracts is strictly forbidden."

Another sign of corporate commitment is the creation of ethics training programs—and even departments—by many companies, including some that have been rocked by scandals. In the past few years, we've seen companies like Union Carbide, Boeing, McDonnell Douglas, and Chemical Bank set up programs to help employees deal with ethical conflicts.

These activities show that—despite the headlines we occasionally see—ethics plays an important role in business. But whether that trend continues will not depend solely on corporations.

Character and Values

Despite the codes of ethics, the ethics programs, and the special departments—*corporations* don't make the ultimate decisions about ethics. Ethical choices are made by *individuals*. And that brings us to the second concept of ethics that I'd like to talk about—character.

Just as the *custom* of ethics directs our attention to *society*, *character* points us to the *individual*. Character can be described as the combined moral or ethical *strength* of the individual.

Much of this strength comes from values—and the choices an individual makes as a result of those values. That's why we become concerned when we read about talented athletes who die from a drug overdose. Or about well-educated Wall Street workers who go to jail for insider trading.

These are the choices—the values—of individuals. And they raise a logical question: do we see a *shift* in the values of young men and women entering the work force today?

To answer that question, we might begin by looking at the values that we see reflected on television. One popular image of those values—and of your generation—is the Michael J. Fox character, Alex Keaton, on *Family Ties*.

If you watch the show, you know Alex as the ultimate, pre-yuppie conservative. In school, he prefers business courses to the liberal arts and—in politics—President Reagan to any other politician. His favorite possessions are an attaché case, a pocket calculator, and a copy of *The Wall Street Journal*.

But do Alex's values—values like money, success, and career—also mirror those of many young people today? A recent survey of college students tells us that they do.

According to that survey, "developing a meaningful philosophy of life" declined as a main goal among college freshmen—from 85 percent in 1968, to less than 50 percent today. On the other hand, 71 percent of today's freshmen see "being well off financially" as an important life goal. In 1968, only 39 percent of the freshmen chose the financial goal.

So, we do see a shift toward values that are more money and success oriented. But what's wrong with that?

To answer this question, let me begin by agreeing—money, career, and success *are* important values. But I must also add that those values aren't the *most* important ones.

They cannot replace more fundamental ethical values—values like truthfulness, honesty, and integrity. These values strengthen the *character* of individuals to make the tough choices. They steady us when outside pressures push us in the wrong direction.

How Do We Develop Character?

Think about the force those pressures can exert. How many of you, for example—when staring at a deadline—have used a "Cliff's Notes"-type summary instead of reading a book? How many of you—despite all of the well-publicized tragedies—have abused drugs or alcohol?

137

And let me warn you, the forces that weigh on you now will not fade when you join the work force. In the yuppified, fast-track jobs that some of you will enter, the pressures will be enormous.

You'll have to make difficult decisions about money. You'll face pressure to increase sales to clients—or to place larger orders with suppliers. Managers will ask you to cut costs—and stockholders will demand higher profits.

Top-level management will impose bottom-line pressures. And upwardly-mobile families will want more of the finer things of life.

No, it won't get any easier. And so you'll need to keep your sights set on solid values. You'll need to develop strength of character as the engine that powers you toward ethical action.

But how do we develop character? Isn't character something we get mostly from our parents during the formative years of childhood?

Of course, character development *begins* in childhood. But we can't afford to let ethical education end there.

Right now, you have an opportunity to continue that process by getting a broad, well-balanced education. Business students who also elect to take some liberal arts courses draw from a richer background than those who limit themselves to marketing, finance, and accounting.

Students, for example, who've seen the dark side of ambition in *Macbeth* bring a perspective to business and to ethics that others miss. And students who've traced the causes of the French Revolution—or wrestled with important concepts of philosophy—or walked in Willy Loman's worn-out shoes in *Death of a Salesman*—gain wisdom that can protect them like ethical armor.

But we must also remember the wisdom of the ancients: knowledge *isn't* virtue. Even with a good education, we'll still need to do more to build strong character.

As adults, we can sharpen those ethical tools and add new ones. We can read, think, and reflect. We can develop habits that form familiar paths to right conduct. And many find it helpful to draw on the resources of religion—the wellspring of much of the world's ethical teaching.

We can also hold up heroes to inspire us. We can look to examples of people who have stood up under pressure and acted honorably—from Socrates to Solzhenitsyn—from Joan of Arc to Anne Frank—from Galileo to Gandhi.

The Example of South Africa

But even with all of these character tools—with a good education—with solid values—with sound habits—and with heroes to hold up as models—it *still* won't be easy to make the tough choices. It won't be easy because—with the really tough choices—the *right* course of action may not be the one that seems obvious at first glance. Let me raise an example that gets a lot of attention in the media these days—South Africa.

What is the ethical course of action for business in that country? Popular opinion holds that American business should disinvest as a protest against apartheid. And several large companies—including IBM, General Motors, and Coca-Cola—have done so.

But *is* disinvestment the ethical answer? What if I contend that disinvestment merely gives a few people—sitting in comfortable offices in this country—a quick and easy dose of moral superiority? What if I argue that it doesn't do a thing to end apartheid? And suppose that I say it shows a very cavalier attitude toward black South Africans?

What happens to the black workers who lose their jobs and the effect that has on their families? What happens to the black managers who are left behind to deal with new South African owners—owners who don't give a hoot about the Sullivan Code? And what about the boost disinvestment gives to the radicals—the people who, in every revolution, won't be satisfied until a country goes through a violent blood bath?

The example of South Africa, I believe, points out the danger of ethical solutions that cost *us* very little—and other people a great deal. And it also points out the difficulty we face as individuals in making choices that go against the grain of popular opinion.

Conclusion

And so, in making the tough choices, what we are left with—and what we cling to like an ethical life buoy—is character. But that should be no small comfort.

Long ago, the Greeks had a saying about character. They said, "Character is *destiny.*" By that saying, they expressed the belief that individuals could shape the ultimate direction of their own lives.

You can take the spirit of that wisdom and make it your own. You can choose values that give you strength to bear up under pressure. You can build character in yourself that powers you through life like a tank—whose treads create a path across any terrain, no matter what the obstacles.

By building the inner light of character, you can shape your own destiny as a better *worker*—a better *citizen*—a better *individual*. At the same time, you'll help create a destiny for our *society* that keeps us a free and prosperous people.

Starting with the ember of character, you can grow as individuals until you stand one day like a moral beacon. That beacon can burn so brightly, a modern-day Diogenes will need no lantern to find you.

139

"*Capitalism is the economic system that is consonant with Christianity.*"

Capitalism and Christianity Are Complementary

George Gilder

George Gilder is the author of *Wealth and Poverty*, a book often referred to as the "Reaganomics bible." A contributor to *The Wall Street Journal* and many other publications, he has also written *Sexual Suicide*, *Men and Marriage*, and most recently, *Microcosm*. In the following viewpoint, Mr. Gilder asserts his belief that the fundamental principles of Christian life act to control the moral aspects of America's capitalist economic system. Capitalism, he claims, like Christianity, is an open system where people succeed by serving others.

As you read, consider the following questions:

1. How does the author think the church should respond to the plight of the poor?
2. What does the author mean when he says the poor need "the spur of poverty"? Do you agree?
3. Why does Mr. Gilder think capitalism, rather than socialism, is more compatible with Christianity?

Rodney Clapp, "*Capitalism and Christianity Meet,*" February 4, 1983. © 1983 by CHRISTIANITY TODAY. Reprinted with permission.

Christianity Today: Let's begin with your own words. You recently wrote in the *American Spectator,* "The church should devote itself to its own spiritual and religious cause, upholding the laws of morality and faith, and thus redeem the most crucial conditions of capitalistic giving and entrepreneurship." Is the church then subordinated to a supportive role in maintaining the capitalist economy? Is that its place in society?

Gilder: No. Like every other human activity, capitalism can succeed to the extent that it accords with the deeper principles that inspire religion. God comes first, obviously. Capitalism comes second. But when churches abandon God through various secular fads and enthusiasms, they are betraying God. When they maintain there's something inherently antagonistic between Christianity and capitalism, they're being obtuse. In other words, the church is perfectly capable of betraying God, and when it does, it betrays its deepest purpose in the world.

Christianity Today: How does that purpose work out in a concrete, practical manner? What exactly should the church be doing?

Gilder: The church should be evangelizing and persuading people of the truth of the Christian message. To the extent that it succeeds in performing that function it can save the world, and to the extent that it abandons that role it will both destroy itself—as many established churches are beginning to do—and destroy the world as well. Ultimately, the world can only work to the extent that it responds to God and is ordered by God's truth. So it's essential that the church propagate those truths rather than get involved in political conflicts. . . .

Christianity Today: So you would see the primary political involvement of the church to be individual Christians and not the church as an organization or body?

Gilder: I think Jerry Falwell makes that distinction very clearly. He is a preacher of the gospel much of the time, but he also performs a political role. He collaborates with a number of people of all faiths, propagating moral propositions that are upheld by many other religions as well as Christianity. I think that distinction is legitimate. The World Council of Churches and the National Council of Churches routinely accept a lot of socialist propositions and try to infuse them with a kind of holy light they don't deserve—helping the poor, for example. This is a practical problem, not something that can be done through good intentions alone. But the liberal policies some churches have endorsed have hurt the poor in America. The essential proposition of the church has been that anything that's done in the name of helping the poor is holy—as long as it doesn't focus on their spiritual or moral condition. . . .

Christianity Today: You've noted, "the poor know their condition is to a great degree their own fault or choice" and that "in

141

order to succeed, the poor need most of all the spur of poverty." One critic wrote that Gilder's theology of capitalism is long on faith and hope and short on charity. How do you respond to that?

Gilder: I reject that proposition. I reject the idea that it's good to the poor to destroy their motivation, to destroy their families, and to destroy their moral integrity. These social programs that are allegedly charitable are in fact profoundly destructive. I reject all the assumptions that underlie that particular criticism. But when I say they need the spur of their poverty, I don't mean that they need the spur of destitution.

A welfare system is indispensable to capitalism, because capitalism is based on freedom, on voluntary participation, on voluntary response to the need of others. A society that's based on forcing people to work under the pain of starvation is just as coercive as one that forces them to work at the point of a gun. Welfare is indispensable to capitalism, and capitalist societies generate welfare systems. We have a much more elaborate welfare state than the Soviet Union, which does force people to work under the pain of starvation. However, when the benefits of the welfare state far exceed the needs of subsistence or the possible earnings of an employee at an entry-level job, then it

---

America's Strengths

The history of this country makes it clear that those two basic strengths, political stability and the best economic system in the world, have combined to make possible more freedom, more choice, more leisure, and more opportunity for development of self and soul than anywhere else in the world.

John J. Riccardo, former president of Chrysler Corporation

---

becomes destructive. It violates the principle of moral hazard, which underlies all insurance schemes, and essentially a welfare system is an insurance scheme.

Take fire insurance, for example. When the payoff becomes more valuable than the house, arson often occurs. This has happened in many cities where the houses have become less and less valuable, until the fire insurance payoff is higher. Fire insurance may foster fires. In the same way, where a social insurance system, or welfare, offers benefits far more valuable than work, the welfare state causes poverty. That's what we're doing now: we're causing poverty by paying for it.

Christianity Today: Back to the "spur of poverty" not meaning destitution—what exactly do you mean?

Gilder: In contemporary American society it means income and benefits are less valuable than working at an entry-level job.

When the combination of welfare benefits the poor receive are about equivalent to the median family income, it's catastrophic for them.

As experienced by the poor, our current welfare state rewards family breakdown, unemployment, and consumption. If you save anything, you're immediately forced to spend that savings in order to retain your welfare benefits. It cultivates exactly the pattern of behavior that assures failure in a capitalist system. The spur of poverty means that the welfare state cannot be a cradle-to-grave cushion.

Christianity Today: Is the capitalist system open to the poor anyway?

Gilder: A capitalist system has millions and millions of small businesses. There are 16 million small businesses in the U.S. In Japan, which has been a more successful capitalist system in recent years, there are as many small businesses as there are in the U.S. with only a little more than half our population. A small business is the crux of a capitalist society, and it's accessible to anybody who doesn't follow the pattern of existence the welfare state prescribes—which is to break down the family into as many welfare-receiving components as possible, forgo all savings, and avoid any kind of regular employment.

There's also something about this dependence on the state that tends to erode religious belief. People begin to orient themselves toward belief in and dependence on the state. The state can become God.

Christianity Today: You have said capitalism thrives on religious faith and that it decays without it, and that capitalist progress is based on risk "that cannot be demonstrated to pay off in any one lifetime, thus it relies on faith in the future and in providence." How specific can you get about the kind of faith that's required here? Must capitalism be Jewish or Christian?

Gilder: Not necessarily. Though Eastern religions lack the help of Jesus, they do manage to capture some of the essential truths. If you analyze their moral teaching, they often correspond very closely to Christian teachings. Capitalism can thrive in that environment. Christianity offers a deeper and more inspiring exposition of those values, but through a glass darkly other religions can also descry the essential outlines of God and his truth, so I don't exclude them.

Christianity Today: Why is capitalism, from a religious standpoint, more acceptable than other economic systems?

Gilder: The central truth in capitalism is that its progress is unpredictable. The attempt to predetermine returns, to arrogate to the human mind the capacity to know the future, to calculate carefully its precise outlines and exploit this knowledge in some prescriptive way, leads to catastrophe. Capitalism, because it is based on the unknowability of the future and the conduct of continual experiments that reveal facets of the truth, can in fact partake of providence. The great sin of *hubris* is to imagine that without the help of God we can create a better future through some sort of human planning. It's this desire to have a master plan based on secular analysis that underlies socialism and makes it an evil system. Capitalism is an open system, where people succeed by serving others.

In order to serve others they have to understand others, and this requires that they have an outgoing temperament—an altruistic orientation, if you wish. And what others want is dependent on their values, which in turn is derived from the religious orientation of the society. If the society is irreligious and oriented chiefly toward hedonistic gratifications and sensuous fulfillment, then the operations of capitalism—in attempting to respond to others—will be depraved by these values. . . .

Christianity Today: Some Christians believe Jesus taught and embodied an ethic that can't be comprehended by any economic system—capitalism, socialism, or whatever. Thus, through the church, he stands in judgment over these temporal systems. Do you agree with that view?

Gilder: No. Obviously, Jesus' teachings far transcend particular economic processes, but I think that his teachings cannot be fulfilled in a socialist system. A planned, socialist system has to be ruled by experts who prescribe the activities of individuals and thus deny to them the moral freedom that is crucial to both Christian behavior and a successful social order. You can't give if the government controls all the property and essentially plans the modes of charity.

"Give and you'll be given unto" is the fundamental practical principle of the Christian life, and when there's no private property you can't give it because you don't own it. When all the returns of enterprise are captured by the state, you can't continue to expand your enterprise in response to your vision of the needs of the society. So socialism is inherently hostile to Christianity and capitalism is simply the essential mode of human life that corresponds to religious truth.

Christianity Today: So Christ, or the church, does not have to stand in judgment or be a potential critic of capitalism?

Gilder: There are two ways to view it. Capitalism is the economic system that is consonant with Christianity. But it obviously does not in itself produce a good society. You can have a hopelessly corrupt, evil society that's actually capitalistic. Capitalism is dependent on the church for the moral values that redeem it, so clearly the church has to stand in judgment. But it should not imagine that there is some other social system that partakes of Christianity in a better way than capitalism itself.

"Capitalism as we know it puts a high premium on the possession of material goods. . . . The gospel commands us to share material goods, not to amass them."

Capitalism and Christianity Are Contradictory

Eugene C. Bianchi

Eugene C. Bianchi is professor of religion at Emory University in Atlanta. Bianchi is the author of *Aging As a Spiritual Journey*, *From Machismo to Mutuality*, and numerous articles for such publications as *The Christian Century* and *America*. In the following viewpoint, Dr. Bianchi stresses his belief that the values of capitalism create greed and aggression. He calls for a revival of the fundamental values of social democracy in America to create equality between Christian and American ideals.

As you read, consider the following questions:

1. In the author's opinion, how are individualism and communal consciousness examples of the tension between capitalism and Christianity?
2. How does the author distinguish between capitalist individualism and healthy individualism?
3. What other examples does the author use to point out the contradictions between capitalism and Christianity?

I would like to point out some of the incompatibilities between gospel Christianity and capitalism as we know them. By capitalism, I mean not simply an economic system but the great productive network that spreads over our social, political and cultural life. That is, I understand capitalism as a total environment in which we are reared and conditioned. . . . I maintain that certain general but essential orientations of the Gospel Way and the American Way are contradictory. . . .

Individualism Versus Community

Capitalism, as an economic system geared mainly to maximizing profits, fosters intense individualism. On the other hand, the core beliefs of the Judeo-Christian tradition stress communal consciousness. Thus, to say that men won't exercise productive initiative without the profit motive to drive them solves nothing *religiously.* For the dangling carrot seems to lure them on toward greater self-centeredness, toward ever more ruthless manipulation of nature and fellow humans for personal (or at best familial) aggrandizement. Corporations are not community-oriented; they are utilitarian aggregates of individuals organized for maximizing *private* profits. The criterion for determining one's self-identity necessarily implies invidiousness and material superiority over others—key motivating elements of capitalism's handmaid, the advertising industry. In brief, if capitalism, as we know it, did not create the Hobbsian war of all against all, it certainly cultivates the seeds of such enmity. The self is supreme over/against others.

Look now at the Judeo-Christian heritage. As mirrored in pivotal documents and holy personalities, it centers on the creation of community. The Hebrew scriptures stress a social conception of God and man. The covenants between Yahweh and his people emphasize community in which the person of God is extended into communal human relationships. The corporate person of Israel rejected individualism with its glorification and isolation of the self—for example, in the controversy over kingship. The prophets also voice the strong ethical demands of the covenantal pact. They call Israel to turn away from the pursuit of private wealth and power and to renew the covenant of social justice and communal responsibility.

The Gospels carry on this theme of community-building as against the individualistic emphases of the Roman imperial world. The master image of early Christianity is the selfless Jesus who dedicates himself in suffering love to the creation of a new people. The Pauline literature develops this anti-individualism into the establishment of church communities where the common good is uppermost. The community (portrayed in Acts) of brothers and sisters lovingly committed to a corporate ministry of worship and action became a model for

Christian living. . . .

There is a healthy kind of individualism—the kind that is resistant to group tyranny and therefore accords with the Christian ideal of community. But capitalist individualism is not concerned about promoting the growth of the person into emotional, intellectual, ethical and cultural fullness; rather, it fosters the development of individual traits only so far as these are useful for maximizing profits. Thus, ironically, capitalist individualism turns into a group despotism under which personal becoming is sacrificed to the external tyrannies of material gain.

Capitalism's Negative Traits

Capitalism as we know it puts a high premium on the possession of material goods. . . . The gospel commands us to share material goods, not to amass them.

Money Is In

Remember when parents, teachers, poets and preachers said things like: "Money isn't everything," "Some things money can't buy," "The love of money is the root of all evil," "Who steals my purse steals trash," "Money can't buy love"? In those days "materialism" had a bad reputation. But our latest bout with hard times seems to have toppled the precarious balance between puritan restraint and pioneer greed—and turned materialism into a national virtue. Lately anyone who questions that the economy comes first sounds just a little treasonous. Money is *in*; by comparison, all other values are *out*.

Judith Paterson, *The Christian Century*, p. 1304, December 16, 1981.

But our technocratic capitalism is still destructively rooted in a primitive attitude toward things. Social Darwinism's stress on the "survival of the fittest" has been but slightly muted as American society's dominant tenet. Among us, possession of material goods is still the clearest sign of "fitness." To possess more is to be more worthy as a person. The great majority of our people still cling to the Horatio Alger myth that the goal of life is to make lots of money. This acquisitive spirit is confirmed in the American attitude toward the poor, who are condemned as willful or unwitting failures at becoming individual possessors—that is, in American terms, "persons.". . .

Capitalism depends on intense competitiveness coupled with overt and covert forms of violence. Family and school inculcate the spirit of rugged individualism, of getting ahead and rising to the top. Whether in athletics, academe, business or profession, competition requires that the neighbor be more or less violently

147

put down. Ethical lip service is paid to the means employed in becoming "successful," while individual responsibility for the humaneness of the means is minimized or eliminated. The compulsion to compete and achieve is all pervasive. In this milieu, to be human is to be violent toward nature, self and others. For only the respectably aggressive will possess goods, status and selfhood.

Abroad, our economic-political-military entanglements assure the spread of competitive violence. Political spheres of influence become vital for economic expansion and financial gain. The cold-war mentality, with its attitude of distrustful rivalry for pre-eminence, can turn into a hot war whenever our politico-economic interests are threatened. That so-called communist countries behave much as we do may help us to assess the world situation, but it does not justify the American style of competitive violence.

That style is a home brew whose ingredients, stirred together over more than two centuries, include the self-righteous notion of "manifest destiny" (with its concomitant racism), a passion for and enslavement to technology, and the all-enveloping ideal of getting rich. The consequences are destructive violence to nature and self and to less advantaged races and classes. Competitive America is raping its land, fouling its air and water for the purpose of making money. Those who compulsively engage in the routine of competition must deny themselves inward growth, for contemplation of spirit or beauty, or yielding to feelings of tenderness, would distract them. Thus they have no compunctions about keeping oppressed groups (e.g., women, blacks) at menial levels to service the competitive machine for the benefit of the master aggressors.

Basic American Ideals and Christianity

This picture of our culture is not a balanced one, but I stress the negativities of America because I believe they are now clearly in the ascendancy. The competitive ethos with its undercurrents of violence is diametrically opposed to Judeo-Christian teaching. The Hebrew religious ideal gradually evolved into that of redemptive suffering. Isaiah's "suffering servant" symbolizes Israel's mission to the nations. The prophets not only preached a more just society but exemplified nonviolent forms of resistance. Jesus commanded sensitivity and service to the needs of one's fellow men. The Jesus of the Beatitudes has always stood as a contradiction to the Christ of the Crusades invented by the church.

Our time has seen new models of suffering love in Gandhi, Martin Luther King and others. Their life style of nonviolent, prophetic resistance to the powers of death and injustice offers a singular hope for authentic rebirth in Christianity. But it is

148

doubtful that the entrenched churches will discover the sources of courage and commitment needed to realize this ideal. Perhaps the way of nonviolent resistance will always be that of the few. . . .

How do we as Christians face the contradictions between our milieu and our deepest commitments? Is there a constructive way to pattern a truly Christian life today? Certainly the first need is to recognize our situation—to recognize it at the gut level of our self-perception as struggling Christians in a hostile environment. It is no solution to import other sociopolitical systems which suffer from many of the same defects that mar ours, though they be called socialist or communist. Second, we must admit our daily complicity in oppressive systems and attitudes. This confession, rather than depressing and immobilizing us, can dispose us for the kind of change of heart and action that conduces new life styles.

As for positive action, we can strive through whatever channels are available to re-establish in our national life the principles of the Bill of Rights and the Declaration of Independence. These foundational American ideals are compatible with Christianity, though today they are merely themes for Fourth of July orators. We can also try to revive the better elements of native American populism and at the same time keep ourselves open to new forms of democratic socialism, whether these appear at home or abroad. Finally, we must do our best to incorporate into our own lives the Judeo-Christian tradition of cooperation and equality.

"Business is today the most significant force shaping American life and the strongest influence determining the everyday values of the average citizen."

Business Is the Source of America's Values

Otto A. Bremer

Otto A. Bremer is the former campus pastor at the Lutheran Campus Ministry, in Goleta, California. At the time the following viewpoint was written he was Newcomen Society Fellow in Business History at the University of Southern California Graduate School of Business Administration. Mr. Bremer contends that the traditional sources of values have lost their influence in American society. Without other strong values to replace them, he claims business has become the prime factor influencing American culture today.

As you read, consider the following questions:

1. What is the author's primary claim?
2. How does the author support his claim in discussing the family and pension funds?
3. In the author's opinion, why do traditional value sources have less influence in American society today? Do you agree?

Otto A. Bremer, "Is Business the Source of New Social Values?" *Harvard Business Review*, November-December 1971, pp. 121-26. © 1971 by the President and Fellows of Harvard College; all rights reserved. This reading consists of segments of the original article.

Business is today the most significant force shaping American life and the strongest influence determining the everyday values of the average citizen; the operative values in the management of a corporate enterprise tend to become the operative values in the daily life of society. . . .

The present student generation has grown up with less value input from traditional sources than any previous one. It is also the first to have had a lifelong exposure to nontraditional values through television. My experience with these students has convinced me that, more than any older generation, they are keenly aware of the dominant influence of business on society. . . .

The purpose of this article is to show why I am firmly convinced that the future of our society is going to be determined more by the day-to-day decisions of corporate managers—and the values that dictate these decisions—than by any other single influence. This conclusion is reached after 25 years as a student of business, a pastor to businessmen, and a campus pastor. . . .

Supporting Evidence

Of all our institutions, the family is most vulnerable to the influence of business values spilling over society in general. In my marriage and family counseling I often encounter people who look upon the family as primarily a financial institution—usually without being aware this is happening. Success is judged by the amount of capital accumulation and the expansion of assets. Difficulties, such as divorce and the rejection of younger members, frequently have their roots in the charge that someone is "unproductive" or "does not contribute to family success." Unconditional love, in the traditional, religious sense, has given way in these families to the standards of accountability appropriate to business.

Increasingly, other institutions are adopting business methods and the values that support them, such as efficiency, profitability, productivity, and quantitative criteria. There is no campaign by businessmen to bring this about, but demands to put public schools, universities, social service agencies, and churches on a "sound business basis" are receiving more and more support these days. In most cases I find myself approving, but should we not think long and hard about the future effects? . . .

Think about the way an average citizen invests in a pension fund. The value message he gets from the fund manager is most likely focused at maximizing his return on the investment in financial terms; he watches the fund closely and identifies his future with it. But are there not other returns on this investment, based on other values that are being overridden by the solely economic one? The investor thinks in economic terms about his future because he has been influenced in that direction. But what about his future in terms of a clean environment, racial

*"Religious freedom is my immediate goal,
but my long-range plan is to go into real estate."*

equality, and individual dignity? There are corporations which further these virtues and make a profit, and corporations which do not further them and make a profit. Why not invest in the former to insure a more "valuable" future? Most people don't think of this because economic values are dominating the others. . . .

The United States has traditionally depended on the interplay of various "value input sources"—farm life, communities, churches, business, education, and so on—to shape the values of each individual and, in sum, the values of society. The outcome, on the whole, has been very good. Each institution (or what I am calling value input source) made its contribution, but society—individually and collectively—made the final decision as to which values would prevail. . . .

There has always been the unspoken assumption that no one source will dictate the values of the whole society, that somehow the final mix of generally accepted values will be a balanced combination of the best from all value input sources. . . .

A Competitive Advantage

Today, the foregoing scenario is no longer applicable. In the language of our parallel in economic theory, the competition between the various value input sources has become quite "imperfect." The influence of education, family, community, church, and so on, in forming the values that individuals live by, is greatly diminished, and the influence of business is consequently stronger than ever before.

Think for a moment about what has happened to the traditional value input sources that influenced the everyday life of Mr. John Q. Citizen a generation or two ago:

Agricultural society—Even when people were leaving the farm in large numbers, they did not do so without having internalized some "down-to-earth" values that lasted a lifetime. Farming itself is now a big business, highly mechanized with daily life influenced more by the values of nearby urban centers than by the agricultural routines of the past.

Family—The extended family of the past helped to secure the passing on of values from generation to generation. Today, few children have daily contact with grandparents who, as Margaret Mead says, "cannot conceive of any future for the children other than their (the grandparents') own past lives."

Town or community—People are now more apt to experience short, rootless residential stops in innumerable, indistinguishable suburbs than to live in the town where they were born and intend to die; thus, assimilation of community mores is considerably weakened.

Religion—One does not really need the results of the many studies showing that people today look less and less to the churches and synagogues as a source of values. It is obvious that religion is not nearly the integrative and normative force that it once was.

Education—I suspect that most readers of this article can recall an elementary school experience characterized by uncritical transmittal of the values of the American way of life. To be sure, these values were usually seen from the perspective of a white, Anglo-Saxon, Protestant middle class imbued with patriotism and the puritan ethic, but the influence was strong. Today, we are more sensitive to the pluralistic nature of society and less willing to impose the values of the majority.

Direct evidence of the demise of traditional value sources is seen in the attempt of many young people to reestablish meaningful contact with contemporary substitutes for them. . . .

While the sources of traditional values decline in influence . . . the influence of business has not declined and now, by default, business finds itself with far more influence on society than ever intended—or desired.

The Emerging Monopolist

We are all familiar with cases where single institutions have dominated the values of other societies. In face, many immigrants to the United States from Prussia and elsewhere sought to escape what they called a "military society." Other immigrants remembered with some nostalgia an "agricultural society" in which the farm, as a living ecosystem, was the pervasive model. For some, this nostalgia almost blotted out the fact that they had left their homelands because the domination by agricultural values stifled new ideas and possibilities for industrial development.

Experience taught both the early settlers and later immigrants that one way to safeguard freedom was to be certain that checks and balances were built into the formal and informal structures of American culture. Few concepts are more deeply embedded in our understanding of what the American way of life is all about.

During the past half-century, however, the description of the United States as a "business society" has been used more and more. The designation expresses a positive and appreciative recognition of the success of the business community in contributing to the highest standard of living in the world. But could "business society" also describe a modern counterpart to the church-dominated society of the middle ages or the military societies, both past and present?. . .

I do not mean to deny the positive influence of business values on society, such as the quality of judging people on the basis of individual competence rather than on wealth, family, or connections. There are many other similar examples, but these should not lull us into complacency about the value crisis confronting us.

As I stated at the outset of this article, the operative values in the management of a corporate enterprise tend to become the operative values of the average citizen. If this is true, it seems clear that the future will be largely shaped by the business community.

"The growing presence of women in the workplace holds forth the greatest promise for a humanizing transformation in American working lives."

Women Are Improving America's Business Values

Elinor Lenz and Barbara Myerhoff

Author Elinor Lenz is an educational consultant and lecturer in Los Angeles. Barbara Myerhoff is a professor of anthropology at the University of Southern California in Los Angeles. In the following viewpoint, Lenz and Myerhoff discuss how the influx of women into workplaces is changing America's business values. They write that management has learned that women's skills at communication and nurturing contribute to companies' success and improve the working environment for men and women.

As you read, consider the following questions:

1. What unique attributes do women bring to corporations, in the authors' opinion?
2. Why do the authors believe many companies have recognized the need for providing day care for employees' children?
3. According to Lenz and Myerhoff, how are female employees affecting male employees?

As women have been moving in ever-increasing numbers into jobs and professions formerly occupied by men, the working environment in which most people spend the major part of their lives has begun to respond to feminine needs and values. As a result, we are seeing a shift to a more humane, more people-centered workplace, a long overdue development that comes in time to counteract a growing discontent with the conditions of work that has been spreading throughout the occupational spectrum.

Discontent and Alienation

The discontents that people are voicing about their work are for the most part connected to a feeling of meaninglessness, a sense of being alienated from what one does during the working day, which afflicts people at all salary levels. Some typical comments from interviews with men and women in the $25,000-$50,000 salary range reflect this:

> I spend most of my time writing ad copy for deodorants and after-shave lotion. Eight to ten hours a day, day after day, year after year, agonizing over stuff I don't give a damn about. When I get home at night after an hour's commute, my kids are in bed and I'm so strung out, all I want is a couple of good stiff scotches, and maybe I'll watch a little TV before I turn in. (Mark Nevelson, forty-five-year-old advertising executive, Chicago)

> I'm just marking time till I get my pension. Twenty years to go, then if I'm not too old, maybe I can do some of the things I've always wanted to do. My job is just a big fat bore, a waste of time. (Helen Jacoby, forty-two-year-old executive secretary to the financial vice-president of a merchandising conglomerate, Dallas)

> I go home on Friday evening, lock the door, and don't leave my apartment until Monday morning. It takes me two days and three nights to calm down so that I can go back on Monday and face five more days of it. I hate my life, I hate myself, I hate what this is doing to me. (Susan Ellis, thirty-year-old program coordinator in a federally funded community project, Detroit)

Underlying much of this unhappiness is the divorce of work from the rest of life, an inevitable outcome of the work-home schism. Work takes on meaning only in a context that provides wholeness and balance and that gives us a feeling of belonging to a community. The notion that the activity at which we spend the most productive years of our lives can be divided off from the rest of us—from our character, aspirations, and cultural heritage—the assumption that a human being can be split in two with one-half placed on hold for forty hours a week is a recent and dangerous idea that is damaging to the individual's sense of self-worth. . . .

The mass movement of women into the workplace has been hailed by social scientists and historians as a social change of momentous proportions, comparable to the industrial revolution or the waves of immigration in the last century. "It's the single most outstanding phenomenon of this century," says Eli Ginzberg, professor at Columbia University and chairman of the National Commission for Manpower Policy. . . .

The feminization of the workplace is transforming more than just the economy. "Women are neurologically more flexible than men," says Eli Ginzberg, "and they have had cultural permission to be more intuitive, sensitive, feeling. Their natural milieu has been complexity, change, nurturance, affiliation, a more fluid sense of time." As these attributes of feminine culture are brought into the workplace, they are providing a much-needed balance to what has been a predominantly male environment, and slowly but steadily they are eroding some of the obsolete practices and prejudices that have dehumanized work and the work environment.

Unique Perspectives

With each passing day, evidence is mounting of the unique skills and perspectives that women, as a group, bring to business. These skills will complement, not replace, the traditional masculine approach to managing. Sometimes, when looked at on an individual basis, these different managerial skills and perspectives may be subtle and difficult to discern. But when viewed in the aggregate, across large numbers of women, the subtleties disappear and the differences become more clearly defined. Women, as a group, truly have their own leadership style, and this style can make an important contribution to American business.

Marilyn Loden, *Feminine Leadership or How To Succeed in Business Without Being One of the Boys,* 1985.

Much of this change is linked to women's deeply rooted need to integrate love and work. The work-home division grates against the feminine sensibility. "Every woman in America leads a double life," says political scientist Emily Stoper. "She is shaped by a double socialization; she is torn apart by a double pull; often she carries a double burden. One side of her duality turns inward to the world of home, children, 'inner feelings'—femininity, in a word. The other side faces outward to the world of work, achievement, power, money, abstract thought—the 'man's world.'"

Challenging Corporate Bureaucracy

Women's efforts to reconcile the two sides of this duality pit them against the structure and rationale of the corporate bureaucracy. As Daniel Boorstin points out in *The End of Ideology,* the contemporary enterprise was set up to obey three "techno-logics": the logic of size, the logic of "metric" time, and the logic of hierarchy. "Each of the three, the product of engineering rationality, has imposed on the worker a set of constraints with which he is forced to wrestle every day." These three technologics, which have defined and delimited work in America for the past century, are giving way—inch by inch, moment by moment, step by step—to the forces of change that are in harmony with feminine culture.

The constraint of "metric time" measurement is loosening as the needs of working mothers challenge rigid work schedules and generate more fluid, flexible time arrangements to include part-time, flexi-time and job sharing. These innovative work patterns, offering more flexibility and the opportunity for choice and self-management on the job, make it possible for women to bring their home and working lives into balance.

But it is not only women who are the beneficiaries of more relaxed work schedules; potential all-around benefits abound: the easing of traffic congestion; the weekday access by employees to shopping, education, recreation; an opportunity for both parents to spend more time with their children. (A 1977 Quality of Employment Survey by the Survey Research Center at the University of Michigan found that 51 percent of wives and 42 percent of husbands with children under eighteen preferred to reduce their work time in order to spend more time with their families.) The time clock may, eventually, be consigned to the ash heap of history as the development of technology converges with new, more leisure-oriented lifestyles to bring about a variety of work schedules that can be adapted to individual needs. . . .

A New Managerial Agenda

Some of the changes being forged in the crucible of feminization could not have been imagined even a decade ago. Bread-and-butter issues—comparable pay, for example—are forcing managers as well as economic theorists to rethink the basic American concept of equality. The Equal Pay Act of 1963 required that women be paid equally with men for the same job; and women's pay, though still a long way from parity, has risen from 57 percent of men's wages in 1973 to 64 percent in 1980. But the concept of comparable worth asks: What if the jobs are not the same but are equal in levels of skill, effort, and responsibility? Should a secretary, for example, be paid as much as a truck driver? The controversy has been heating up, with employers and union representatives, particularly those representing public employees, positioning themselves for a protracted battle. A judicial or legislative resolution does not appear to be in the offing, but in the meantime, the underlying question of what equality is, once a preoccupation mainly of academic philosophers, will continue to be argued at corporate seminars and meetings of public officials.

Other strange new issues are appearing on the managerial agenda, issues unrelated to production quotas or profit margins that seem, oddly enough, to be closer to the homeplace than the workplace. In the 1970s, babies were not a concern of such enterprises as the Caltech Jet Propulsion Laboratory. At that time, the laboratory was mostly male. But in 1973, when the federally funded lab initiated an affirmative action program, the number of women employees began growing, until women constitute a quarter of the 5,000-person work force. And a quarter-mile from the lab is the Child Educational Center of the Caltech/JPL community, which serves 150 preschool children of employees and area residents. Women workers drop in to nurse and play with their children; both mothers and fathers are encouraged to visit.

Women Are Gaining Credibility

In the past, male characteristics were thought to be good in business and female characteristics were considered bad. But I think people are starting to recognize that this was wrong. Today, as the job of managing continues to get more complex and managers realize that they have to be more inclusive of employees, women are gaining credibility. Because of socialization, I think women may have an advantage in this area. They've been taught to be more concerned with people matters.

Carol Bellamy quoted in *Feminine Leadership or How To Succeed in Business Without Being One of the Boys*, 1985.

At present, nearly 3,000 corporations nationwide sponsor day-care centers for their employees, or otherwise assist them in finding reliable day care. A survey funded by the federal government called employer-supported child care "the fastest growing form of child care today." The survey, conducted for the U.S. Department of Health and Human Services, found that although employer-sponsored programs cover less than 1 percent of children in day care, "the trend is accelerating rapidly." . . .

We may justifiably question the value system of a society that spends billions on sophisticated weapons yet skimps on care for its children. But as Eric Nelson, codirector of the Caltech/JPL center puts it, "It's going to take people of vision at the top and bottom getting together to solve the day-care problem. In general, management is older and male. Child care is a problem with which they can't easily identify. Child-care experts have to understand that and be able to convince hard-headed businessmen that they should be interested in babies. The fact that women are out of the home is still a shock to some men, and the thought of babies in the workplace is the last straw."

But the trend is unstoppable, for it reflects a growing public con-sciousness that day care for the children of working parents is a concern not only of the parents but of the entire society. When children are not adequately cared for, as many studies show, the lack is reflected in rising rates of crime, unemployment, and domestic violence. An argument that is proving more persuasive, however, especially among "hard-headed businessmen," is that day care is good for business, reducing absenteeism and boosting morale. Most companies would be hard hit by the loss of those female workers who are mothers of small children, and economic analyses indicate that the economy would go into a severe decline without the earnings and purchasing power of working mothers. The facts of economic life make it safe to predict that by the end of this decade, companies without some form of day care will be regarded as dinosaurs, along with those having no employee benefit plans. . . .

This growing interest in the needs of working parents stems less, as we have suggested, from a sudden surge of corporate solicitude for the two-job family than from the new economic realities that business and industry are facing as a result of women entering the work force. The facts and figures are clear and their implica-tions for the workplace are unmistakable: women now constitute one-half of the work force, and of these women, half will become pregnant at some time in their working lives. The majority of these women are no longer leaving their jobs for an extended time to rear their children. According to U.S. census figures for 1982, almost one-third of mothers with infants under six months are working, and a survey of corporations found that the average length of time off work for new mothers is three months. (This coincides with research in infant psychology, which has found that at three months, the infant can be safely separated from the mother for limited time periods.)

Feminization Is Changing Values

These corporate efforts to meet the needs of working mothers, insufficient as they are at present, represent a radical reordering of an institutional mind-set that has been shaped by "the cult of efficiency." Feminization is forcing that mind-set to extend itself to the larger questions of human values and relationships and how these impinge upon people's working lives. For traditional manage-ment, confronting such questions has had the effect of shock treat-ment. To most men in top management, women are "a foreign country," says organizational psychologist Sandra Florstedt. She attributes the slow pace of reform to women's "different heritage" of values, behavior, and style, acquired over the centuries and often baffling to men in the workplace, accustomed as they are to working in an all-male environment. Having started her career as a high school language teacher, she identifies as the most difficult problem in organizations today the development of a common language to span the communication gap between men and women in the workplace. . . .

The most important influence of women on the workplace, according to Florstedt, is that "they're keeping men honest. I know a lot of men who like working with women because it's the women who are calling it the way they see it, at least privately—maybe it's because they're new to the situation, they're seeing it differently, more clearly." At the same time, she recognizes that women's creative energies, which are now being diverted from housework and babies to business and the professions, need to be channeled properly if women are to achieve their full potential for productivity. "They need to feel a sense of connection to the workplace and not think of it as a male world in which they are intruders."

A Change for the Better

In a few years, women will equal men in numbers as well as in every area of economic activity.

Is society better for this change? Women's exit from the home and entry into the work force has created problems—an urgent need for good, affordable child care; troubling questions about the kind of parenting children need; the costs and difficulties of diversity in the work place; the stress and fatigue of combining work and family responsibilities. Wouldn't we all be happier if we could turn back the clock to an age when male and female roles were clearly differentiated and complementary?

Nostalgia, anxiety and discouragement will urge many to say *yes*. My answer is emphatically *no*. Two fundamental benefits that were unattainable in the past are now within our reach. For the individual, freedom of choice—in this case the freedom to choose career, family or a combination of the two. For the corporation, access to the most gifted individuals.

Felice N. Schwartz, *Los Angeles Times*, March 17, 1989.

It may well be that the growing presence of women in the workplace holds forth the greatest promise for a humanizing transformation in American working lives: the desegregation of the workplace and the restoration in today's egalitarian terms of a working life shared by men and women, which was disrupted by the industrial revolution. "Men and women are rediscovering each other," said a woman who heads a corporate training program. There is still hostility and resentment, she added, by men who see women taking over jobs that were formerly regarded as strictly male occupational territory, but this is lessening as men become accustomed to women in these jobs. Distance may lend enchantment, but it also leads to stereotyping: as the distance between male and female working lives narrows, the stereotype too is waning, and women are appearing less and less as a "foreign country" to their male colleagues. . . .

Boosting Morale

Those men who succeed in developing nonsexual friendships with their female colleagues—and their number increases daily—are experiencing a gratifying sense of personal growth, an ability to look beyond gender at individual competency and accomplishment. Several men who have made this transition report that it has enriched not only their relationships at work but also their personal lives. "I'm finding it easier to make friends, with men as well as women," said one. "Women seem to have some sort of special talent for friendship, and it's rubbing off on me."

The morale-boosting, performance-improving impact of the feminine presence has not escaped the notice of corporate personnel managers. Jane Evans, an executive vice-president of General Mills, reports that corporations are searching for women who know how to help men open up, share their feelings, become comfortable with women. Executive search firms agree, adding that one of the major barriers to the promotion of women is the male executive who does not understand women and can only look on them in such supportive roles as wives, mothers, daughters, and secretaries. This musty attitude is as much a problem for the male executive, whose narrow perspective denies him the productive abilities of qualified women, as it is for the women whose progress he attempts to stall.

Women's Contribution

As women in so-called traditional male jobs cease to be a novelty, men are beginning to recognize the benefits that women bring to the workplace. A survey of male CEOs in Fortune 500 companies on the effects of women in executive positions yielded a generally positive reaction, with a substantial percentage stating that women bring a humanizing quality to the corporate world and are also improving business. The growth of an information/service economy calls for the kind of skills and problem-solving approaches that are essentially feminine. Information and service are, like women's historic culture, processual; and there is a developing awareness in business and industry of the linkage between productivity and what is usually referred to as "human resources," or the relationships among people at work.

Mary Bradley, a former teacher in adult education and now a corporate training director, has this to say on the subject of the feminine influence on technology: "Formerly, my experience and that of most women has consisted of learning how to function in a male system. But in my present work environment, which combines computer technology with education, the situation is reversed: men have to move into what has always been a female system—education, helping people develop new skills, which is what a high-technology economy is all about—and when it comes to education, men whose training has been exclusively in business and industry are totally lost. They understand equipment, marketing, the good old bottom line, but they don't know what goes into the development of a human being. They've never before paid much attention to human needs in their enterprises—they thought that was for social workers. But now they have to pay attention because it means money and expansion and business opportunities." . . .

For many women in influential positions, changing the workplace is at the heart of their commitment to feminism. For Donna Shalala, the practice of feminism is not limited to serving as a role model; it encompasses "thinking of ways in which I can humanize the institution." She believes that women's issues should be integrated into a larger, humanistic agenda. "My single professional focus is to make institutions act better than they ever thought they could act." As assistant secretary at the Department of Housing and Urban Development during the Carter administration, she called the department heads together to conduct a "women's impact study," as a result of which shelters for battered women became eligible for community development grants, and housing units to accommodate large families headed by a woman were included in planning. . . .

A Healthy Workplace

The willingness to listen and the quality of caring and comforting that exists in many women comes through in their work, sometimes without their being aware of it, as they go about their daily tasks in the business and professional world. The cumulative effect of such empathic behavior does not show up in organizational blueprints or financial statements; but in building small, often imperceptible bridges between home and work, this aspect of feminization is performing a function essential to the health of the American workplace.

"A clear majority . . . believe businesses actually strengthen their competitive position by maintaining high ethical standards."

A National Survey of Business Ethics

Touche Ross & Company

Touche Ross is one of the leading eight accounting firms in the nation. Periodically the company publishes reports that it feels will benefit the country. This viewpoint is taken from its report on *Ethics in American Business*. The company received completed questionnaires from 1,082 business and political leaders, business students, educators, and other professionals who shared their thoughts on the current status of ethics in American business practices. Respondents believed almost unanimously that although business is troubled by ethical problems, US business is either highly or reasonably ethical. Only 3 percent said it was unethical. Respondents also thought that companies actually strengthen their competitive position by maintaining high ethical standards.

As you read, consider the following questions:

1. How do survey respondents compare current ethical standards to those of the past?
2. What industries and professions do they think have the highest ethical standards?

Touche Ross & Company, *Ethics in American Business: A Special Report*. New York: 1988. Reprinted by permission of Touche Ross & Company.

It was the ultimate get-rich-quick scheme. Two businessmen conspire with a relative of the President of the United States to corner the available supply of gold in the New York stock market. Believing they have convinced the President not to sell government gold, they drive its share price to dizzying heights, throwing the nation's business into panic. After the Treasury Department unexpectedly steps in and sells government gold, the scheme—and the market—collapse. When the crash comes, on "Black Friday," many innocent investors are ruined. But the principal conspirators escape. One, apparently on the basis of inside information, sells early. The other, who once responded to criticism of his misuse of other people's money by saying, "Nothing is lost save honor," simply repudiates his debts and then hires thugs to threaten his creditors.

To many, this episode may read like a story out of today's newspapers, though it actually took place more than 100 years ago amid the turbulence of the country's post-Civil War years. Yet for all its notoriety, this scandal is but one of many that have contributed to the questionable image against which American business and industry have long struggled. Is the perception of American business beset by scandal fair? Does this image apply to all business people—men and women, young and old? What is the reality today?

Seeking answers to such questions, Touche Ross surveyed 1,082 corporate directors and officers, business school deans, and members of Congress for their views on ethics in American business. Conducted in October 1987, the survey sought opinions on a wide range of topics, from which industries and professions are the most ethical to whether ethics has any effect on a corporation's competitiveness.

Business Ethics Today and in the Past

Does American business have an ethics problem? Based on the survey's findings, the answer clearly is "yes." Indeed, that viewpoint seems to be nearly unanimous. The survey found that 94 percent of respondents think the business community is troubled by ethical problems. Some 95 percent of the corporate directors and officers expressed this belief, as did 99 percent of the business school deans and 77 percent of the lawmakers.

But since this survey came at a time when publicity over American ethics was at its height, could the response be more a reflection of that publicity than a true reading of respondents' actual beliefs? Apparently not. In fact, more than two-thirds (68 percent) of survey respondents said they do not think the issue of business ethics has been overblown in the current public debate. This finding holds true for business leaders in all industry groups except aerospace and defense. Sixty-three percent of those

Profile of the Sample

That key business leaders regard ethics as an important issue today is demonstrated by the large response to the survey. The survey questionnaire was mailed only to directors and top executives of corporations with $500 million or more in annual sales, to deans of business schools, and to members of Congress. Of 8,180 questionnaires mailed in October 1987, 1,107 were completed and returned, 1,082 in time to be included in the tabulation.

Most of the respondents are officers of corporations (65 percent), directors of corporations (58 percent), or both. Seventy percent of them say they are involved with multinational companies. Among the corporate officers, 37 percent give their title as chief executive officer, 15 percent as chairman, 10 percent as chief financial officer, and another 10 percent as chief operating officer.

Nine percent of the respondents are deans of business schools, and 2 percent are members of Congress. Three percent are retired corporate officers or deans.

In professional background, 34 percent of the respondents identify themselves as lawyers, 16 percent as teachers and 16 percent as engineers, 15 percent as accountants, 9 percent as bankers, 3 percent as lawmakers, 2 percent as media professionals, and less than 1 percent each as physicians, military, and clergy. Forty-six percent have a degree from a U.S. school of business.

The respondents' primary industry identifications are: manufacturing 18 percent; banking 10 percent; insurance 6 percent; agriculture and food processing 5 percent; high technology 5 percent; retailing 5 percent; securities 5 percent; and utilities 5 percent. Industries with less than 5 percent representation are aerospace and defense; apparel and textiles; construction; drugs, pharmaceuticals, and cosmetics; energy; media; telecommunications; and transportation.

Fourteen percent of the respondents are under 45 years old. Twenty-seven percent are between 45 and 54, 38 percent are between 55 and 64, and 20 percent are 65 or older. Ninety-six percent are men and 4 percent are women.

Regionally, 26 percent of the respondents live in the East, 26 in the Midwest, 15 percent in the West, 12 percent in New England, 10 percent in the South, 6 percent in the Southwest, and 3 percent in the Northwest.

Touche Ross & Company, *Ethics in American Business*, 1988.

surveyed in this industry said the issue *had* been exaggerated. (Of the 32 percent of all respondents who think the issue has been overblown, 87 percent blame the media and 22 percent blame politicians.)

In stark contrast to these findings, the survey pointed up an apparent contradiction. Although respondents believed almost unanimously that business is troubled by ethical problems, they did not say it suffers from a wholesale breakdown in ethics. Indeed, 97 percent believed U.S. business is either highly or reasonably ethical, and only 3 percent said it is unethical.

Moreover, compared to 100 years ago, business ethics are better today, said 62 percent of those polled. But they are not so sure about the direction that business ethics have taken in the past 25 years. Only 37 percent think that business ethics have improved since the early 1960s, 33 percent said they have declined, and the rest think they have stayed the same.

How Does the US Rank?

What is more, respondents regard the United States as having higher business ethics than any other country in the world. Asked to name and rank the five countries that have the highest standards of ethics, respondents rated the United States first, followed by Great Britain, Canada, Switzerland, and West Germany, in that order. Japan, a close runner-up in the overall ratings, was ranked among the top five by some respondents. Foreigners were not polled.

The main reason for these countries' high ethical standards, most respondents said, is their cultural heritage. Seventy-three percent named this as the primary factor, while only 13 percent pointed to the educational system. Only 9 percent named economic conditions.

Good Ethics Means Good Business

One of the most striking findings of the survey is that a clear majority of respondents (63 percent) believe businesses actually strengthen their competitive position by maintaining high ethical standards. Only 14 percent say companies with high ethical standards are weaker competitors, and 23 percent think that companies' ethical standards have no effect on their competitive position.

What Causes Ethics Problems?

If respondents think that companies having high ethical standards are stronger competitors, the question that arises is: Why is there an ethics problem in the first place? One explanation is that companies, under pressure from the increased concentration on short-term earnings, may turn to unethical measures to achieve the results that shareholders and others desire. Indeed, the pressure for short-term earnings was viewed by all respondents as the second-greatest threat to business ethics, just slightly behind the threat posed by decay in cultural and social institutions. Among business school deans and members of Congress, concentration on short-term earnings ranked first. On an interesting note, although the vast majority of respondents have careers in business or business education, they ranked volatile economic conditions as the least important factor threatening to undermine business ethics.

In contrast, if these factors pose the greatest threat to business ethics, then which factors most effectively encourage ethical business behavior? Thirty-nine percent of those polled cited adoption of business codes of ethics as the best way to inspire ethical behavior; 30 percent recommended a more humanistic curriculum in business education; and 20 percent suggested legislation.

In terms of who plays the biggest role in setting ethical standards for employees, 73 percent of respondents pointed to the company's chief executive officer. Twenty-five percent said it is the employee's immediate supervisor, and 5 percent said it is the board of directors. (Some respondents named more than one.)

Ranking Industries and Professions

Asked which three groups have been the most helpful in improving American business ethics, respondents identified business people themselves, business associations, and the courts, ranked in that order. Academia failed to place among the top three, as did government and the media, both of which were rated much less helpful than academia.

On the issue of whether ethical standards differ from industry to industry, 87 percent of those surveyed think so. And they rank commercial banking; utilities; and drugs, pharmaceuticals, and cosmetics as the most ethical, in that order.

Although these industries are among the most regulated in the country, only 21 percent of the respondents attributed these industries' high ethics to regulation. Instead, they gave the credit to strong existing industry standards.

Five other industries, though not placing among the top three, nevertheless earned good ratings for their ethical standards. Ranked in order, they are high technology, agriculture and food processing, insurance, manufacturing, and telecommunications.

The survey also found that ethical differences are seen not only among industries but also among professions. Ninety-seven percent of respondents think that some professions have higher ethical standards than others. The four professions with the highest standards, they believed, are the clergy, accountants, teachers, and engineers, ranked in that order.

Almost half (48 percent) of the respondents attributed the high ethics of these professions to rigorous standards and accreditation. Twenty-six percent named peer opinion and approval as the main reason, 11 percent said education, and 10 percent pointed to the socioeconomic background of the practitioners.

Geographically, the Midwest, the Northwest, and New England were rated by 58 percent of the respondents as having the highest standards of business ethics. The East—home of Wall Street—was rated the lowest.

Seventy-five percent of respondents said the main reason the Midwest and other Snowbelt regions have high ethical standards is their cultural heritage. Only 10 percent pointed to religious traditions, and 7 percent to educational systems.

Among the survey's other highlights, 78 percent of respondents said ethical standards do not differ between men and women in business. Only 43 of the respondents are women, but 19 of them think that ethical standards do vary—and that women are more ethical. Of the men who think that ethical standards vary between men and women, 82 percent say women are more ethical.

That a person's rules of ethics depend at all on his or her age is believed by slightly more than half of the respondents—52 percent. Of those who do believe this, 82 percent say that older people are more ethical.

The older respondents are, the more inclined they are to believe that ethical standards vary by age. Sixty-five percent of those who are 65 years old or older believe this, but only 39 percent of those who are under 45 agree.

Is big business any more or less ethical than small business? Half of the respondents said there is no difference between the two. Thirty-eight percent said big business is more ethical, and 12 percent said small business is more ethical.

Given that the corporate directors and officers participating in this survey represent companies having $500 million or more in sales, it is notable that 11 percent of them said that small business is more ethical than big; only 40 percent said that big business is more ethical than small; and 49 percent said they see no difference.

a critical thinking activity

Case Study: Economic Democracy

Acme Manufacturing Company is a prosperous firm with fine potential for the future. The owner of Acme has offered to sell the company to the one hundred employees who work there. A group of employees is in favor of the purchase and recommends that all employees contribute equally to the purchase price. The group suggests that the employees own and operate the company according to a plan they call *Economic Democracy*. A copy of the plan is given to each employee to study.

Step 1.   The class should break into groups of four to six students.

Step 2.   Each group should pretend that it represents an advisory council appointed by the employees to study the owner's offer and the plan for Economic Democracy. The advisory council must recommend whether or not it considers it practical for the employees to buy Acme and run it according to the plan for Economic Democracy.

Step 3.   After a majority of the members of each small group has made its decision, it should be able to present its recommendation and reasoning to the whole class.

Plan for Economic Democracy

WE ADVOCATE A NEW ECONOMIC SYSTEM
ECONOMIC DEMOCRACY
—It's neither Capitalism nor Socialism—

Most of us are familiar with Capitalism and Socialism, the two dominant economic systems in the world today. There is, however, a third economic system that is being discussed and experimented with in countries throughout the world. It is a system of self-managed enterprises that operate within a competitive free market economy.

The 5 Defining Characteristics of a "Democratic Economy"

1. A democratic economy is composed of firms controlled and managed by the people who work in them. Employees determine broad company policies and elect management on the principle of one person one vote.

2. In a self-managed firm, all participants share in the net income of the enterprise. The members themselves jointly determine the various income levels for different job tasks in the firm.

The members also jointly determine the amount of undistributed net income that will be used for other purposes, such as investment in new capital and reserve funds.

3. In a democratic economy, the ownership of the capital assets can take one of two forms. Either the working members of that firm directly own the enterprise; or they 'lease' the plant, equipment and other capital assets from an agency of the local or national government, and pay a contractual fee, rental or interest out of the income they generate from the enterprise.

In the latter case, the members of a self-managed firm cannot sell these borrowed assets and distribute the proceeds as current income to the members. The assets are merely being leased and when and if a particular firm decides to go out of business, the capital assets go back to the leasing source. On the other hand, the lenders of financial capital have no right of control over the policies or physical assets of the self-managed firm as long as it is meeting its debt-servicing obligations.

4. A self-managed system always operates in a competitive free market economy. Firms are free to vie with each other in terms of prices, product quality, and types of products and services in the marketplace.

Economic planning and policy may be exercised by the local or National Government through the use of indirect policy instruments, such as special tax incentives, but never through direct orders or interventions.

Natural resources, utilities and public transportation remain outside the free market economy and are publicly owned and administered in a democratic economy.

5. In a democratic economy, there is complete freedom of employment. The individual is free to take or not take a job or to leave a particular job.

What is the motivating force of a self-managed economy?

The financial objective of the self-managed firm is to maximize the income of each of its members.

The social objective is to maximize democratic participation of each of its members.

Peoples Bicentennial Commission, Washington, D.C. 20036

Periodical Bibliography

The following articles have been selected to supplement the diverse views presented in this chapter.

Robert Bachelder
"Have Ethics Disappeared from Wall Street?" *The Christian Century*, July 15-22, 1987.

Robert N. Bellah
"Resurrecting the Common Good," *Commonweal*, December 18, 1987.

Patrick M. Boarman
"Business and Ethics," *Vital Speeches of the Day*, June 15, 1982.

Norman Gall
"When Capitalism and Christianity Clash," *Forbes*, September 1, 1980.

James Glassman
"The Monster That's Eating Wall Street," *Washington Post National Weekly Edition*, January 18-24, 1988.

Ivan Hill
"Honesty, Freedom and Business Ethics," *Vital Speeches of the Day*, May 1, 1982.

James E. Hug
"Call to Cultural Conversion," *New Catholic World*, July/August 1983.

Donna Day Lower
"Reworking the Work Ethic," *The Other Side*, June 1983.

M
"Greed," October 1986.

Myron Magnet
"The Money Society," *Fortune*, July 6, 1987.

Daniel E. Maltby
"The One-Minute Ethicist," *Christianity Today*, February 19, 1988.

George D. O'Brien
"The Christian Assault on Capitalism," *Fortune*, December 8, 1986.

Anthony M. Pilla
"How To Implement 'Economic Justice for All'," *America*, January 31, 1987.

Ronald Reagan
"Free Enterprise," *Vital Speeches of the Day*, January 15, 1973.

Paul O. Sand
"Business Ethics," *Vital Speeches of the Day*, November 15, 1988.

Richard Stengel
"Morality Among the Supply-Siders," *Time*, May 27, 1987.

Michael Thomas
"Michael Thomas on Wretched Excess," *M*, October 1986.

Utne Reader
"Ethical Business: Oxymoron?" January/February 1989.

What Are America's Religious Values?

Chapter Preface

Many people argue that America is a religious society. According to Robert Bellah, a prominent authority on religion, church attendance has stayed at about 40 percent for the last fifty years, and church membership has stayed at around 60 to 70 percent.

The first four viewpoints in this chapter present differing perspectives on America's religious traditions. Reading them will provide some understanding of how these traditions have been so closely interwoven with the political and social values of the society. In addition, the viewpoints lend insight as to why Americans so tenaciously revere their religious heritage. As one academician has claimed, America may be ''a nation with the soul of a church.''

"Five elements . . . are sufficiently widely shared in America and not sufficiently widely shared by other nations or peoples."

America's Religious Tradition Has Five Roots

Martin E. Marty

Martin E. Marty, called by *Time* magazine "the most influential living interpreter of religion in the US," is Fairfax M. Cone Professor of the History of Modern Christianity at the University of Chicago. He is the author of more than thirty books, among them *Righteous Empire, Pilgrims in Their Own Land,* and *Religion & Republic: The American Circumstance.* In this viewpoint, Professor Marty claims that anyone who wants to understand America must first explore its religious traditions. He identifies five elements that he thinks form the distinctive basis of the American tradition. The five elements are pluralism, experimentalism, scripturalism, enlightenment, and voluntaryism.

As you read, consider the following questions:

1. What does the author claim is distinctive about America's brand of religious pluralism?
2. How does he relate the Bible to the concept of scripturalism that he describes?
3. To what does he refer when using the term the "American Enlightenment?"

From *Religion & Republic: The American Circumstance* by Martin E. Marty. Copyright © 1987 by Martin E. Marty. Reprinted by permission of Beacon Press.

Paul Tillich . . . argues that religion is the soul of culture and culture the form of religion. One would not think of interpreting cultures that derive from Buddhist, Islamic, Hindu, or similar influences without some awareness of their religious grounding. Every visitor to American shores who wishes to make sense of life in this nation also finds it important to reexplore the religious roots of this culture, as many natives do not. While we cannot write "religion equals tradition," we can see that the deepest sanctions for the tradition are religious. . . .

There is no claim here that the five elements to which I shall point are unique to America. They are distinctive. They are sufficiently widely shared in America and not sufficiently widely shared by other nations or peoples who are apart from or who preceded the American precedent to warrant some measure of identification.

Pluralism

Pluralism is the obvious fact about America, and it is certainly distinctive. With the spread of technology, mobility, and mass media, an increasing pluralism is known all over the world today, in many nations. America is not the first country to include more than one religious grouping, to be sure. But nowhere before or elsewhere has there been variety on the scale experienced here, or such a widespread acceptance of the grounding of that diversity, or such celebration of its positive values. No foreign visitor fails to observe it. In a sense, to say that our tradition is pluralistic seems to say that America has no tradition: how can the "many" be a "one"? Yet Americans have dealt with their "many" in a way that has caused a kind of "one" to emerge.

On the fact of the variety one need not long dwell. *The Yearbook of American and Canadian Churches* annually lists between 220 and 230 widely recognized church bodies. Some Roman Catholic authors who want to perpetuate an old tradition that finds Protestantism to be false because it is both diverse and divided provide longer lists. Israeli scholars, who have to keep tabs on every millennial or apocalyptic sect in America because so many of them have their eye on Israel's role in the plot of history's end time, can list hundreds more. And those listings refer only to more or less formal groups. They do not even begin to reach out to the attitudes of private citizens, or to the ephemeral clusters, cells, movements, and impulses that can be discerned in the index to *Coming Apart.*

What is further distinctive about American pluralism in the religious tradition, beyond its sheer quantity and scope, is the fact that it has generated an assumption: "Any number can play." Most pluralisms have been based on the idea that there should be a host culture and then there can be guest cultures. First there is an official, legal establishment, and then dissenters are allowed to exist in the society on some terms or other. Assent is present so that there can also be dissent; conformity is present so that there can be nonconformity. . . .

Experimentalism

While pluralism in religion has been at the heart of the tradition, experimentalism or the experimental spirit has been what has made it interesting. If less obvious, it is no less important. I consider it the basic element in the American experience of spirituality. When we use the word experiment, we refer to the fact that in religion, as in so many other respects, Americans are always ready with "Plan B." But Plan B is not argued on purely pragmatic grounds; it is seen to derive out of a consistent set of principles. There is always room for testing, for trying again, for changing.

The American Tradition

Contemporary American religious pluralism develops within a continuity that we may fairly describe as "The American Tradition."

Martin E. Marty, *Religion & Republic: The American Circumstance*, 1987.

Are not all nations religiously experimental? Some of them may be turning toward this temper. Change is the law of life, and people can be dragged into it almost anywhere. But that change is usually slow and subtle, and yielded to grudgingly. It is important to look at characteristic ways of regarding religion elsewhere and in the past. In primitive religion the task was to adhere to the cosmos and the universe of meanings that were already given. The witch doctor, the shaman, and the priest all existed to monitor the ceremonies and ritual acts that grew out of a myth that explained the world. There was no thought of change, only of conformity. While biblical messianism should have meant change in the European world, that world which provided American ancestry, the establishment of Christianity in the fourth century and the forcing of Judaism into the ghetto (while Islam was kept at bay geographically), led people again to see religion as fixed, never to be tampered with. The European tradition of sociology of religion, because it converged, with Émile Durkheim, on "the elementary forms of religious life" or because it drew on Europe's traditionalist religious construct, tended to regard religion only as an apprehension of a given world. . . .

Yet the American religious tradition *was* malleable. Change may be disguised under what sociologist J. Milton Yinger called "symbols of nonchange." "Changes are . . . obscured by the continuity of symbols." That means that American religionists characteristically have had to refer to a script, to a code or canon. They have had to reassure themselves that their changes were in line with a past that had come to them by revelation. But in the context of that revelation were endless possibilities for adaptation and innovation. They might even despise the term *innovation*—as New Englanders in colonial times most certainly did. Then they innovated. . . .

The Americans invented the denominational system and the voluntary pattern, lacking precedent for both. They changed their polities on the basis of both practical necessity and ecumenical encounter, and then went on to explain how the changed version was what God had had in mind all along. Fortunately for all of them in all these moves, their scriptures were sufficiently deep, obscure, and manifold to permit many interpretations and impulses!

Scripturalism

This whole discussion of experimentalism so far relied on a sense that American religious life was somehow pre-scripted. It was from a holy Word that God's further truth and light was to break. Jerald C. Brauer linked "a constant free experimentation and search for a fuller manifestation of God's truth and will" with "a sustained effort to avoid going beyond the truth and light already known in the Bible and codified in certain basic beliefs and confessions." Such resort to the scripted and the codified went far beyond Protestantism.

It has often been pointed out that even in the radically non-Christian counterculture of the 1960s, young Americans who wanted to leave the Bible far behind were also scriptural people. The Hare Krishna youth hawked their scriptures in airports and exegeted them endlessly. The followers of Sun Myung Moon in his Unification church had their own scriptures. So did the radical Americans who possessed the writings of Chairman Mao. People who lived in communes read the *Whole Earth Catalog* not as literary critics read a text, nor as aesthetes do for enjoyment, but as a kind of canon. So to move beyond the Bible does *not* mean to move beyond a scripture.

Scripturalism did first come to America, however, on biblical terms. Despite all the subsequent changes in our national life, nothing has displaced the Hebrew Scriptures and the New Testament from their positions of privilege. The antecedency helps; the people who give names to a culture hold power for an indefinite period. Americans may be increasingly biblically illiterate, but biblical lore is so bonded to their heritage that whenever they become thoughtful, whenever they reach deeply into their political lore (as with Abraham Lincoln) or into their literature (as with

Nathaniel Hawthorne, or Herman Melville, or even William Faulkner), they are going to come across biblical nuances and promises. . . .

Enlightenment

The Bible did not hold a unique position at the time of the birth of the nation, that moment from which so much later American life derives. For it happens that in the quarter-century surrounding the birth of the nation a new set of ideas had come to prominence. We refer to them as an "American Enlightenment." Europe, of course, had an Enlightenment at the same time, a more extensive, consistent, full-blown event. But the European Enlightenment ordinarily worked *against* religious claims and opposed the standard religious tradition. In America the Enlightenment was absorbed into the religious claims and either supported or had to coexist with the religion of the churches and subgroups.

Americanism

What is it, then, that binds us? The answer can be found in a set of ideals and myths pervading our national consciousness that has been growing for two centuries. Whether we admit it or not, and even if we claim we are not religious, we frequently tend to operate according to the prophetic vision, dogma, and rituals of a generally unacknowledged religious tradition. Our behavior belies this as we take pilgrimages to this tradition's shrines, view its relics, sing its songs, celebrate its holy days, show respect to its saints and martyrs, and respond to its symbols. The United States is indeed a religious nation, but its unifying religion is not Christianity or any other world faith—not even "the religion of secular humanism," as has been claimed of late. It is instead a unique national belief system best called *Americanism*.

Frederick Edwords, *The Humanist*, November/December 1987.

In 1749 Benjamin Franklin, despairing of the churches' ability to get themselves together enough to give basis to the nation or to provide it with morals and virtue, spoke of "the necessity of a *Publick Religion*." That public religion was grounded not simply in the Scriptures—though Franklin, Washington, Jefferson, and their kith and kind showed respect for them apart from their supernaturalism. Now religion was also to be grounded in social process, in a reason and nature that were both accessible to all people of thought and good will or good intentions. Here was a modified deism, a post-Christian style of religious philosophy. While it was soon countered by Protestant revivalists and Catholic or Jewish immigrants and fled from by secular folk who did not want to be identified with the excesses of the French Revolution, the Enlightenment did leave its stamp on American institutions. Taught as the truth about life by no known philosophy department in America, and seen as the creed in no church today, it still provided the basis for the nearest thing there is to a national creed—the Declaration of Independence—and was an element in the forming of the constitutional, legal, political, and educational systems in America. It provided the public with just enough hint of ideology to make it possible for them to adhere both to their particular faiths and the general ethos or code. . . .

That Enlightenment ethos, whose detail never had much following, but whose outline remains strong in our institutions, is therefore seen in America to be a religious positive, even though in Europe it was regarded negatively, as a displacement of historic faith. In America the two kinds of faith are seen not as contradictory (which they sometimes are), but as complementary, overlapping, mutually supportive, and—in the minds of the most reflective—both grounded in a still deeper order of Being that may always elude mortals who in their finitude cannot reach its extent or depth. But from fundamentalism to Unitarianism, in highly varied ways, Americans celebrate and live out many of the intentions of Enlightened religion. . . .

Voluntaryism

I have chosen to characterize the American style of experience and affiliation as *voluntaryism*. Note the *y*. It is not *voluntarism*— "one or other theory or doctrine which regards will as the fundamental principle or dominant factor in the individual or in the universe" (*Oxford English Dictionary*). Voluntaryism, instead, is "the principle or tenet that the Church and educational institutions should be supported by voluntary contributions instead of by the State; any system which rests upon voluntary action or principles." The accent is on volunteering, not on the will. And while the dictionary definition accents the fiscal and legal implications, voluntaryism in America carries with it a heavy burden of assumptions about the personal agent and his religious experience along with reference to the character of the associations that are formed by the experiencers.

Included in the concept of voluntaryism is a competitive spirit. Daniel J. Boorstin has shown how encompassing such a spirit is, for it also includes Judaism, which has seen itself as being in no way missionary or evangelistic, nor given to advertising. Yet what Boorstin calls "Instrumentalism" has taken over. "Even Judaism— or at least its reformed branch—has become pretty well assimilated to this instrumental emphasis. One Jewish congregation has for the motto of its Sunday School, 'Sinai never does anything halfway.'" When the revivalist calls the potential convert out of the world, he is not really asking the evangelized one to turn his back on it. He is offering a ticket to the "OK world," and is participating in a cultural initiation rite wherever evangelism has been pervasive.

The voluntary style is not necessary where there is no pluralism. There all citizens would be, virtually by the fact of birth, members of the single church. It is not plausible where there is no experimentalism, for it represents the opposite of the sense of fixity and fate that has characterized so much of what was called primitive and what was ancestral and is even now European religion. It draws on scripturalism, but scriptures are commended more "for the services they perform than for the truths they affirm," to use Boorstin's summary of the theme. (That is not to say the truths are not affirmed; they simply are not pushed forward as the main advantage for followers of a code or an invitation.) And voluntaryism draws heavily on the Enlightenment gift of toleration, for it assumes that, religiously, "any number can play," and that support for such playing exists in our law and ethos. Further, voluntaryists tend to rely on a second American Enlightened presupposition: that the separate churches can go about their business without disrupting the commonweal, that the various groups share enough ideas or beliefs to make possible a society, and not a jungle.

"The Old and New Testaments are not only infallible guides to personal salvation; they contain the prescriptions for just laws and a good society."

America's Roots Are in Judeo-Christian Values

Patrick J. Buchanan

A nationally-syndicated columnist and television commentator who has served Presidents Nixon and Reagan, Mr. Buchanan is one of the most visible and articulate conservatives in the country. The following viewpoint is taken from his recent book, *Right from the Beginning*, in which he lays out a conservative's agenda for America. Mr. Buchanan believes that the issues that divide the country today are, at bottom, religious disagreements. He claims that America's religious consensus, historically based on Judeo-Christian values and traditions, has deteriorated due to the influence of secularism. He argues that America's best hope lies in the renewed ascendance of Judeo-Christian values, and that traditionalists have as much right to promote their values as do secularists.

As you read, consider the following questions:

1. What point does the author make when claiming that "the resolution of America's social crisis may be beyond the realm of politics and government?"
2. What is his view of the role of religious values in America's schools?

Though a wealthier people than our forefathers could ever have dreamed of our becoming, we Americans are today as divided as we have been in our modern history; and the divisions are far deeper and more profound than those that separated us, say, in the 1950s. We no longer share the same religious faith, the same code of morality, the same public philosophy. It is not simply about the role and responsibility of government that we disagree; today, our ideas of freedom and virtue and patriotism collide. As the conflict between the Communists in Managua and the *contras* in the hills reveals, we Americans no longer even agree on who our enemies are. And because our disagreements go far beyond the old political question of how we divide the pie, of "who gets what," our politics have taken on a new aspect. Our political and social quarrels now partake of the savagery of religious wars because, at bottom, *they are religious wars*. The most divisive issues in American politics are now about our warring concepts of right and wrong, of good and evil. In a way the Kerner Commission never predicted, we have indeed become "two nations."

What I offer, then, is an agenda on which Americans must necessarily disagree, not only about the means proposed, but about the ends. It is an agenda, then, only for those who wish to see Judeo-Christian values ascendant again in American society and undergirding American law. . . .

The Destruction of America's Judeo-Christian Roots

Half a century ago, during a depression in which a third of America's wealth would be wiped out and a fourth of her labor force left idle, Franklin Roosevelt said our difficulties, thank God, "concern . . . only material things." That time is gone. . . .

Materially, we have never been better off; the United States is the most vibrant, energetic society on earth. . . .

Yet, beneath the glittering prosperity of a $4 trillion economy, there is a deepening social crisis in America. Between 1960 and 1985 funds for income support in the United States rose from $20 billion to almost $400 billion, from 4 percent of the Gross National Product to 10 percent. Yet, this spectacular explosion of the Welfare State was accompanied, writes Dr. Roger Freeman of the Hoover Institution, by an equally "spectacular rise in all forms of crime, family abandonment, child neglect, widespread adoption of ruinous lifestyles and destructive behavior, and an exponential growth of drug and alcohol use. . . ."

Then, there is AIDS. Has ever there been a more telling example of the mental confusion and moral cowardice of our time than the timidity of our Lords Temporal and Lords Spiritual in refusing to condemn the perpetrators of this epidemic that will kill more Americans than Korea and Vietnam?

Compassion for the victims of this dread disease does not relieve us of the obligation to speak the truth: Promiscuous sodomy—unnatural, unsanitary sexual relations between males, which every great religion teaches is immoral—is the cause of AIDS. Anal sex between consenting adults is spreading the virus from one homosexual to another, thence into the needles of addicts and the blood supply of hemophiliacs.

American Law Is Based on Christianity

True law necessarily is rooted in ethical assumptions or norms; and those moral principles are derived, in the beginning at least, from religious convictions. When the religious understanding, from which a concept of law arose in a culture, has been discarded or denied—well, the laws may endure for some decades, through what sociologists call "cultural lag"; but in the long run, the laws also will be discarded or denied, after having been severed from their ethical and religious sources.

With this hard truth in mind, I venture to suggest that the corpus of English and American laws—for the two arise for the most part from a common root of belief and experience—cannot endure forever unless it is animated by the spirit that moved it in the beginning: that is, by religion, and specifically by the Christian religion. . . .

Christian belief is not the only source of ethical principle behind our laws; but it is the most powerful and popular source. If all connection between the Christian religion and the verdicts of courts of law is severed in this country, the law must become erratic and unpredictable at best (when it is supposed to be regular in its operation), and tyrannical rather than protective.

Russell Kirk, *Imprimis*, April 1983.

When I wrote that New York City, on the eve of that celebration of sodomy known as "Gay Pride Week," should shut down the squalid little "love" nests called bathhouses, the incubators of the disease, I was denounced as a "homophobe" by the Governor and Mayor of New York. Because these men were morally confused, men and boys continued infecting one another in the bathhouses, and continued killing one another. And, today, nine-year-olds are being educated in the use of condoms. But, it is not nine-year-olds who are buggering one another with abandon, spreading this deadly virus; it is not nine-year-olds who threaten doctors, dentists, health workers, hemophiliacs, and the rest of society by their refusal to curb their lascivious appetites. By the way in which they define themselves, the militant homosexuals are killing themselves. What, precisely, is "gay" about that?

To destroy a country, Solzhenitsyn wrote, you must first cut its roots. If America's roots are in Judeo-Christian values and traditions, they have, in large measure, been severed.

To some Americans, the rise of the Religious Right, a decade ago, was an ominous development; to others of us, however, it was the natural, healthy reaction of a once-Christian country that has been force-fed the poisons of paganism. As Bernanos wrote of another time, to be a reactionary today may simply mean to be alive, because only a corpse does not react any more—against the maggots teeming upon it.

Religion Is at the Root of Morality

Religion is at the root of morality; and morality is the basis of law. Many decades ago, America's intellectual elite privately uttered its *non serviam* to the God of Christianity. America, meanwhile, continued to live off the inherited capital of the old faith. Now, the dissent from, and disbelief in, traditional Hebrew and Christian values and proscriptions is widespread. The routine deference once accorded the traditional churches is no longer proffered. In books and plays and films, priests and pastors and rabbis are mocked for the amusement of modernity. The Secular City is brimming with self-confidence.

And, here, we come close to the heart of America's social crisis. The United States is divided not only between Left and Right. What is social progress to secular America is advancing decadence to traditionalist America. . . .

The hard truth with which conservatives must come to terms is that the resolution of America's social crisis may be beyond the realm of politics and government, in a democratic society. If men have come to believe homosexuality is a "legitimate" and even commendable "life-style," that abortion is a matter of personal choice, that "pornography" exists only in the eye of the beholder, no federal law will dissuade them. If a woman has come to believe that divorce is the answer to every difficult marriage, that career comes before children, that the day-care center is the proper place for infants and toddlers and the boarding school for the younger children, no democratic government can impose another set of values upon her. If half of America has given up "the old-time religion," no political party and no national administration can reconvert that half of a country. If our traditional pastors and priests and rabbis and preachers have lost their congregations, even the most brilliant of political communicators or leaders will not retrieve the lost sheep. Politics alone cannot change the human heart. Much of what ails America, then, is not a "problem" that can be "solved" by political action; it is a predicament with which we must learn to live.

Whose Morality Shall We Consult?

But this necessity—that we understand and accept the limits of politics in a democratic society—is not an argument for quietism.

Traditionalists and conservatives have as much right as secularists to see our values written into law, to have our beliefs serve as the basis of federal legislation.

"Why are you trying to impose your values on the rest of us?" Among too many raised in the Judeo-Christian tradition, that taunt has engendered a moral disarmament and political paralysis. But the underlying premise is that a democratic society may be constructed upon values and beliefs found in the books of Rachel Carson, Ralph Nader, Betty Friedan, and Alfred Kinsey, but not upon values and beliefs found in the Pentateuch and the New Testament. To accept that argument is to permit ourselves to be driven permanently from the public square.

America's Debt to Judeo-Christian Traditions

Americans . . . should appreciate how much the Jewish and Christian traditions have provided the vision and context for creating and maintaining a society of ordered liberty. The belief that every human person possesses unalienable rights to liberty derives from a vision first introduced into history by Judaism and then taught to Christianity. Both Judaism and Christianity, despite historical sins and failures, cherish the religious liberty of even those who say No to their revelations. Both believe that true faith arises only in voluntary consent. Conscience can be neither feigned nor coerced. And the perfectionism to which Judaism and Christianity are committed is always both realistic and progressive.

Michael Novak, *The Christian Century*, July 6-13, 1986.

Someone's values are going to prevail. Why not ours? Whose country is it, anyway? Whose moral code says we may interfere with a man's right to be a practicing bigot, but must respect and protect his right to be a practicing sodomite? Why should the moral code of modern secularism prevail? Simply because the militant homosexuals have come marching out of their closets is no reason for the saints to go marching in.

The Old and New Testaments are not only infallible guides to personal salvation; they contain the prescriptions for just laws and the good society—for building a city set upon a hill.

Again, religion is at the root of morality; and morality is the basis of law. The only questions are whose religion, and whose morality, shall we consult. Environmentalism, feminism, humanism, consumerism, secularism, and socialism have all taken on the aspect of religious faiths in our time, but these "isms" have no greater preemptive claim to serve as the basis of law than the tenets of Judaism, Catholicism, Mormonism, or Protestant Fundamentalism.

The only option the traditionalist and the conservative have, then, is never to cease struggling—until we have re-created a government and an America that conforms, as close as possible, to our image of the Good Society, if you will, a Godly country. That struggle will be endless; and it will define us, test us, and likely provide us the only temporal reward we shall know. . . .

America's Schools Teach Secularism

When the Baltimore Conference of Catholic Bishops of 1884 mandated the parochial school system, the hierarchy did not walk away because the public schools were anti-Christian. To the contrary, they viewed those schools as militantly Christian; but a Protestant Christianity pervaded, and the Catholic bishops wanted Catholic children brought up in their own faith.

In the intervening century, the curricula of these public schools have been systematically drained of all Christian content; they have lost all trace of their original character. Neither Catholic nor Protestant today, they have become, in the late Will Herberg's description, "secularist and even militantly so."

"Children in public schools are under an influence with which the churches cannot compete and which they cannot counteract," writes Charles Clayton Moore of *Christian Century.* "The public school presents the church with a generation of youth whose minds have been cast in a secular mold." . . .

Secularism remains a minority faith; and more and more Americans are aware that the expulsion of traditional religion and ethical instruction from the public schools has gone hand in hand with a decline in public education and a collapse in public morality. Nor is that collapse difficult to understand. Those who have captured the heights of modern education have no conclusive, convincing answer to the age-old question of youth: "Why not?" Why not casual sex? Why not smoke marijuana? Why not use drugs? Why not steal a pair of Adidas? Why not cheat in class?

Even by utilitarian and pragmatic standards, secularism does not work.

If secularist ideology continues to mandate the permanent expulsion of traditional religious teaching from the public schools, we should probably get on with the building of new prisons. For external force is the only line of defense left, when the internal constraints of an informed conscience and religious belief no longer bind.

Someone's values, someone's beliefs, someone's concept of morality, will be transmitted during the education of the child. . . .

Democracy Is Not Enough

While democratic rule is in the bones of every American, democracy is not enough. Democracy is an empty vessel into which a corrupt and decadent society may be fitted quite as well as a just and good one.

Today, many Christians, emulating the Catholics of a century ago, are walking away from the public schools, creating their own Christian schools. While these efforts merit sustenance and support—through vouchers and tuition tax credits—there is no reason to raise the white flag and forever surrender the public schools; they can be recaptured.

Why should a secularist minority, rather than a believing majority, see its values dominant? Whose schools are they, anyway? . . .

If tolerance is a necessary virtue in our democratic society, there must be tolerance for the views of the majority. The village atheist has the right to be heard; he has no right to be heeded. While he has a right not to have his own children indoctrinated in what he believes are false and foolish teachings, he has no right to dictate what other children shall and shall not be taught.

The way to bring permanent peace to the war over public education is to replace autocratic, with democratic, decisionmaking. Parents and teachers, not judges and bureaucrats, should decide what the schools shall and shall not teach. Let the character of each public school reflect the character of the neighborhood and the community in which it is located; and let the schools compete with one another for the allegiance, the tax dollars, and the vouchers of parents and taxpayers.

There is no more important battle shaping up in America than for the hearts and minds of the next generation. Whether that generation will be traditionalist and Christian, or agnostic and atheist, whether its code of morality and ethics will be based on Judeo-Christian beliefs or in the secular nostrums of the moment, will be largely determined by America's public schools. And Christianity, too, has the right to compete. . . .

Conclusion

Like a modern hospital, with all the technological advances of the modern age, good government can help restore to health a nation taken ill; it cannot give meaning in life to a people who have lost their faith; it cannot forever restrain a generation that wishes to "live fast, die young, and leave a good-looking corpse." Democracy really has no answer to decadence. Churchill, after all, could halt neither the decline of Great Britain nor the dissolution of an empire whose time had come; and Marcus Aurelius could not save Rome.

Unlike the crisis of "material things" FDR confronted in 1933, our crisis of the spirit in 1988 may be beyond the ken of politics, and beyond government solution. The duty of the political conservative, then, is to do our best to make ourselves, and our government, the allies of our Judeo-Christian values, to make government again the protector and friend of the permanent things, to do the best we can in the times in which we live. And to put our trust and faith, ultimately, not in ourselves alone.

"There actually exists alongside of and rather clearly differentiated from the churches an elaborate and well-institutionalized civil religion in America."

America Has a Civil Religion

Robert N. Bellah

Robert N. Bellah is Elliott Professor of Sociology at the University of California in Berkeley. In 1967 he published an essay that brought the phrase "civil religion" into the public dialogue about the place of religion in American culture. In the following viewpoint, taken from that essay, he describes America's civil religion and how its values parallel those of Christianity. His many publications include *The Broken Covenant*, *Habits of the Heart*, and most recently, *Uncivil Religion: Interreligious Hostility in America.*

As you read, consider the following questions:

1. What does the author mean by the term "civil religion"?
2. In the author's opinion, how does America's civil religion relate to Christianity?
3. What does Bellah believe the Civil War contributed to America's civil religion? What role does Abraham Lincoln play according to the author?
4. How does the author relate America's civil religion to its role in the world?

Robert N. Bellah, "Civil Religion In America," *Daedalus*, Winter 1967, pp. 1-21. Reprinted by permission of *Daedalus*, Journal of The American Academy of Arts and Sciences, Boston, Massachusetts. Winter 1967, Religion In America.

While some have argued that Christianity is the national faith, and others that church and synagogue celebrate only the generalized religion of "the American Way of life," few have realized that there actually exists alongside of and rather clearly differentiated from the churches an elaborate and well-institutionalized civil religion in America. This article argues not only that there is such a thing, but also that this religion—or perhaps better, this religious dimension—has its own seriousness and integrity and requires the same care in understanding that any other religion does.[1]. . .

The Founding Fathers and Christianity

The words and acts of the founding fathers, especially the first few presidents, shaped the form and tone of the civil religion as it has been maintained ever since. Though much is selectively derived from Christianity, this religion is clearly not itself Christianity. For one thing, neither Washington nor Adams nor Jefferson mentions Christ in his inaugural address; nor do any of the subsequent presidents, although not one of them fails to mention God.[2] The God of the civil religion is not only rather "unitarian," he is also on the austere side, much more related to order, law, and right than to salvation and love. Even though he is somewhat deist in cast, he is by no means simply a watchmaker God. He is actively interested and involved in history, with a special concern for America. Here the analogy has much less to do with natural law than with ancient Israel; the equation of America with Israel in the idea of the "American Israel" is not infrequent.[3] What was implicit in the words of Washington. . .becomes explicit in Jefferson's second inaugural when he said: "I shall need, too, the favor of that Being in whose hands we are, who led our fathers, as Israel of old, from their native land and planted them in a country flowing with all the necessaries and comforts of life." Europe is Egypt; America, the promised land. God has led his people to establish a new sort of social order that shall be a light unto all the nations.[4]. . .

What we have, then, from the earliest years of the republic is a collection of beliefs, symbols, and rituals with respect to sacred things and institutionalized in a collectivity. This religion—there seems no other word for it—while not antithetical to and indeed sharing much in common with Christianity, was neither sectarian nor in any specific sense Christian. At a time when the society was overwhelmingly Christian, it seems unlikely that this lack of Christian reference was meant to spare the feelings of the tiny non-Christian minority. Rather, the civil religion expressed what those who set the precedents felt was appropriate under the circumstances. It reflected their private as well as public views. Nor was the civil religion simply "religion in general." While generality was undoubtedly seen as a virtue by some. . .the civil religion was specific enough when it came to the topic of America. Precisely because of this specificity, the civil religion was saved from empty formalism and served as a genuine vehicle of national religious self-understanding. . . .

Civil War and Civil Religion

Until the Civil War, the American civil religion focused above all on the event of the Revolution, which was seen as the final act of the Exodus from the old lands across the waters. The Declaration of Independence and the Constitution were the sacred scriptures and Washington the divinely appointed Moses who led his people out of the hands of tyranny. The Civil War, which Sidney Mead calls "the center of American history,"[5] was the second great event that involved the national self-understanding so deeply as to require expression in the civil religion. In 1835, Tocqueville wrote that the American republic had never really been tried, that victory in the Revolutionary War was more the result of British pre-occupation elsewhere and the presence of a powerful ally than of any great military success of the Americans. . . .

The Founding Fathers Words

The words and acts of the founding fathers, especially the first few presidents, shaped the form and tone of the civil religion as it has been maintained ever since.

Robert N. Bellah

With the Civil War, a new theme of death, sacrifice, and rebirth enters the civil religion. It is symbolized in the life and death of Lincoln. Nowhere is it stated more vividly than in the Gettysburg Address, itself part of the Lincolnian "New Testament" among the civil scriptures. Robert Lowell has recently pointed out the "insistent use of birth images" in this speech explicity devoted to "these honored dead": "brought forth," "conceived," "created," "a new birth of freedom." He goes on to say:

> The Gettysburg Address is a symbolic and sacramental act. Its verbal quality is resonance combined with a logical, matter of fact, prosaic brevity. . . . In his words, Lincoln symbolically died, just as the Union soldiers really died—and as he himself was soon really to die. By his words, he gave the field of battle a symbolic significance that it had lacked. For us and our country, he left Jefferson's ideals of freedom and equality joined to the Christian sacrificial act of death and rebirth. I believe this is a meaning that goes beyond sect or religion and beyond peace and war, and is now part of our lives as a challenge, obstacle and hope.[6]

Lowell is certainly right in pointing out the Christian quality of the symbolism here, but he is also right in quickly disavowing any sectarian implication. The earlier symbolism of the civil religion had been Hebraic without being in any specific sense

191

Jewish. The Gettysburg symbolism (". . .those who here gave their lives, that that nation might live") is Christian without having anything to do with the Christian church.

The symbolic equation of Lincoln with Jesus was made relatively early. Herndon, who had been Lincoln's law partner, wrote:

> For fifty years God rolled Abraham Lincoln through his fiery furnace. He did it to try Abraham and to purify him for his purposes. This made Mr. Lincoln humble, tender, forebearing, sympathetic to suffering, kind, sensitive, tolerant; broadening, deepening and widening his whole nature; making him the noblest and loveliest character since Jesus Christ. . . . I believe that Lincoln was God's chosen one.[7] . . .

The new symbolism soon found both physical and ritualistic expression. The great number of the war dead required the establishment of a number of national cemeteries. Of these, the Gettysburg National Cemetery, which Lincoln's famous address served to dedicate, has been overshadowed only by the Arlington National Cemetery. Begun somewhat vindictively on the Lee estate across the river from Washington, partly with the end that the Lee family could never reclaim it,[8] it has subsequently become the most hallowed monument of the civil religion. . . .

Memorial Day, which grew out of the Civil War, gave ritual expression to the themes we have been discussing. As Lloyd Warner has so brilliantly analyzed it, the Memorial Day observance, especially in the towns and smaller cities of America, is a major event for the whole community involving a rededication to the martyred dead, to the spirit of sacrifice, and to the American vision.[9] Just as Thanksgiving Day, which incidentally was securely institutionalized as an annual national holiday only under the presidency of Lincoln, serves to integrate the family into the civil religion, so Memorial Day has acted to integrate the local community into the national cult. Together with the less overtly religious Fourth of July and the more minor celebrations of Veterans Day and the birthdays of Washington and Lincoln, these two holidays provide an annual ritual calendar for the civil religion. The public-school system serves as a particularly important context for the cultic celebration of the civil rituals. . . .

The American civil religion was never anticlerical or militantly secular. On the contrary, it borrowed selectively from the religious tradition in such a way that the average American saw no conflict between the two. In this way, the civil religion was able to build up without any bitter struggle with the church powerful symbols of national solidarity and to mobilize deep levels of personal motivation for the attainment of national goals.

Such an achievement is by no means to be taken for granted. It would seem that the problem of a civil religion is quite general in modern societies and that the way it is solved or not solved will have repercussions in many spheres. One needs only to think of

France to see how differently things can go. The French Revolution was anticlerical to the core and attempted to set up an anti-Christian civil religion. Throughout modern French history, the chasm between traditional Catholic symbols and the symbolism of 1789 has been immense. . . .

The civil religion has not always been invoked in favor of worthy causes. On the domestic scene, an American-Legion type of ideology that fuses God, country, and flag has been used to attack nonconformist and liberal ideas and groups of all kinds. Still, it has been difficult to use the words of Jefferson and Lincoln to support special interests and undermine personal freedom. The defenders of slavery before the Civil War came to reject the thinking of the Declaration of Independence. Some of the most consistent of them turned against not only Jeffersonian democracy but Reformation religion; they dreamed of a South dominated by medieval chivalry and divine-right monarchy.[10] For all the overt religiosity of the radical right today, their relation to the civil religious consensus is tenuous, as when the John Birch Society attacks the central American symbol of Democracy itself.

Average American Saw No Conflict

The American civil religion was never anticlerical or militantly secular. On the contrary, it borrowed selectively from the religious tradition in such a way that the average American saw no conflict between the two.

Robert N. Bellah

With respect to America's role in the world, the dangers of distortion are greater and the built-in safeguards of the tradition weaker. The theme of the American Israel was used, almost from the beginning, as a justification for the shameful treatment of the Indians so characteristic of our history. It can be overtly or implicitly linked to the idea of manifest destiny which has been used to legitimate several adventures in imperialism since the early-nineteenth century. Never has the danger been greater than today. The issue is not so much one of imperial expansion, of which we are accused, as of the tendency to assimilate all governments or parties in the world which support our immediate policies or call upon our help by invoking the notion of free institutions and democratic values. Those nations that are for the moment "on our side" become "the free world." A repressive and unstable military dictatorship in South Viet Nam becomes "the free people of South Viet Nam and their government." It is then part of the role of America as the New Jerusalem and "the last best hope on earth" to defend such governments with treasure and eventually with blood. When our soldiers are actually dying, it becomes possible to consecrate the struggle further by invoking the great theme of sacrifice. . . .

The Third Time of Trial

In conclusion it may be worthwhile to relate the civil religion to the most serious situation that we as Americans now face, what I call the third time of trial. The first time of trial had to do with the question of independence, whether we should or could run our own affairs in our own way. The second time of trial was over the issue of slavery, which in turn was only the most salient aspect of the more general problem of the full institutionalization of democracy within our country. This second problem we are still far from solving though we have some notable successes to our credit. But we have been overtaken by a third great problem which has led to a third great crisis, in the midst of which we stand. This is the problem of responsible action in a revolutionary world, a world seeking to attain many of the things, material and spiritual, that we have already attained. . . .

Out of the first and second times of trial have come, as we have seen, the major symbols of the American civil religion. There seems little doubt that a successful negotiation of this third time of trial—the attainment of some kind of viable and coherent world order—would precipitate a major new set of symbolic forms. So far the flickering flame of the United Nations burns too low to be the focus of a cult, but the emergence of a genuine transnational sovereignty would certainly change this. It would necessitate the incorporation of vital international symbolism into our civil religion, or, perhaps a better way of putting it, it would result in American civil religion becoming simply one part of a new civil religion of the world. . . .

Behind the civil religion at every point lie Biblical archetypes: Exodus, Chosen People, Promised Land, New Jerusalem, Sacrifical Death and Rebirth. But it is also genuinely American and genuinely new. It has its own prophets and its own martyrs, its own sacred events and sacred places, its own solemn rituals and symbols. It is concerned that America be a society as perfectly in accord with the will of God as men can make it, and a light to all the nations. . . .

It does not make any decision for us. It does not remove us from moral ambiguity, from being, in Lincoln's fine phrase, an "almost chosen people." But it is a heritage of moral and religious experience from which we still have much to learn as we formulate the decisions that lie ahead.

1. Why something so obvious should have escaped serious analytical attention is in itself an interesting problem. Part of the reason is probably the controversial nature of the subject. From the earliest years of the nineteenth century, conservative religious and political groups have argued that Christianity is, in fact, the national religion. Some of them have from time to time and as recently as the 1950's proposed constitutional amendments that would explicitly recognize the sovereignty of Christ. In defending the doctrine of separation of church

and state, opponents of such groups have denied that the national policy has, intrinsically, anything to do with religion at all. The moderates on this issue have insisted that the American state has taken a permissive and indeed supportive attitude toward religious groups (tax exemption, et cetera), thus favoring religion but still missing the positive institutionalization with which I am concerned. But part of the reason this issue has been left in obscurity is certainly due to the peculiarly Western concept of "religion" as denoting a single type of collectivity of which an individual can be a member of one and only one at a time. The Durkeimian notion that every group has a religious dimension, which would be seen as obvious in southern or eastern Asia, is foreign to us. This obscures the recognition of such dimensions in our society.

2. God is mentioned or referred to in all inaugural addresses but Washington's second, which is a very brief (two paragraphs) and perfunctory acknowledgment. It is not without interest that the actual word **God** does not appear until Monroe's second inaugural, 5 March 1821. In his first inaugural, Washington refers to God as "that Almighty Being who rules the universe," "Great Author of every public and private good," "Invisible Hand," and "benign Parent of the Human Race." John Adams refers to God as "Providence," "Being who is supreme over all," "Patron of Order," "Foundation of Justice," and "Protector in all ages of the world of virtuous liberty." Jefferson speaks of "that Infinite Power which rules the destinies of the universe," and "that Being in whose hands we are." Madison speaks of "that Almighty Being whose power regulates the destiny of nations," and "Heaven." Monroe uses "Providence" and "the Almighty" in his first inaugural and finally "Almighty God" in his second. See **Inaugural Addresses of the Presidents of the United States from George Washington 1789 to Harry S. Truman 1949,** 82nd Congress, 2d Session, House Document No. 540, 1952.

3. For example, Abiel Abbot, pastor of the First Church in Haverhill, Massachusetts, delivered a Thanksgiving sermon in 1790, **Traits of Resemblance in the People of the United States of America to Ancient Israel,** in which he said, "It has been often remarked that the people of the United States come nearer to a parallel with Ancient Israel, than any other nation upon the globe. Hence 'Our American Israel' is a term frequently used; and common consent allows it apt and proper." Cited in Hans Kohn, **The Idea of Nationalism** (New York, 1961), p. 665.

4. That the Mosaic analogy was present in the minds of leaders at the very moment of the birth of the republic is indicated in the designs proposed by Franklin and Jefferson for a seal of the United States of America. Together with Adams, they formed a committee of three delegated by the Continental Congress on July 4, 1776, to draw up the new device. "Franklin proposed as the device Moses lifting up his wand and dividing the Red Sea while Pharaoh was overwhelmed by its waters, with the motto 'Rebellion to tyrants is obedience to God.' Jefferson proposed the children of Israel in the wilderness 'led by a cloud by day and a pillar of fire at night.' " Anson Phelps Stokes, **Church and State in the United States,** Vol. 1 (New York, 1950), pp. 467-468.

5. Sidney Mead, **The Lively Experiment** (New York, 1963), p. 12.

6. Allan Nevins (ed.), **Lincoln and the Gettysburg Address** (Urbana, Ill., 1964) pp. 88-89.

7. Quoted in Sherwood Eddy, **The Kingdom of God and the American Dream** (New York, 1941), p. 162.

8. Karl Decker and Angus McSween, **Historic Arlington** (Washington, D.C., 1892), pp. 60-67.

9. How extensive the activity associated with Memorial Day can be is indicated by Warner: "The sacred symbolic behavior of Memorial Day, in which scores of the town's organizations are involved, is ordinarily divided into four periods. During the year separate rituals are held by many of the associations for their dead, and many of these activities are connected with later Memorial Day events. In the second phase, preparations are made during the last three or four weeks for the ceremony itself, and some of the associations perform public rituals. The third phase consists of scores of rituals held in all the cemeteries, churches, and halls of the associations. These rituals consist of speeches and highly ritualized behavior. They last for two days and are climaxed by the fourth and last phase, in which all the separate celebrants gather in the center of the business district on the afternoon of Memorial Day. The separate organizations, with their members in uniform or with fitting insignia, march through the town, visit the shrines and monuments of the hero dead, and, finally enter the cemetary. Here dozens of ceremonies are held, most of them highly symbolic and formalized." During these various ceremonies Lincoln is continually referred to and the Gettysburg Address recited many times. W. Lloyd Warner, **American Life** (Chicago, 1962), pp. 8-9.

10. See Louis Hartz, "The Feudal Dream of the South," Part 4, **The Liberal Tradition in America** (New York, 1955).

"Religious conservatives and liberals offer competing versions of American civil religion that seem to have very little of substance in common."

America Has
Two Civil Religions

Robert Wuthnow

Robert Wuthnow is professor of sociology at Princeton University and the author of several books on American culture and religion. In the following viewpoint, taken from his most recent book, The Restructuring of American Religion, *Professor Wuthnow identifies two versions of America's civil religion, labeling one conservative and the other liberal. In describing the characteristics of each, he claims the lack of consensus caused by the two different traditions has created a vacuum in contemporary America from which a new set of values is emerging. He argues that America's new creed may resemble secular values, partially because of the inability of the two religious camps to develop a unifying consensus.*

As you read, consider the following questions:

1. What characteristics does the author attribute to conservative civil religion?
2. What characteristics does he attribute to liberal civil religion?
3. What two values does he claim are components of America's new secular ideology?

Robert Wuthnow, *The Restructuring of American Religion: Society and Faith Since World War II*. Copyright © 1988 by Princeton University Press. Excerpt, pp. 244-257, reprinted with permission of Princeton University Press.

Robert Bellah has written that the key ingredients of America's legitimating myth include a civil religion and a highly utilitarian secular ideology. The civil religion consists of Judeo-Christian symbols and values that relate the nation to a divine order of things, thus giving it a sense of origin and direction. The utilitarian ideology, emanating from Enlightenment political philosophy, provides the nation with a sense of proper governmental procedure, as well as fundamental guiding values such as life, liberty, and the pursuit of happiness. Together, these cultural traditions have at various times in the past legitimated great national crusades. Periodically, they have combined to check the excesses of political expediency by subjecting the nation's programs to the harsh light of transcendent values. But they have also contended with one another for political supremacy.

Civil religion continues to serve as an extremely visible dimension of American culture. In recent election campaigns presidential candidates have often appeared to stumble over one another in their haste to demonstrate loyalty to some branch of the Judeo-Christian tradition. Inaugural addresses, now as in the past, pay ritual obeisance to the divine judge; prayers at all major political functions invoke God's presence and blessing; and, despite constitutional restrictions, much mixing of religious and political symbols continues on major holidays. America's civil religion portrays its people, often in comparison with people in other countries, as God-fearing souls, as champions of religious liberty, and in many instances as a nation that God has consciously chosen to carry out a special mission in the world.

American Civil Religion Is Divided

American civil religion is, nevertheless, deeply divided. Like the religion found more generally in the nation's churches, it does not speak with a single voice, uniting the majority of Americans around common ideals. It has instead become a confusion of tongues speaking from different traditions and offering different visions of what America can and should be. Religious conservatives and liberals offer competing versions of American civil religion that seem to have very little of substance in common.

Conservative Civil Religion

On the conservative side, America's legitimacy seems to depend heavily on a distinct "myth of origin" that relates the nation's founding to divine purposes. According to this interpretation of American history, the American form of government enjoys lasting legitimacy because it was created by Founding Fathers who were deeply influenced by Judeo-Christian values. Although their personal convictions on occasion may have strayed from this standard, men like Washington, Franklin, Witherspoon, and Adams

197

knew the heart of man from a biblical perspective so that they understood what kind of government would function best. . . .

One Nation Under God

A favorite theme was the slogan "One Nation Under God," which carried more than one level of meaning, connoting both a unified nation and an "only," "best," "leading," or "special" nation under God. Norman Vincent Peale, in a book with this slogan as its title, argued that America had received a unique calling from God at the beginning of its history which continued to be expressed in the special zeal and spiritual quality of its people. In another book by the same title, evangelical writer Rus Walton arrived at the conclusion that even the American constitution had been "divinely inspired." . . .

In emphasizing the close historical connection between America and God, evangelicals and fundamentalists assert the importance of religious values which they themselves still uphold. Their version of American history points to a time when such values were evidently taken quite seriously. By implication—and sometimes directly—the proponents of this interpretation suggest that these values should again be taken more seriously, thus restoring a way of life in America with which evangelicals and fundamentalists could feel comfortable. . . .

America's Civil Religion Has Become Divided

The civil religion to which we so blithely pay homage has, however, become deeply divided. Like the fractured communities found in our churches, our civil religion no longer unites us around common ideals. Instead of giving voice to a clear image of who we should be, it has become a confusion of tongues. It speaks from competing traditions and offers partial visions of America's future. Religious conservatives offer one version of our divine calling; religious liberals articulate one that is radically different.

Robert Wuthnow, *The Christian Century*, April 20, 1988.

Priorities generally focus on personal salvation, spiritual growth, biblical knowledge, and the affairs of local religious communities instead of God's providence in American history. Even Jerry Falwell alludes only occasionally in his books and sermons to America's collective relation to God. Insofar as conservative civil religion can be associated with evangelicals and fundamentalists, therefore, it appears to consist of a background assumption rather than an explicit object of devotion. . . .

Yet conservative civil religion generally grants America a special place in the divine order. Falwell goes on to say, "The United States is not a perfect nation, but it is without doubt the greatest and most influential nation in the world. We have the people and the resources to evangelize the world in our generation." Tim LaHaye, head of the American Coalition for Traditional Values, makes the same point negatively: were it not for America, he asserts, "our contemporary world would have completely lost the battle for the mind and would doubtless live in a totalitarian, one-world, humanistic state."

The idea of America evangelizing the world is in fact a much-emphasized theme in conservative civil religion. God's purpose for America is to use its advantaged position to preach Christianity to all nations—a task that in some evangelical eschatologies represents the final work that must be accomplished in order to hasten the "second coming" of Christ to this earth. America's wealth and power is thought to be God's supply of resources for carrying out this important task, as well as a token of divine "good faith" to those willing to shoulder the task. This view is particularly prominent among conservative Christian groups with a strong missionary emphasis. . . .

Divine Authority

Despite formal separation between the kingdom of God and the kingdom of man, the "two kingdoms" doctrine in conservative civil religion also confers a strong degree of divine authority on the existing mode of government. Although no human government can ever fully conform to God's ideal, government is nevertheless established by God as a means of maintaining social order. Thus ordained, it should not be questioned or openly challenged, except in those rare instances when it violates the Christian's right to worship. . . .

The Supremacy of Capitalism

In addition to its views on government, conservative civil religion generally includes arguments about the propriety of the U.S. economic system. These arguments grant capitalism a high degree of legitimacy by drawing certain parallels between capitalist economic principles and biblical teachings. Economist George Gilder, who identifies himself as an evangelical Christian, has argued, "'Give and you'll be given unto' is the fundamental practical principle of the Christian life, and when there's no private property you can't give it because you don't own it. . . . Socialism is inherently hostile to Christianity and capitalism is simply the essential mode of human life that corresponds to religious truth." Elsewhere he remarks, drawing a calculated reference to the apostle Paul's teaching on love, "the deepest truths of capitalism are faith, hope, and love." . . .

On the other side, few spokespersons for the liberal version of American civil religion make reference to the religious views of the Founding Fathers or suggest that America is God's chosen nation. References to America's wealth or power being God's means of evangelizing the world are also rare and religious apologetics for capitalism seem to be virtually taboo. A liberal version of American civil religion does exist, but it draws on a different set of religious values and portrays the nation in a very different light from the conservative version.

America's Secular Ideology

One of the most frequently voiced secular arguments that has been advanced to legitimate America links the nation with the value of freedom. The American system, simply put, is good and decent because it upholds individual freedom. Both democracy and capitalism are said to provide necessary conditions for the survival of freedom. . . .

As a legitimating value, freedom is often combined with some version of American civil religion. In the conservative view, it is likely to be included as one of the biblical principles that the Founding Fathers built into the Constitution or as one of the conditions which the American system upholds so that religious people may worship as they choose without fear of intervention by any secular authority. In the liberal view, freedom may be colored by other religious connotations, such as freedom from fear or freedom from want, either of which may be interpreted as manifestations of the redemptive process outlined in the Christian gospel. Freedom is a concept sufficiently inclusive to be easily incorporated into these other worldviews. . . .

But there is also another component to the secular legitimating ideology currently prevalent in America. As if freedom were not in itself enough—or perhaps because other more tangible reminders are necessary to convince us of our virtues as a people—a materialistic ideology is frequently advanced in defense of America's position in the world. This ideology is blatantly pragmatic, like much of the culture more generally. It asserts simply that America is right because it is rich. Undisguised by any references to historic values or cultural ideals, the pragmatic myth asserts that we are virtuous because we are so successful.

Robert Wuthnow, *The Restructuring of American Religion*, 1988.

The liberal view of America focuses less on the nation as such, and more on humanity in general. According to this interpretation, America has a role to play in world affairs, not because it is a chosen people, but because it has vast resources at its disposal, because it has caused many of the problems currently facing the world, and because it is, simply, part of the community of nations and, therefore, has a responsibility to do what it can to alleviate the world's problems. Rather than drawing specific attention to the distinctiveness of the Judeo-Christian tradition, liberal civil religion is much more likely to include arguments about basic human rights and common human problems. Issues like nuclear disarmament, human rights, world hunger, peace, and justice tend to receive special emphasis. The importance attached to these issues is generally not legitimated with reference to any particular sacred mandate, but simply on the assumption that these are matters of life and death—perhaps for us all. Nevertheless, religious faith often plays an important part in the discussion, differentiating liberal civil religion from purely secular or humanist beliefs. Faith plays a role chiefly as a motivating element, supplying strength to keep going against what often appear as insuperable odds. The example of the biblical prophets, who spoke out for peace and justice, is frequently mentioned as a source of strength and hope. . . .

Opposition to Nuclear Weapons

Because of their awesome destructive potential, nuclear arms have occupied an especially prominent place in liberal civil religion. As one writer has acknowledged, "In virtually every large gathering of mainline or liberal Protestants these days, preoccupation with the awful possibility of nuclear war sooner or later rises to overshadow whatever the meeting was supposed to be about." Liberal clergy have so often taken the lead in seeking solutions to the arms race that the peace movement has come to be identified in many circles as a religious issue. In a 1982 survey of a national sample of Presbyterians, for example, two-thirds agreed strongly with the statement "peacemaking is not simply 'another political issue' but is a basic aspect of the Christian faith.'' . . .

Other crusades that have typified the liberal version of American civil religion include civil rights, international justice, and ecology. Liberal religious periodicals have kept these issues in the forefront of their readers' attention. . . .

The rhetoric of liberal religious leaders often includes references to the biblical tradition in support of its concern with peace and justice. Addressing more than 3,000 clergy and lay leaders gathered in Washington to protest the nuclear arms race in 1983, Jim Wallis, editor of *Sojourners* magazine, alluded repeatedly to the Christian values on which their movement was founded: "As the crisis we face becomes ever more clear, so do biblical passages about the oppression of the poor, the arrogance of power, and the idolatry of military might. Christians are remembering that the Gospel is to be good news to the poor and that the children of God are to live in the world as peacemakers." Yet in making these appeals, liberal religious leaders offer little that specifically legitimates America as a nation. Instead, they appeal to broader values that transcend American culture and, indeed, challenge some of the more nationalistic assumptions it incorporates. As Father John

Langan of the Woodstock Theological Center suggests, what seems to be needed most is a "clear delineation of the moral claims of the solidarity that binds us together as human beings sharing a common destiny under God. Such a delineation necessarily involves a critique of individualism and self-reliance in our national culture." . . .

Two Competing Visions for America

Both the liberal and conservative wings of American religion, therefore, have a vision of where America should be heading. But the two visions frequently appear to be at fundamental odds with one another. Each side inevitably sees itself as the champion of higher principles, against which present conditions often seem wanting.

The two sides, in fact, appear to have become differentiated along a fracture line that has long been apparent in discussions of civil religion. That line reflects the inherent tension between symbols expressing the unique identity of a nation and those which associate the nation with a broader vision of humanity. As Bellah notes in his initial essay on the subject, civil religion in America seems to function best when it apprehends "transcendent religious reality . . . as revealed through the experience of the American people"; yet, the growing interdependence of America with the world order appears to "necessitate the incorporation of vital international symbolism into our civil religion."

Perhaps it is not terribly surprising that these twin objectives can be accomplished more easily by two, relatively distinct civil religions than by one. The conservative tradition has in recent decades made clearest use of those symbols which are unique to the American experience; e.g., the mythologies of the Founding Fathers, of God's calling to the nation, of America's heroic accomplishments, and of the unique mission which America has to fulfill in the world. The liberal tradition, in contrast, has often been accused of neglecting these uniquely American symbols, but has given concerted emphasis to the international symbols that derive from a vision of the commonality of humanity.

The Lack of Consensus

The two versions of America also correspond in a general way with the ambivalent character of the American state. On the one hand, the relatively long period in American history during which the nation was able to enjoy virtual isolation from the rest of the world has resulted in the orientation of a segment of the bureaucratic state toward nationalistic concerns. On the other hand, America's rise to global power in the twentieth century has forced the state to act not only on behalf of narrow U.S. interests, but also as a potential contributor to the common good in global terms. These dual functions have sometimes been sufficiently different that particular agencies have come to be identified clearly with one or the other. But more commonly the two have been ambiguous enough that different advisory groups, administrators, and policy proposals have provided their chief manifestation. Under these circumstances, both versions of American civil religion have found proponents within the state who were willing to exploit them for purely political purposes.

In consequence, the two visions of America have been the subject of disagreement and polarization more than they have of consensus and mutual understanding. . . .

Neither side can claim effectively to speak for consensual values. Each represents a constituency, but holds—especially in the other's view—no assumptions on which all can agree. Any claim one side makes is likely to be disputed, leaving much of the public in doubt about the credibility of either. Religion, therefore, becomes (as indeed it has often been characterized in the press) "sectarian" rather than providing a basis of unity. . . .

Shared Assumptions

Conflicting interpretations notwithstanding, large segments of American culture continue to presuppose certain shared assumptions about religion and about the place of religion in the democratic process. The competing interpretations of American civil religion actually converge at a number of points. They agree with one another in asserting the importance of religious values to the political process; both assume the existence and importance of transcendent values in relation to which the nation may be judged; they agree on the relevance of certain biblical principles, such as compassion, equity, and liberty (while disagreeing on the priorities given to these principles); and they in fact draw on a common heritage of Judeo-Christian symbols and stories. . . .

The Emergence of a New Secular Ideology

Where the rub comes is that American civil religion does not operate in a vacuum. In a society which is not only deeply religious but also decidedly secular, other values and assumptions stand as ready alternatives to the civil religion. Faced with conflicting interpretations based on religious premises, spokespersons for the American creed have the option of turning to other arguments on which there may be greater consensus. Indeed, religious leaders themselves may fall back on purely secular values in attempting to find firmer ground from which to launch their religious arguments.

As the debate in American religion has intensified, the different versions of civil religion, therefore, have continued to be voiced as motivational appeals and as alternative stories of America.

"Four main themes emerge from this status report on where America stands on religion in the public arena."

A Survey on Religion and Public Life

The Williamsburg Charter Foundation

The following survey was commissioned by The Williamsburg Charter Foundation, an organization that describes itself as a "private, non-partisan, non-sectarian public policy group concerned with the place of religion in American public life." Foundation supporters include prominent national leaders from politics, religion, business, education, and the media, including Republican Senator Mark Hatfield and former Democratic presidential candidate Michael Dukakis. The survey explores such questions as how do the American people view the place of religion in public life today. Where do Americans currently draw the line between church and state? Are there significant limits to tolerance? Are there important differences between the general public and key leadership groups? Is there less religious tolerance today than twenty or thirty years ago?

As you read, consider the following questions:

1. What four main themes emerged from the survey?
2. What evidence does the survey present to support its conclusion that Americans are not becoming less tolerant?
3. What does the survey reveal about the public's beliefs on the separation of church and state?

The Williamsburg Charter Foundation, *The Williamsburg Charter Survey on Religion and Public Life.* Washington, DC: 1988. Reprinted with permission.

Four main themes emerge from this status report on where America stands on religion in the public arena after nearly 200 years of life under the First Amendment:

1. *Expanding Tolerance*: Contrary to widespread belief and charges in recent public disputes, Americans are not becoming less tolerant. In fact, there is a broad approval or acceptance of religion in public life, whether of its general place and importance or of its diverse expressions. As pluralism has expanded, toleration has expanded with it.

But there are noteworthy exceptions:

2. *Deep Ambivalences*: There is a notable ambivalence in the general public between theory and practice on church-state issues. Rhetorical assent to the separation of church and state is contradicted by nearly constant approval of less rigid separation in practice.

3. *Definite Limits*: While broad toleration is accorded to the main religious faiths, Americans still draw a clear line in their toleration of atheism and alternative life styles in political leaders and show a marked insistence on legal sanctions to curb unusual religious practices as well as more traditional groups when their activism is considered threatening.

4. *Significant Polarities*: Underlying the surface appearance of broad toleration, profound tensions and divergences are apparent. On a wide range of policy issues the rifts between the general public and certain leadership groups are pronounced, and even within the general public between different communities of faith.

These broad themes are supported by the following findings:

Presidential Candidates

The overwhelming majority of Americans are willing to vote for presidential candidates of different faiths which are part of the Judeo-Christian heritage.

- Only 8% of Americans would refuse to vote for a Catholic on the basis of religion.

- Only 10% would refuse to vote for a Jew.

- Only 13% would refuse to vote for a "born-again Baptist."

> These numbers show increasing toleration: In 1958, 28% told a Gallup poll they would not vote for a Jew; 25% said they would not vote for a Catholic. The only movement toward intolerance was an increase from 1958 when 3% were hostile to a Baptist candidate to the current 13% who say they would not vote for a "born-again" Baptist.

- Only 13% would refuse to vote for a Greek Orthodox candidate.

205

Tolerance of Religious Activism in American Politics

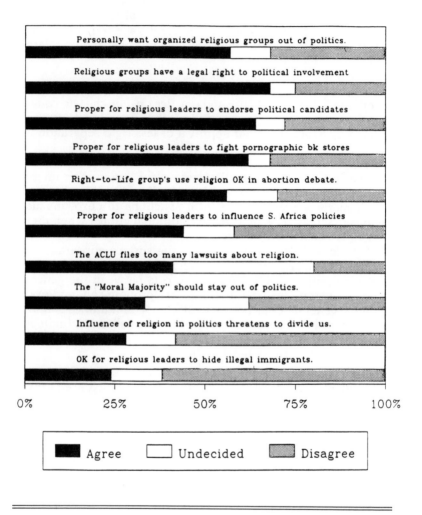

Personally want organized religious groups out of politics.

Religious groups have a legal right to political involvement

Proper for religious leaders to endorse political candidates

Proper for religious leaders to fight pornographic bk stores

Right-to-Life group's use religion OK in abortion debate.

Proper for religious leaders to influence S. Africa policies

The ACLU files too many lawsuits about religion.

The "Moral Majority" should stay out of politics.

Influence of religion in politics threatens to divide us.

OK for religious leaders to hide illegal immigrants.

0%   25%   50%   75%   100%

■ Agree   □ Undecided   ▨ Disagree

- 70% say it is important that the President have strong religious beliefs.
- However, about one-fifth (21%) said they would be unwilling to vote for a candidate who has been a minister of a church.
- 62% say they would be unwilling to vote for an atheist for President.

- 65% say they would be unwilling to vote for a homosexual for President.
- Traditional moral values were expected in candidates for the President. 65% would be unwilling to vote for a homosexual (26% would be willing) and 43% would be unwilling to vote for a married candidate who "has been having other love affairs" (43% would be willing).

Religious Activism and Public Life

There is an expanding tolerance of diverse religious expressions and a general, though qualified, acceptance of religious activism in public life.

- About two-thirds (68%) agree that "religious groups should have a legal right to get involved in politics," but most people (57%) say that "personally," they would prefer "to see organized religious groups stay out of politics."
- 62% think it is proper for religious leaders "to try to close pornographic book stores."
- 56% do not fault the Right to Life movement for injecting religious issues into the abortion debate.
- But, religious activism to try to influence U.S. foreign policy toward South Africa produces a more divided response (44% pro; 42% con).
- Only 24% support church protection of immigrants whom the government says are illegal.
- A plurality, 40% to 34%, believes that the "Moral Majority should stay out of politics."
- 67% of those familiar with the American Civil Liberties Union believe that "the ACLU files too many law suits regarding religion."

Church and State

The public tends to favor a strict separation of church and state in theory, while accepting a strong blending of the two in practice.

- A majority of Americans (51%) prefer a "high wall of separation between church and state," while 32% favor "special steps" by government "to protect the Judeo-Christian heritage."
- However, when asked which of these statements came closest to their opinion: "The government should not provide support to any religion" or "The government should support all religions equally," 44% wanted no support for any religion; 52% wanted government support equally.
- Most Americans support the idea of having Congress open

Acceptance of Government
Support of Religious Expression

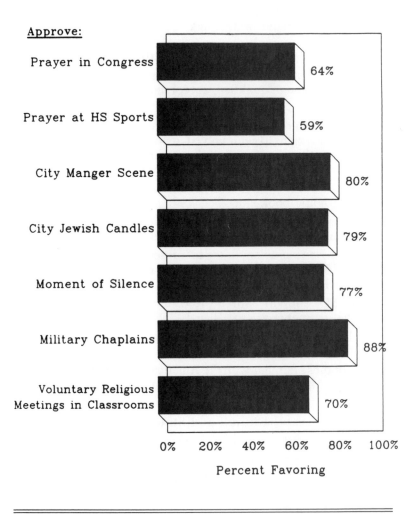

Approve:

Prayer in Congress — 64%

Prayer at HS Sports — 59%

City Manger Scene — 80%

City Jewish Candles — 79%

Moment of Silence — 77%

Military Chaplains — 88%

Voluntary Religious Meetings in Classrooms — 70%

0% 20% 40% 60% 80% 100%

Percent Favoring

with a prayer (64%), public prayers before high school sporting events (59%) and a moment of silence in schools for voluntary prayer (77%).

- But most opposed the idea that "the government should require that Judeo-Christian values be emphasized in public schools." (52% disagreed; 30% agreed).

- Most want Biblical perspectives about creation included with discussions of evolution (69%), with minorities favoring the teaching of creationism only (11%) or the teaching of evolution only (11%).

- 70% say that public schools should allow student religious groups to hold voluntary meetings in classrooms, when classes are not in session.

- Most Americans are unfamiliar with the term "secular humanism," but those who are aware of it (26%) are divided as to whether the schools are teaching it (11% of the total sample think they are; 8% think they aren't). Of those familiar with secular humanism, roughly half think it is "bad" for the country, one-fourth think it is "good" and the rest have no opinion.

- The public is deeply divided on whether the government should provide financial help to parochial schools: 41% said yes; 50% said no.

- 80% agree that "it's OK for a city government to put up a manger scene on government property"; 79% agree that it's OK to put up candles for Jewish celebrations.

The Limits of Tolerance

While tolerance is expanding to the non-Western religions, certain limits remain.

- Only 13% felt that "there is no place in America for the Moslem religion," while 71% disagreed.

- 60% approved of having Buddhist chaplains in the armed forces.

- But two-thirds (65%) agree that "it should be against the law for unusual religious cults to try to convert teenagers."

- 57% said "there should be laws to prevent groups like Hare Krishna from asking people for money at airports."

- 54% endorse "laws against the practice of Satan worship."

- A majority (57%) believe that "the FBI should keep a close watch on new religious cults."

- 40% said they would support laws prohibiting preachers from using TV shows to raise money (49% said no).

- Nearly one-fourth (23%) said that "followers of the Rev. Sun Myung Moon should not be allowed to print a daily newspaper in Washington, D.C." (56% disagreed).

Toward Polarization?

Among the many tensions within the communities of faith, the widest divergence is between the secularists and the Evangelicals.

- 61% of all secularists agree that "churches should have to pay taxes on all their property" compared to 34% of all Evangelicals.
- Only 18% of secularists agree that "the government should require that Judeo-Christian values be emphasized in public schools" compared with 52% of Evangelicals.
- 17% of secularists said that Evangelicals, more than any other group, "had too much power and influence"; while one out of 10 said that Evangelicals are "a threat to democracy."
- A plurality of all Americans, 45% to 41%, believe there is less religious tolerance today than there was 20 to 30 years ago.
- A plurality, 45% to 44%, believe that there are religious groups which are "a threat to democracy."

Two age groups of young people—15-to-19 and 19-to-22—were surveyed. With only minor exceptions, there is no generation gap on religious issues.

Knowledge of the Constitution

As in the past, attitudes to the Constitution are marked by a high level of esteem but a low level of knowledge.

- For example, only one in three (33%) knew that the freedom of religion is guaranteed by the First Amendment.

Leadership Contrasts

On a broad number of policy issues there are profound divergences between the general public and certain leadership groups and between those leadership groups.

- One out of every five academics said that Evangelicals, more than any other religious group, had "too much power and influence."
- Nearly one out of three academics (34%) said that Evangelicals are "a threat to democracy." This sentiment was shared by 27% of the rabbinate.
- While just over half of the general public (52%) believes that the government should support all religions equally, the majority of leaders in business (76%), government (78%), universities (87%), the media (64%), the Protestant ministry (62%) and the rabbinate (78%) believe that "the government should not provide any support to any religions."
- While roughly half (52%) of the public disagrees that "the government should require that Judeo-Christian values be emphasized in public schools," strong majorities in business (66%), government (84%), the university (89%), the media (79%), and the rabbinate (68%) disagreed with that statement.

a critical thinking activity

Distinguishing Between Fact and Opinion

This activity is designed to help develop the basic reading and thinking skill of distinguishing between fact and opinion. Consider the following statement as an example. "Both the United States and the Soviet Union have nuclear weapons in their arsenals." The preceding statement is a fact which no historian or diplomat, of any nationality, would deny. But let us consider a statement which makes a judgement about the current nuclear arms race. "The aggressive foreign policy of the Soviet Union is the major cause of the arms race." Such a statement is clearly an expressed opinion. Attributing blame concerning the cause of the arms race obviously depends upon one's point of view. A citizen of the Soviet Union will view the arms race from a far different perspective than will a citizen of the United States.

When investigating controversial issues it is important that one be able to distinguish between statements of fact and statements of opinion.

Most of the following statements are taken from the viewpoints in this book. Some have other origins. Consider each statement carefully. *Mark O for any statement you feel is an opinion or interpretation of facts. Mark F for any statement you believe is a fact.*

If you are doing this activity as the member of a class or group, compare your answers with those of other class or group members. Be able to defend your answers. You may discover that others will come to different conclusions than you. Listening to the reasons others present for their answers may give you valuable insights in distinguishing between fact and opinion.

If you are reading this book alone, ask others if they agree with your answers. You too will find this interaction very valuable.

O = *opinion*
F = *fact*

1. Business is today the most significant force shaping American life.
2. Capitalism puts a high premium on the possession of material goods.
3. Work is one way of justifying our existence to Our Creator.
4. The role of government is already excessively intrusive in the lives of our citizenry and the operation of our economy.
5. In our Constitution, the Founding Fathers created a structure of government based on the separation of powers between President and Congress.
6. Sport has displaced religion, dislodged citizenship and even further dislocated communication between the sexes.
7. The pressure to win can breed corruption.
8. No man can live and no society can survive for very long without a religion and a faith of some sort that explains man's nature and the meaning of his life and death.
9. There actually exists alongside of and rather clearly differentiated from the churches an elaborate and well-institutionalized civil religion in America.
10. Capitalism is the economic system that is consonant with Christianity.
11. The fundamental and paramount role of the church is to transmit moral, inspirational teachings to the poor.
12. Jesus' teachings far transcend particular economic processes.

Periodical Bibliography

The following articles have been selected to supplement the diverse views presented in this chapter.

Robert Bellah   "The Sacred and the Political in American Life," *Psychology Today*, January 1976.

Harry C. Boyte   "The Secular Left, Religion & the American Commonweal," *Christianity and Crisis*, May 1983.

Charles W. Colson   "The Spiritual State of the Union," *Moody Monthly*, July/August 1986.

Edd Doerr   "Religion in Public Education," *The Humanist*, November/December 1987.

William Edelen   "America's Founders Rejected Orthodox Christianity," *Free Inquiry*, Fall 1985.

Frederick Edwords   "The Religious Character of American Patriotism," *The Humanist*, November/December 1987.

Free Inquiry   Special issue on "Religion in American Politics," Summer 1983.

Nicholas F. Gier   "Humanism As an American Heritage," *Free Inquiry*, Spring 1982.

Lawrence W. Hyman   "Humanists and Traditional Moral Values," *The Humanist*, March/April 1987.

Kirk Kidwell   "Back to God," *The New American*, June 20, 1988.

Everett Carl Ladd   "Secular and Religious America," *Society*, March/April 1987.

John Lawing   "Are America's Moral Values Stable or Sliding?" *Eternity*, June 1982.

Warren B. Martin   "American Values in a Revolutionary World," *Vital Speeches of the Day*, July 15, 1965.

Martin E. Marty   "Public Religion: The Republican Banquet," *Phi Kappa Phi Journal*, Winter 1988.

Gabriel Moran   "Taking Offense: Civil Religion in America," *America*, September 30, 1978.

Jon G. Murray   "Religion and Democracy," *American Atheist*, April 1986.

Richard J. Neuhaus   "Who, Now, Will Shape the Meaning of America?" *Christianity Today*, March 19, 1982.

Michael Novak   "Religion and Liberty: From Vision to Politics," *The Christian Century*, July 6-13, 1988.

H.W. Prentis Jr.   "The Faith of Our Fathers," *Vital Speeches of the Day*, December 15, 1941.

W. Stanley Rycroft   "America—Secular or Christian?" *The Churchman*, March 1987.

Curtis J. Sitomer   "Religion in US: Many Beliefs, a Common Morality," *The Christian Science Monitor*, April 21, 1988.

Terry Sommerville   "Did America's Founding Fathers Really Stand on the Word of God?" *Christianity Today*, June 17, 1983.

James M. Wall   "A Moral Tone Shapes the Nation's Soul," *The Christian Century*, June 8-15, 1983.

Kenneth L. Woodward   "How the Bible Made America," *Newsweek*, December 27, 1982.

Robert Wuthnow   "Divided We Fall: America's Two Civil Religions," *The Christian Century*, April 20, 1988.

5 CHAPTER

What Is Patriotism?

AMERICAN
V·A·L·U·E·S

Chapter Preface

The *Random House Dictionary of the English Language* defines the patriot as "a person who loves, supports, and defends his or her country and its interests with devotion." This definition seems clear on the surface, but beneath, roiling emotions and different interpretations create a contentious issue. One side is represented by Stephen Decatur's famous dinner toast, made in 1816: "Our country! In her intercourse with foreign nations may she always be in the right; but our country right or wrong." Thirty-one years later, a former president, John Quincy Adams, identified the opposite side with the following statement: "And say not thou 'My country right or wrong,' nor shed thy blood for an unhallowed cause." Which of these two statements bests represents the true patriot?

The five viewpoints in this chapter offer different perspectives on patriotism. From advocacy of tribal-like loyalty to a disavowal of national patriotism, experts defend different positions. The central issue being debated is the characteristics of true patriotism. After concluding this chapter, readers should be able to construct their own definition of the word patriot.

"I want to talk to you about a vanishing species—the American patriot."

America Must Return to Patriotism

Max Rafferty

Max Rafferty was the superintendent of public instruction for the state of California from 1963 to 1971. The author of several books, including *What They Are Doing to Your Children*, *Max Rafferty on Education*, and *Classroom Countdown*, he was awarded the George Washington Honor Medal by the Freedom Foundation at Valley Forge for a speech on patriotism. The following viewpoint is excerpted from that speech. In it, Mr. Rafferty blames the American educational system for raising a nation of cowards. He contends that America must dedicate itself to teaching the young about the glorious attributes of heroism and patriotism.

As you read, consider the following questions:

1. Why does the author claim the American patriot is a vanishing species?
2. Why does he think American schools are to blame for the decline in patriotism? Do you agree?

Max Rafferty, "The Passing of the Patriot," reprinted with the author's permission.

I want to talk to you about a vanishing species—the American patriot. I hope to show you what you and I have done . . . to make possible—nay, to render inevitable—this dwindling decline of a once noble breed. And, at the end, I shall propose to you a simple question: "Is this what we want?"

Our Country, Right or Wrong!

First, go back with me in time. . . . Our country is in a strange sort of undeclared war against the forces of despotism, then as now. A young man volunteers to go behind the enemy lines to collect information. He is captured and tried as a spy and publicly questioned. Surrounded by the jeering foe, cut off beyond all hope of rescue, the rope already knotted around his bared throat and the pallor of approaching death already on his cheek, he breaks his steadfast silence. With the wind of another world cold upon his forehead, he speaks one short sentence, and his words echo down the corridors of time to us today, ringing and light-hearted and magnificent: "I only regret that I have but one life to give for my country."

His statue, with the throat still bared, stands today gazing with blind stone eyes across the green park in New York City, where I saw it not too long ago. He was a schoolmaster—God rest his soul—and he did not live to see his twenty-second birthday.

What were those blind eyes looking for a few years ago, I wonder, when for the first time in our history a substantial number of young men sold out their fellow American soldiers, and licked the boots of brutal Chinese and North Korean invaders, and made tape recordings praising Communism? What do those stone ears make of the other young men and women who seem to spend every waking moment agitating against ROTC, booing authorized Congressional committees, and parading in support of Fidel Castro?

Whether we like it or not, ladies and gentlemen, this is our doing—yours and mine. For the past twenty years, the great mistake has been made by my profession, and by the voters and taxpayers who permitted it.

This sizable minority of spineless, luxury-loving, spiritless characters came right out of our classrooms. They played in our kindergartens, went on field trips to the bakery, and studied things called "social living" and "language arts" in our junior high schools. They were "adjusted to their peer groups." They were taught that competition was bad. They were told little about modern democratic capitalism. They were persuaded that the world was very shortly to become one big, happy family. They were taught to be kind, and democratic, and peaceful.

These last are praiseworthy goals. What went wrong?

There were two things, you see, that we *didn't* teach them. And oh! how they needed to learn these.

Do You Remember . . .

When *riots were unthinkable.*
When *you left front doors open.*
When *socialism was a dirty word.*
When *ghettos were neighborhoods.*
When *the Flag was a sacred symbol.*
When *criminals actually went to jail.*
When *you weren't afraid to go out at night.*
When *taxes were only a necessary nuisance.*
When *a boy was a boy, and dressed like one.*
When *a girl was a girl, and dressed like one.*
When *the poor were too proud to take charity.*
When *the clergy actually talked about religion.*
When *clerks and repairmen tried to please you.*
When *college kids swallowed goldfish, not acid.*
When *songs had a tune, and the words made sense.*
When *young fellows tried to join the Army or Navy.*
When *people knew what the Fourth of July stood for.*
When *you never dreamed our country could ever lose.*
When *a Sunday drive was a pleasant trip, not an ordeal.*
When *you bragged about your hometown and home state.*
When *everybody didn't feel entitled to a college education.*
When *people expected less and valued what they had more.*
When *politicians proclaimed their patriotism, and meant it.*
When *everybody knew the difference between right and wrong.*
When *things weren't perfect—but you never expected them to be.*
When *you weren't made to feel guilty for enjoying dialect comedy.*
When *our Government stood up for Americans, anywhere in the world.*
When *you knew that the law would be enforced, and your safety protected.*
When *you considered yourself lucky to have a good job, and proud to have it.*
When *the law meant justice, and you felt a shiver of awe at sight of a policeman.*
When *you weren't embarrassed to say that this is the best country in the world.*
When *America was a land filled with brave, proud, confident, hardworking people!*

Undated circular by Americanism Educational League

One was that most of the inhabitants of this big, bad-tempered, battling planet hate our American insides. This is hard to teach, and unpleasant to learn. It is the simple truth, nevertheless.

The other should have been simpler. It was to teach the children the real meaning of Decatur's great toast: "Our country! In her intercourse with foreign nations, may she always be right, but our country, right or wrong!"

Had they been taught these things, they would not now be wondering what all the fuss is about. They would know that their country was in danger, and that would be enough. It was enough in 1898, and 1917, and 1941. It's not enough today. Too many of them neither know nor care.

It's our own fault. What will History have to say of my generation of educators—the generation of the '30s, the '40s, and the '50s? We were so busy educating for "life adjustment" that we forgot that the first duty of a nation's schools is to preserve that nation.

Words that America had treasured as a rich legacy, that had sounded like trumpet calls above the clash of arms and the fury of debate, we allowed to fade from the classrooms and the consciousness of the pupils. "Liberty and Union, now and forever, one and inseparable. . ." "We have met the enemy and they are ours. . ." "Millions for defense, but not one cent for tribute. . ."

Search for these towering phrases in vain today in too many of our schools, in the hearts and minds of too many of our children. . . . We have no further need of Websters—nor of Nathan Hales.

Our Schools Teach Trivia Not Patriotism

Our sin was greater than this, however. Patriotism feeds upon hero-worship, and we decided to abolish heroes. Even the fairy tales and nursery rhymes, beloved by generations of children, we pronounced too "violent" and "brutal" for the children to hear until after we had tinkered with them. Hansel and Gretel we neutralized to the status of children on a Sunday School picnic, and Jack the Giant-Killer to a schoolboy swatting flies. Everything that was fearful and wonderful, we leveled off to the lowest *common* denominator.

Ulysses and Penelope have been replaced by Dick and Jane in the textbooks of our schools. The quest of the Golden Fleece has been crowded out by the visit of Tom and Susan to the zoo. The deeds of the heroes before Troy are now passe, and the peregrinations of the local milkman as he wends his way among the stodgy streets and littered alleys of Blah City are deemed worthy of numberless pages in our readers. The sterile culture of the Pueblo Indians looms large in our curriculum, but the knightly Crusaders are glossed over. Bobby and Betty pursue their insipid goal of a ride in the district garbage truck with good old crotchety Mr. Jones, while the deathless ride of Paul Revere goes unwept, unhonored, and unsung. It is interesting and significant, I think, that education has deliberately debunked the hero to make room for the jerk.

Today's hero—if there is one—is fashioned in the blasphemous image of Ourselves.

He is "Daddy" in the second reader, who comes mincing

Americans Must Sacrifice

I want to propose just one large category of concept and activity which, I believe, is contributing to an attitude of hostility toward the American Dream. It is the spreading preoccupation, particularly among the youth, with one's own comfort, one's own physical gratification, one's right to do whatever he pleases as long as he doesn't significantly harm someone else, one's own security, one's own immediate desires, and the corollary belligerent intolerance of any laws, customs, or considerations for other people which might prevent me from doing my thing right now. Protest has become a way of life. If the individual's comfort and convenience are not at a maximum, then whatever is thwarting them should be attacked.

The government inaugurated in 1789 was committed to maximizing the dignity of all citizens. It recognized the eternal need for change in the governing process and the governing personnel and it created the mechanisms for orderly change. It guaranteed to all citizens certain privileges and devised a judiciary to try to assure that those privileges were fairly interpreted and properly maintained. However, in attending to all aspects of maximizing human dignity, the whole structure of the government was posited upon the requirement that the citizens, every citizen, would have to make some very great sacrifices. Each would have to pay duly levied taxes in order to sustain the authorized operations of the government. Each citizen would have to forego his other activities when called to jury duty. Each would submit peacefully to the will of the majority when it was expressed by vote, directing his own disappointments and dissatisfactions when thwarted by the majority vote, into legal and appropriate channels with the hope of subsequently making his own, the majority vote.

This form of government was entirely dependent upon a universal commitment to certain superior goals which necessitated personal sacrifices, acceptance of restrictions and conformity where the public weal was engaged. To achieve a new level of freedom for all, certain aspects of personal freedom had to be sacrificed by all.

Against this necessity for sacrifice, the current enthusiasm for total personal freedom, the current insistence upon exercising one's own whims with a disregard for the sensitivities of others, the quickening readiness to pronounce one's own particular objectives as uniquely moral and therefore beyond the purview of publicly established limits—all of these attitudes and actions stand in hostility to what this country is all about, and contribute to the disenchantment with America.

John Howard, "Patriotism Revisited," *Vital Speeches of the Day*, September 17, 1969, pp. 27-28. Reprinted with permission.

home with his eternal briefcase from his meaningless day in his antiseptic office just in time to pat Jip the dog and carry blonde little Laurie into the inevitable white bungalow on his stylishly padded shoulders.

He is "Mommy" in the third grade books, always silk-stockinged and impeccable after a day spent over the electric range, with never a cross word on her carefully made-up lips and never an idea in her empty head.

He is all the insufferable nonentities who clutter up the pages of our elementary textbooks with their vapid ditherings about humdrum affairs which could never be of conceivable interest to anybody. . . .

When I think of the doors we've closed upon the children! The wonderful pantheon of youthful gods and goddesses that my generation knew and loved; the great parade of heroes who made old Earth a magic place for boys and girls!

Wilfred of Ivanhoe rode stirrup to stirrup with Richard the Lion-Hearted, and the evil hold of Torquilstone burned eternal witness to the power of youth and goodness. Laughing and shouting in the same great company rode Arthur with his Table Round, forever splintering their lances in the cause of Right. Roistering and invincible swaggered Porthos, Athos, and Aramis, with the young D'Artagnan, ever ready to draw those magic blades for truth and glory and the Queen. . . .

The horn of Roland echoed through the pass at Roncevalles, and somehow caught and mingled in our memories with the far-off blast of Robin Hood, calling down the misty years upon his merry men of Sherwood.

Were not these fit heroes for the children?. . .

It remained for our generation to turn its back upon the heroes of the children. For Siegfried in the lair of Fafnir, we have substituted Muk-Muk the Eskimo Boy, and we have replaced Horatius at the Bridge with Little Pedro from Argentina.

Mark this. Until. . .a few years ago, most schools on all levels were teaching trivia. Today, too many—especially on the elementary level—are still doing so.

If you doubt this, don't take my word for it. Visit classroom after classroom in widely separated regions of this country, as I have done.

Watch the abler pupils grow dull and apathetic, bored and lackluster, as they yawn over Bill and Tom's Trip to the Farm, or Sally's Fun at the Orange Grove. Then, suddenly—as though opening an enchanted window upon a radiant pageant—give them the story of the wrath of Achilles. Let them stand with Casabianca upon the burning deck. Trek with them in spirit to the Yukon, and with glorious Buck let them answer the call of the wild. Place them upon the shot-swept shrouds of the Bonhomme Richard, and let them thrill to those words flashing like a rapier out of our past, "I have not yet begun to fight." Kneel with them behind the cotton bales at New Orleans with Andy Jackson at their side, as the redcoats begin to emerge from the Louisiana mists and the sullen guns of Lafitte begin to pound.

Watch their faces. See the eyes brighten and the spirits ruffle. See the color come, the backs straighten, the arms go up. They dream, they live, they glow. Patriotism will come easily to them now, as it does to all of us who know our nation's past—and love it.

Teach them the grand old songs. How long has it been since California children learned to sing "Columbia, the Gem of the Ocean"? And why was it dropped? Probably because someone decided that the lines which end, "The Army and Navy forever! Three cheers for the Red, White and Blue!" were hopelessly out of place in our brave new world of foreign aid and peaceful coexistence and collaboration.

I say that we had better thank God for the army and navy! And—with half the world at our throats—we had better teach our children that it is not a disgrace, but a priceless privilege, to wear our country's uniform!. . .

The Sad Results

The results are plain for all to see: the worst of our youngsters growing up to become. . .Slobs, whose favorite sport is ravaging little girls and stomping polio victims to death; the best of our youth coming into maturity for all the world like young people fresh from a dizzying roller-coaster ride, with everything blurred, with nothing clear, with no positive standards, with everything in doubt. No wonder so many of them welsh out and squeal and turn traitor when confronted with the grim reality of Red military force and the crafty cunning of Red psychological warfare.

We as a people have been taunted and reviled and challenged in the last few years as we thought no one would ever challenge us. A soulless Thing slavers at us today on all the continents, under all the seas, and out into the void of interplanetary space itself—a rotten, hateful, vicious entity. Our national nose has been first tweaked and then rubbed contemptuously into the dirt. The flag for which our ancestors bled and died has been torn down and unspeakably defiled by a dozen little pipsqueak comic-opera countries emboldened by our spinelessness and encouraged by our sneering Enemy. I don't know when at long last the American people will rise in all the power and majesty of their great tradition to put an end to this role of international doormat which we have assumed of late, and which becomes us so poorly.

But I do know one thing. When that time comes—and it cannot be too far distant—we educators had better not be caught short.

We had better not be caught withholding from the nation's children the wonderful, sharp-edged glittering sword of Patriotism.

What is the alternative? You see that all about you now, in all the headlines. Do you like it? As I said in the beginning, "Is this what we want?"

Or rather, do we want our young people informed and disciplined and alert—militant for freedom, clear-eyed to the filthy menace of Communist corruption? Do we want them happy in their love of country?

If your answer is "Yes," then go home and get busy. It is to this that I propose that we dedicate ourselves in the years to come. We have not an hour to spare. If Almighty God grants us the time and the will, we may still be able to preserve this lovely land of ours as it once was and—please God—will yet be again; a nation fit for heroes—serene in the knowledge of our past—confident and ready for whatever the future may bring—stretching in warmth of heart and unity of purpose "from sea to shining sea."

"It was not until the Indochina War that we began to search for a new kind of patriotism."

America Needs a New Patriotism

Ralph Nader

Ralph Nader is a Washington, DC attorney and a champion crusader for the US consumer. Educated at Princeton and Harvard, he is the founder of the Center for Responsive Law and Public Interest Research Group. He is the author of *Who's Poisoning America?* and a contributing editor to *Ladies Home Journal*. In the following viewpoint, Mr. Nader claims that America must search for a new kind of patriotism that is built on behavior patterns that advocate world peace rather than abstract militaristic symbols of war.

As you read, consider the following questions:

1. In the author's opinion, why was patriotism important during the early days of American history?
2. Why does he feel America now needs a new kind of patriotism? Do you agree?
3. What four points does Mr. Nader suggest Americans use as guidelines in searching for a new kind of patriotism?

Ralph Nader, "We Need a New Kind of Patriotism," *The Saturday Evening Post*, July 1, 1971, pp. 4-5. Reprinted with permission from *The Saturday Evening Post* © 1971 The Curtis Publishing Company.

At a recent meeting of the national PTA, the idealism and commitment of many young people to environmental and civil rights causes were being discussed. A middle-aged woman, who was listening closely, stood up and asked: "But what can we do to make young people today patriotic?"

In a very direct way, she illuminated the tensions contained in the idea of patriotism. These tensions, which peak at moments of public contempt or respect for patriotic symbols such as the flag, have in the past few years divided the generations and pitted children against parents. Highly charged exchanges take place between those who believe that patriotism is automatically possessed by those in authority and those who assert that patriotism is not a pattern imposed but a condition earned by the quality of an individual's, or a people's, behavior. The struggle over symbols, epithets and generalities impedes a clearer understanding of the meaning and value of patriotism. It is time to talk of patriotism, not as an abstraction steeped in nostalgia, but as behavior that can be judged by the standard of "liberty and justice for all."

Patriotism can be a great asset for any organized society, but it can also be a tool manipulated by unscrupulous or cowardly leaders and elites. The development of a sense of patriotism was a strong unifying force during our Revolution and its insecure aftermath. Defined then and now as "love of country," patriotism was an extremely important motivating force with which to confront foreign threats to the young nation. It was no happenstance that *The Star Spangled Banner* was composed during the War of 1812 when the Redcoats were not only coming but already here. For a weak frontier country beset by the competitions and aggressions of European powers in the New World, the martial virtues were those of sheer survival. America produced patriots who never moved beyond the borders of their country. They were literally defenders of their home.

As the United States moved into the 20th century and became a world power, far-flung alliances and wars fought thousands of miles away stretched the boundaries of patriotism. "Making the world safe for democracy" was the grandiose way Woodrow Wilson put it. At other times and places (such as Latin America) it became distorted into "jingoism." World War II was the last war that all Americans fought with conviction. Thereafter, when "bombs bursting in air" would be atomic bombs, world war became a suicidal risk. Wars that could be so final and swift lost their glamour even for the most militaristically minded. When we became the most powerful nation on earth, the old insecurity that made patriotism into a conditioned reflex of "my country right or wrong" should have given way to a thinking process; as expressed by Carl Schurz; "Our country. . .when right, to be kept right. When wrong, to be put right." It was not until the Indochina war that we began the search for a new kind of patriotism.

If we are to find true and concrete meaning in patriotism, I suggest these starting points. *First,* in order that a free and just consensus be formed, patriotism must once again be rooted in the individual's own conscience and beliefs. Love is conceived by the giver (citizens) when merited by the receiver (the governmental authorities). If "consent of the governed" is to have any meaning, the abstract ideal of country has to be separated from those who direct it; otherwise the government cannot be evaluated by its citizens. The authorities in the State Department, the Pentagon, or the White House are not infallible; they

"It was designed as a flag, Buddy—not as a blindfold."

have been and often are wrong, vain, misleading, shortsighted or authoritarian. When they are, leaders like these are shortchanging, not representing, America. To identify America with them is to abandon hope and settle for tragedy. Americans who consider themselves patriotic in the traditional sense do not usually hesitate to heap criticism in domestic matters over what they believe is oppressive or wasteful or unresponsive government handling of their rights and dignity. They should be just as vigilant in weighing similar government action which harnesses domestic resources for foreign involvements. Citizenship has an obligation to cleanse patriotism of the misdeeds done in its name abroad.

The Meaning of Patriotism

In the '80s, patriotism and its symbols increasingly have become media extravaganzas for commercial and political exploitation. Such shows and speeches, disassociated as they are from contemporary deeds and national missions, have become refuges for holders of power who seek to define and control the nation's patriotic sentiments. . . .

The challenge is to find activities in our own daily lives that give meaning to our patriotic slogans, and that allow us to define our love for our country through civic achievement. Patriotism is a powerful idea, and one that should be defined by citizens, not by their rulers alone. For me, the meaning of patriotism lies in working to make America more lovable.

Ralph Nader, *Manchester Guardian Weekly,* July 13, 1986.

The flag, as the Pledge of Allegiance makes clear, takes its meaning from that "for which it stands"; it should not and cannot stand for shame, injustice and tyranny. It must not be used as a bandanna or a fig leaf by those unworthy of this country's leadership.

Second, patriotism begins at home. Love of country in fact is inseparable from citizen action to make the country more lovable. This means working to end poverty, discrimination, corruption, greed and other conditions that weaken the promise and potential of America.

Third, if it is unpatriotic to tear down the flag (which is a symbol of the country), why isn't it more unpatriotic to desecrate the country itself—to pollute, despoil and ravage the air, land and water? Such environmental degradation makes the "pursuit of happiness" ragged indeed. Why isn't it unpatriotic to engage in the colossal waste that characterizes so many defense contracts? Why isn't it unpatriotic to draw our country into a mistaken war and then keep extending the involvement, with untold casualties to soldiers and innocents, while not telling Americans the truth? Why isn't the deplorable treatment of returning veterans by government and industry evaluated by the same standards as is their dispatch to war? Why isn't the systematic contravention of the U.S. Constitution and the Declaration of Independence in our treatment of minority groups, the poor, the young, the old and other disadvantaged or helpless people crassly unpatriotic? Isn't all such behavior contradicting the innate worth and the dignity of the individual in America? Is it not time to end the tragic twisting of patriotism whereby those who work to expose and correct deep injustices, and who take intolerable risks while doing it, are accused of running down America by the very forces doing just that? Our country and its ideals are something for us to uphold as individuals and together, not something to drape, as a deceptive cloak, around activities that mar or destroy these ideals.

Fourth, there is no reason why patriotism has to be so heavily associated, in the minds of the young as well as adults, with military exploits, jets and missiles. Citizenship must include the duty to advance our ideals actively into practice for a better community, country and world, if peace is to prevail over war. And this obligation stems not just from a secular concern for humanity but from a belief in the brotherhood of man—"I am my brother's keeper"—that is common to all major religions. It is the classic confrontation—barbarism *vs.* the holy ones. If patriotism has no room for deliberation, for acknowledging an individual's sense of justice and his religious principles, it will continue to close minds, stifle the dissent that has made us strong, and deter the participation of Americans who challenge in order to correct, and who question in order to answer. We need only to recall recent history in other countries where patriotism was converted into an epidemic of collective madness and destruction. A patriotism manipulated by the government asks only for a servile nod from its subjects. A new patriotism requires a thinking assent from its citizens. If patriotism is to have any "manifest destiny," it is in building a world where all mankind is our bond in peace.

3

"Patriotism . . . means that you place the welfare of your nation ahead of your own, even if it costs you your life."

America's Survival Depends on Patriotism

Robert A. Heinlein

Robert A. Heinlein, (1907-1988), is famous for his science fiction. The author of dozens of books, he was a four-time Hugo Award recipient for his books *Double Star, Starship Trooper, Stranger in a Strange Land,* and *The Moon Is a Harsh Mistress.* He was also awarded the first Grand Master Nebula award by the Science Fiction Writers of America. Mr. Heinlein was a naval officer and a graduate of the US Naval Academy. The following viewpoint is an excerpt from a speech to the Brigade of Midshipmen at the US Naval Academy. In it, Mr. Heinlein compares the instinctive behavior of baboons to that of humans, and claims that patriotism, or moral behavior on a national level, means "women and children first."

As you read, consider the following questions:

1. Why does the author think many American intellectuals sneer at patriotism?
2. How does the author define moral behavior? Do you agree?
3. In Heinlein's opinion, what can be learned from baboons about patriotism?

Robert A. Heinlein, "The Pragmatics of Patriotism," *Human Events,* January 26, 1974, pp. 84-85. © 1973—Robert A. Heinlein. All rights reserved.

Today, in the United States, it is popular among self-styled "intellectuals" to sneer at patriotism. They seem to think that it is axiomatic that any civilized man is a pacifist, and they treat the military profession with contempt. "Warmongers"—"Imperialists"—"Hired killers in uniform"—you have all heard such sneers and you will hear them again. One of their favorite quotations is: "Patriotism is the last refuge of a scoundrel."

What they never mention is that the man who made the sneering wisecrack was a fat, gluttonous slob who was pursued all his life by a pathological fear of death.

I propose to prove that a baboon on watch while his herd grazes is morally superior to that fat poltroon who made that wisecrack.

Patriotism is the most practical of all human characteristics.

But in the present decadent atmosphere patriots are often too shy to talk about it—as if it were something shameful or an irrational weakness.

But patriotism is not sentimental nonsense. Nor something dreamed up by demagogues. Patriotism is as necessary a part of man's evolutionary equipment as are his eyes, as useful to the race as eyes are to the individual.

A man who is *not* patriotic is an evolutionary dead end. This is not sentiment but the hardest sort of logic.

Fundamentals of Patriotism

To prove that patriotism is a necessity we must go back to fundamentals. Take any breed of animal—for example, *tyrannosaurus rex*. What is the most basic thing about him? The answer is that *tyrannosaurus rex* is dead, gone, extinct.

Now take *homo sapiens*. The first fact about him is that he is not extinct, he is alive.

Which brings us to the second fundamental question: Will *homo sapiens* stay alive? Will he survive?

We can answer part of that at once: Individually, *homo sapiens* will *not* survive. It is unlikely that anyone here tonight will be alive 80 years from now; it approaches mathematical certainty that we will all be dead a hundred years from now as even the youngest plebe here would be 118 years old then—if still alive.

Some men do live that long, but the percentage is so microscopic as not to matter. Recent advances in biology suggest that human life may be extended to a century and a quarter, even a century and a half—but this will create more problems than it solves. When a man reaches my age or thereabouts, the last great service he can perform is to die and get out of the way of younger people.

Very well, as individuals we all die. This brings us to the second half of the question: Does *homo sapiens as a breed* have to die? The answer is: No, it is *not* unavoidable.

231

We have two situations, mutually exclusive: Mankind surviving, and mankind extinct. With respect to morality, the second situation is a null class. An extinct breed has *no* behavior, moral or otherwise.

Since survival is the sine qua non, I now define "moral behavior" as "behavior that tends toward survival." I won't argue with philosophers or theologians who choose to use the word "moral" to mean something else, but I do not think anyone can define "behavior that tends toward extinction" as being "moral" without stretching the word "moral" all out of shape.

We are now ready to observe the hierarchy of moral behavior from its lowest level to its highest.

America's Rebirth of Patriotism

During the 1960s and early 1970s, patriotism fell into disrepute. Young people—and some older ones—felt that love of country was a barbaric and philistine emotion. For the first time in our history, large numbers of Americans viewed their own country as "the enemy." Flags were burned, military service was resisted, many proudly waved the flags of the enemies of their country.

Now. . .all of this seems to be a thing of the distant past. Patriotism is once again an acceptable attitude, even in "sophisticated" circles. Tedd Christensen, owner and manager of Copeland Company, a major flag maker in Virginia, says: "Ten years ago they bought a flag only to step on it or to spit on it. Now, the pendulum is swinging towards patriotism."

Allan C. Brownfeld, "America's Healthy Rebirth of Patriotism," *Manchester Union Leader*, August 27, 1981.

The simplest form of moral behavior occurs when a man or other animal fights for his own survival. Do not belittle such behavior as being merely selfish. Of course it is selfish, but selfishness is the bedrock on which all moral behavior starts and it can be immoral only when it conflicts with a higher moral imperative.

An animal so poor in spirit that he won't even fight on his own behalf is already an evolutionary dead end; the best he can do for his breed is to crawl off and die, and not pass on his defective genes.

The next higher level is to work, fight, and sometimes die for your own immediate family. This is the level at which six pounds of mother cat can be so fierce that she'll drive off a police dog. It is the level at which a father takes a moonlighting job to keep his kids in college—and the level at which a mother or father dives into a flood to save a drowning child—and it is still moral behavior even when it fails.

232

Moral Behavior Tested

The next higher level is to work, fight, and sometimes die for a group larger than the unit family—an extended family, a herd, a tribe—and take another look at that baboon on watch; he's at that moral level. I don't think baboon language is complex enough to permit them to discuss such abstract notions as "morality" or "duty" or "loyalty"—but it is evident that baboons *do* operate morally and *do* exhibit the traits of duty and loyalty; we see them in action. Call it "instinct" if you like—but remember that assigning a name to a phenomenon does not explain it.

But that baboon behavior can be explained in evolutionary terms. Evolution is a process that never stops. Baboons who fail to exhibit moral behavior do not survive; they wind up as meat for leopards. Every baboon generation has to pass this examination in moral behavior; those who bilge it don't have progeny. Perhaps the old bull of the tribe gives lessons, but the leopard decides who graduates—and there is no appeal from his decision. We don't have to understand the details to observe the outcome: Baboons behave morally—for baboons.

The next level in moral behavior higher than that exhibited by the baboon is that in which duty and loyalty are shown toward a group of your own kind too large for an individual to know all of them. We have a name for that. It is called "patriotism."

Behaving on a still higher moral level were the astronauts who went to the Moon, for their actions tend toward the survival of the entire race of mankind. The door they opened leads to the hope that *homo sapiens* will survive indefinitely long, even longer than this solid planet on which we stand tonight. As a direct result of what they did, it is now possible that the human race will *never* die. . . .

I must pause to brush off those parlor pacifists I mentioned earlier, for they contend that *their* actions are on this highest moral level. They want to put a stop to war; they say so. Their purpose is to save the human race from killing itself off; they say that, too. Anyone who disagrees with them must be a bloodthirsty scoundrel—and they'll tell you that to your face.

I won't waste time trying to judge their motives; my criticism is of their mental processes: Their heads aren't screwed on tight. They live in a world of fantasy.

Let me stipulate that, if the human race managed its affairs sensibly, we could do without war.

Yes—and if pigs had wings, they could fly.

I don't know what planet those pious pacifists are talking about, but it can't be the third one out from the Sun. Anyone who has seen the Far East—or Africa—or the Middle East—knows or certainly should know that there is *no* chance of abolishing war in the foreseeable future. . . .

233

Our Basic Problem

Our basic problem is the intellectual frame of mind that considers it unsophisticated and narrow-minded to love one's country. The diagnostic mark of a sophisticated person in the United States is the ability to be very skeptical of his own society but very tolerant and open-minded of all others, so long as they are not right-wing allies of the United States.

We are imperiled when the endeavor to be holier than one's country is an important mechanism of intellectual and social status. Self-criticism, which includes criticism of one's country, is a refined way of talking about oneself that undermines American confidence. Those who care little of the struggle for the world, but know at least that they are indifferent to the good opinion of what they see as the rednecked patriot class strung out on Rambo and Bruce Springsteen, will turn their voices where they know they can hurt.

This disposition can only deprive the United States of its intellectual resources. Edward Teller has expounded the unwillingness of the American scientific community to cooperate with former President Reagan's Strategic Defense Initiative. In other words, Soviet disinformation doesn't have to work, because our intellectuals don't need to be led down the garden path. They can find the way on their own. Indeed, they have a way of laying out their own garden that always leads to the defense of the enemy and a denunciation of their own country.

I do not believe that a country that is more skeptical of itself than it is of its opponent can survive. It is unclear what will shake loose this frame of mind. We have to ask ourselves if we are any longer a serious nation when the American sophisticate is, as in the verse of Alexander Pope, "A steady patriot for the world alone, a friend of every country but his own."

Paul C. Roberts, *Vital Speeches of the Day*, January 15, 1987.

Patriotism—moral behavior at the national level. *Non sibi sed Patria.* Nathan Hale's last words: "I regret that I have but one life to give for my country." Torpedo Squadron Eight making its suicidal attack. Four chaplains standing fast while the water rises around them. Thomas Jefferson saying, "The Tree of Liberty must be refreshed from time to time with the blood of patriots." A submarine skipper giving the order, "Take her *down!*" while he himself is still topside. Jonas Ingram standing on the steps of Bancroft Hall and shouting, "The Navy has no place for good losers! The Navy needs tough sons of bitches who can get out there and *win!*"

Patriotism—an abstract word used to describe a type of behavior as harshly practical as good brakes and good tires. It means that you place the welfare of your nation ahead of your own, even if it costs you your life.

Men who go down to the sea in ships have long had another way of expressing the same moral behavior tagged by the abstract expression "patriotism." Spelled out in simple Anglo-Saxon words, "Patriotism" reads "Women and children first!"

And that is the moral result of realizing a self-evident biological fact: Men are expendable; women and children are not. A tribe or a nation can lose a high percentage of its men and still pick up the pieces and go on, as long as the women and children are saved. But if you fail to save the women and children, you've had it, you're done, you're *through!* You join *tyrannosaurus rex*, one more breed that bilged its final test. . . .

Nevertheless, as a mathematical proposition in the facts of biology, children and women of child-bearing age are the ultimate treasure that we must save. Every human culture is based on "Women and children first"—and any attempt to do it any other way leads quickly to extinction.

Possibly extinction is the way we are headed. Great nations have died in the past; it can happen to us.

Nor am I certain how good our chances are. To me it seems self-evident that any nation that loses its patriotic fervor is on the skids. Without that indispensable survival factor the end is only a matter of time. I don't know how deeply the rot has penetrated—but it seems to me that there has been a change for the worse in the last 50 years. Possibly I am misled by the offensive behavior of a noisy but unimportant minority. But it does seem to me that patriotism has lost its grip on a large percentage of our people.

I hope I am wrong—because if my fears are well grounded, I would not bet two cents on this nation's chance of lasting even to the end of this century.

But there is no way to force patriotism on anyone. Passing a law will not create it, nor can we buy it by appropriating so many billions of dollars. . . .

I said that "patriotism" is a way of saying "Women and children first." And that no one can force a man to feel this way. Instead, he must embrace it freely. I want to tell about one such man. He wore no uniform and no one knows his name, nor where he came from; all we know is what he did.

In my home town 60 years ago when I was a child, my mother and father used to take me and my brothers and sisters out to Swope Park on Sunday afternoons. It was a wonderful place for kids, with picnic grounds and lakes and a zoo. But a railroad line cut straight through it.

One Sunday afternoon a young married couple were crossing these tracks. She apparently did not watch her step, for she managed to catch her foot in the frog of a switch to a siding and could not pull it free. Her husband stopped to help her.

But try as they might they could not get her foot loose. While they were working at it, a tramp showed up, walking the ties. He joined the husband in trying to pull the young woman's foot loose. No luck.

Out of sight around the curve a train whistled. Perhaps there would have been time to run and flag it down, perhaps not. In any case both men went right ahead trying to pull her free—and the train hit them.

The wife was killed, the husband was mortally injured and died later, the tramp was killed—and testimony showed neither man made the slightest effort to save himself.

The husband's behavior was heroic, but what we expect of a husband toward his wife: his right, and his proud privilege, to die for his woman. But what of this nameless stranger? Up to the very last second he could have jumped clear. He did not. He was still trying to save this woman he had never seen before in his life, right up to the very instant the train killed him. And that's all we'll ever know about him.

This is how a man dies.

This is how a *man*. . .lives!

4

"Patriotism, that emotion that feeds our tribal thinking, must die if the human enterprise is to survive."

America's Survival Depends on Patriotism's Death

John S. Spong

John S. Spong is Bishop of the Episcopal Diocese of Newark, New Jersey. The author of ten books, he most recently wrote *Living in Sin: A Bishop Rethinks Human Sexuality*. In the viewpoint that follows, Bishop Spong claims that patriotism is a destructive force. He argues that loyalty to the tribe was the essential key to survival in the past, but as the necessity for the tribe fades, so does the need for loyalty. Patriotism, in his view, is not only becoming obsolete, it is an impediment to a new international mindset that is needed to solve regional and international problems.

As you read, consider the following questions:

1. Why does the author think patriotism has become obsolete?
2. What does he claim will cause the death of patriotism around the world?

John S. Spong, "The Twilight of Patriotism," *The Witness*, September 1987. Reprinted with permission.

Throughout the summer of 1987 we have seen a version of "patriotism" extolled by a series of witnesses in the Iran-Contra hearings. The star "patriot" was surely the beribboned Marine, Lt. Col. Oliver North. His words had an old-fashioned ring and the patriotism he espoused sounded like something out of the 19th century, when national self-interest was almost always identified with divine providence or manifest destiny.

Patriotism Is a Destructive Force

But this is the 20th century and patriotism, despite the Norths and the Poindexters, is no longer a virtue; indeed, patriotism has become a destructive force that cannot be allowed to survive. These are startling words that just a generation ago would have surely brought a sharp and hostile response. Indeed they still will from those whose consciousnesses have not been raised by the necessities of the human struggle for survival—those who still divide the world into "us" and "them." For the same patriotism that once served as the means for romanticizing the life and values which bind a people together must now increasingly be seen as undergirding a view of reality that is destined to die.

The Origin of Patriotism

In the early days of civilization, the human family lived in small nomadic tribal units where the struggle for survival demanded a division of labor among the tribal members. Life was hard and insecure. Food could not be preserved so it had to be found daily to feed hungry mouths. Enemies, both human and subhuman, had to be fought off on a regular basis. Death was ever present. Preserving and defending the corporate life was a tribal responsibility.

In that era no sense of individualism could be encouraged or sustained. The individual was too fragile, too susceptible to disease, infection, accident, or to an overtly hostile act to be the important unit of life. Value could not be placed on the individual. Rather, it had to be vested in the tribe whose corporate preservation was the overriding human concern. The tribe alone provided its members with identity, worth and the ability to cope in a dangerous environment. Loyalty to the tribe was thus the essential key to survival, so this value was placed at the very heart of the human emotions. That was the origin of what we now call patriotism, and it accounts for the continuing power and emotional hold of patriotism on life.

The Rise of Nations

As the patterns of society became more and more intricate and complicated, tribal units came together to form larger entities, first organized as cities and later as nations. But the emotions originally attached to the tribe were always transferred to the larger unit for there identity and security could be found. To the nation fell the traditional tribal responsibilities. Survival was the first task, and the need to defend itself against all external threats still lies behind every nation's armed forces and arsenals. The second task was to insure the well-being of the tribe's internal life. Today's various national social welfare programs are the modern versions of this ancient tribal duty.

We Must Become World Patriots

Ever since I can remember, people have been telling me what a good thing it is to be a patriotic American. As a result, patriotism is one of those powerful core values I've accepted, without question, as part of my social and cultural heritage. But lately, there is too much evidence contrary to the wisdom of my parents, former teachers, military leaders, and fellow Americans to continue my old business-as-usual way of thinking. It's now apparent that failure to revise our old thought and behavior patterns will be hazardous to our survival. It's clear that common sense must overrule our assumptions, our blind faith, in this old-time religion we call patriotism. . . .

We are individual people in this world before we are Canadian, Vietnamese, French, Libyan, Soviet, Kenyan, or American. We no longer have the luxury of falsely protective political boundaries. We are in mortal danger as a species if we continue to behave in this fashion. Science and technology have made anachronisms of national boundaries, and we will all perish if we fail to broaden our outlook.

So that's what's wrong with nationalistic patriotism. It is technologically, not to mention morally, bankrupt. We therefore must all broaden our visions and understand that we are a world of one species, interdependent brothers and sisters who must replace patriotism with humanism. We must become world-patriots, which simply means we must become humanists.

Phillip Butler, *The Humanist*, March/April 1986.

In the sweep of human history, the emergence of trans-tribal nations is a relatively new experience, starting no earlier than 1000 years ago, and continuing even today. The United States was born near the end of the 18th century. Italy and Germany did not become nation states until well into the 19th century. India and Pakistan were born after World War II. As the era of western colonialism died, new nations roughly determined by ancient tribal boundaries were born in Africa and other heretofore underdeveloped regions of the world.

Most people cannot imagine a world without nations. We are unable to define identity apart from the ingrained feeling of the tribe. Our citizenship tells us who we are, determines in large measure our values, sets our limits and shapes our world view.

However, slowly but surely, the necessity that created tribes and nations in the first place is fading. Modern technology has linked the world more deeply than our grandparents could ever have imagined. Television has brought such things as the tragedies of Vietnam, African starvation, and the international scope of our covert operations into our living rooms daily. We have been made to understand our human interdependence in the oil crisis of the '70s and the terrorist activities of the '80s.

Organizations have been established, such as the European Common Market, in which smaller nations have allowed their economics to become so interdependent that regional thinking has begun to replace national thinking in those areas. Businesses the world over have become multinational. Jet travel has brought the diverse continents of the world together in a way that even neighboring kindred tribes were not linked in the past.

The Bonding Effect of Environmental Crisis

The final human bonding experience that will apply the coup de grace to nation states will be an awareness of the threat to the environment that will dawn as we recognize that all human beings share a common destiny in the air we breathe, the water we drink, and the oceans that feed us, and that no nation state is capable of addressing these concerns alone. When the world's ozone layer is damaged by the chemical gases from the industries of any nation, all life is at risk. When a nuclear accident occurs in Pennsylvania or in the Ukraine, all the people of the world are endangered. When polluted rivers empty their poisons into the oceans, the ability of the sea to feed the world's population either directly or indirectly is called into question. Suddenly, we begin to be aware that nation states cannot fulfill their purposes. They can no longer do the things they were created to do.

When any institution loses its purpose it is doomed to death. The death of nation states will not be instantaneous because deeply ingrained cultural needs attached to that institution will continue to carry the concept for some long time, but death is nonetheless inevitable. Nation states will quickly become an anachronism and will not survive in a radically interdependent world. As states' rights gave way in this country to national needs, so national sovereignty will finally give way to international needs.

All wars of the past have been fought to insure the vested interests of the tribe or the nation states. Today, however, no nation's vested interests can be served by a war. No nation today can guarantee its people protection against the threat of an enemy. There is no one villain we can oppose when destruction comes to our environment, our atmosphere, our food supply and even to the safety of a nursing mother's milk. A nuclear accident pours radioactivity into the common atmosphere.

This means that my life and my survival are now radically dependent on someone else in a nation halfway around the world. My destiny is human destiny; it is no longer an American destiny.

Patriotism Is Absurd

The notion that one owes an obligation to one's country is absurd. Like the defenders of family, church, and community, the champions of the modern nation state want us to believe that inanimate objects—mere social sandboxes—deserve to command our respect, love, and loyalty. This is reification of the highest order.

Our obligations should be to ourselves and our fellow living beings, not to some bloodless concoction of bygone rulers. Our identities should be of our own making, not imposed by an ancient cartographer. And our loyalties should not stop at the border.

Once we recognize this, we won't fall into the good old American trap of caring solely for U.S. citizens and not a whit for inhabitants of other countries. The United States can kill two million Indochinese, but Americans concern themselves only with the less than 60,000 U.S. soldiers who fell in the fetid conflict of Vietnam. Something's not right about that, and that something is patriotism.

Matthew Rothschild, "Put Out No Flags," *The Progressive*, July 1986.

Patriotism, that emotion that feeds our tribal thinking, must die if the human enterprise is to survive. What we need is a world consciousness, a world agreement, a worldwide security system, a sense of human interdependence that transcends nation, race, ethnic origin, religion and every other defining human barrier by which we have in the past determined who we are. To achieve that requires an enormous leap of consciousness that will ultimately be required of all of us. The ability on the part of all the people of the world to make such a leap is the prerequisite to survival of the human enterprise.

Throughout history it has often been a disaster that has caused the development of such new consciousness and created the context in which new values can arise. We have now had Three Mile Island and Chernobyl to jolt our security. The AIDS epidemic shows a capacity to leap every barrier that we hoped would enclose it. Scientists warn us that the earth's atmosphere is heating up at an alarming rate due to the burning of fossil fuels and the release of chlorofluorocarbons into the ozone.

Inevitably, another devastating ecological disaster will afflict the earth; a disaster severe enough to create a worldwide willingness to lay aside the barriers of the past and to seek a new understanding of our common destiny. The victims of that disaster may not be able to rejoice in this benefit but perhaps in time those who survive will begin to realize that this is one world, with one human family, in which all nationalism is simply inappropriate. It is strange to imagine that only an ecological calamity might save a portion of humanity. It is also a depressing prospect. I wish I thought my government in Washington had even the slightest inkling of this reality.

"If our democracy is to flourish it must have criticism; if our government is to function, it must have dissent."

True Patriotism Demands Dissent

Henry Steele Commager

Henry Steele Commager has been Simpson Lecturer at Amherst College since 1972. A historian and educator, he earned his M.A. and Ph.D. degrees from the University of Chicago and holds many honorary degrees. Dr. Commager is the author of numerous books including *The Heritage of America, The Spirit of Seventy-Six,* and *The Rise of the American Nation.* In the following viewpoint, Dr. Commager states that American philosophies were created by nonconformists whose ideals were to maintain the concept of liberty for all. He contends that true loyalty is displayed by those who question, criticize, and rebel, thus enabling Americanism to flourish.

As you read, consider the following questions:

1. What does the author refer to with the term "the new loyalty" and how does he relate it to conformity?
2. How does the author define loyalty?
3. In the author's opinion, who are those who are really disloyal in America? Do you agree?

Henry Steele Commager, "Who Is Loyal to America?" *Harper's*, September 1947, pp. 195-99. Reprinted with permission from the author.

What is the new loyalty? It is, above all, conformity. It is the uncritical and unquestioning acceptance of America as it is—the political institutions, the social relationships, the economic practices. It rejects inquiry into the race question or socialized medicine, or public housing, or into the wisdom or validity of our foreign policy. It regards as particularly heinous any challenge to what is called "the system of private enterprise," identifying that system with Americanism. It abandons evolution, repudiates the once popular concept of progress, and regards America as a finished product, perfect and complete.

It is, it must be added, easily satisfied. For it wants not intellectual conviction nor spiritual conquest, but mere outward conformity. In matters of loyalty it takes the word for the deed, the gesture for the principle. It is content with the flag salute, and does not pause to consider the warning of our Supreme Court that "a person gets from a symbol the meaning he puts into it, and what is one man's comfort and inspiration is another's jest and scorn." It is satisfied with membership in respectable organizations and, as it assumes that every member of a liberal organization is a Communist, concludes that every member of a conservative one is a true American. It has not yet learned that not everyone who saith Lord, Lord, shall enter into the Kingdom of Heaven. It is designed neither to discover real disloyalty nor to foster true loyalty. . . .

Conformity Is Not Loyalty

The concept of loyalty as conformity is a false one. It is narrow and restrictive, denies freedom of thought and of conscience, and is irremediably stained by private and selfish considerations. "Enlightened loyalty," wrote Josiah Royce, who made loyalty the very core of his philosophy,

> means harm to no man's loyalty. It is at war only with disloyalty, and its warfare, unless necessity constrains, is only a spiritual warfare. It does not foster class hatreds; it knows of nothing reasonable about race prejudices; and it regards all races of men as one in their need of loyalty. It ignores mutual misunderstandings. It loves its own wherever upon earth its own, namely loyalty itself, is to be found.

Justice, charity, wisdom, spirituality, he added, were all definable in terms of loyalty, and we may properly ask which of these qualities our contemporary champions of loyalty display.

Above all, loyalty must be to something larger than oneself, untainted by private purposes or selfish ends. But what are we to say of the attempts by the NAM and by individual corporations to identify loyalty with the system of private enterprise? Is it not as if officeholders should attempt to identify loyalty with their own party, their own political careers? Do not those corporations which pay for full-page advertisements associating Americanism with the competitive system expect, ultimately, to profit from that association? Do not those organizations that deplore, in the name of patriotism, the extension of government operation of hydroelectric power expect to profit from their campaign?

Certainly it is a gross perversion not only of the concept of

---

Why Is It Important To Be Number One?

I hear that Carl Porter, Chicago's pre-eminent flagmaker, says that U.S. flag sales picked up after the American invasion of Grenada; they also did so after the release of the hostages in Iran and after the American bombing of Libya. Porter: "Americans are sick of getting their rear ends kicked from around the world." When we kick back, up go flag sales, and flags.

What psychological impulse insists on connecting patriotism with superiority and egotism—or with military acts? I am loyal to the Marty family, the Lutheran Church, the University of Chicago, *The Christian Century*. But only if I have a weak ego or something to prove to myself must I insist that these are the uniquely superior family, church, university or magazine. And who is listening? Does anyone out there still need convincing that we think we are Number One?

Martin E. Marty, *The Christian Century*, July 16-23, 1986.

---

loyalty but of the concept of Americanism to identify it with a particular economic system. . . .

There is, it should be added, a further danger in the willful identification of Americanism with a particular body of economic practices. . . .If Americanism is equated with competitive capitalism, what happens to it if competitive capitalism comes a cropper? If loyalty and private enterprise are inextricably associated, what is to preserve loyalty if private enterprise fails? Those who associate Americanism with a particular program of economic practices have a grave responsibility, for if their program should fail, they expose Americanism itself to disrepute.

The effort to equate loyalty with conformity is misguided because it assumes that there is a fixed content to loyalty and that this can be determined and defined. But loyalty is a principle, and eludes definition except in its own terms. It is devotion to the best interests of the commonwealth, and may require hostility to the particular policies which the government pursues, the particular practices which the economy undertakes, the particular institutions which society maintains. "If there is any fixed star in our Constitutional constellation," said the Supreme Court in the Barnette case, "it is that no official, high or petty, can prescribe what shall be orthodox in politics, nationalism, religion, or other matters of opinion, or force citizens to confess by word or act their faith therein. If there are any circumstances which permit an exception they do not now occur to us.''

True Loyalty

True loyalty may require, in fact, what appears to the naive to be disloyalty. It may require hostility to certain provisions of the Constitution itself, and historians have not concluded that those who subscribed to the "Higher Law" were lacking in patriotism. We should not forget that our tradition is one of protest and revolt, and it is stultifying to celebrate the rebels of the past—Jefferson and Paine, Emerson and Thoreau—while we silence the rebels of the present. "We are a rebellious nation," said Theodore Parker, known in his day as the Great American Preacher, and went on:

> Our whole history is treason; our blood was attainted before we were born; our creeds are infidelity to the mother church; our constitution, treason to our fatherland. What of that? Though all the governors in the world bid us commit treason against man, and set the example, let us never submit.

Those who would impose upon us a new concept of loyalty not only assume that this is possible, but have the presumption to believe that they are competent to write the definition. We are reminded of Whitman's defiance of the "never-ending audacity of elected persons." Who are those who would set the standards of loyalty? They are Rankins and Bilbos, officials of the D.A.R. and the Legion and the NAM, Hearsts and McCormicks. May we not say of Rankin's harangues on loyalty what Emerson said of Webster at the time of the Seventh of March speech: "The word honor in the mouth of Mr. Webster is like the word love in the mouth of a whore.''

What do men know of loyalty who make a mockery of the Declaration of Independence and the Bill of Rights, whose energies are dedicated to stirring up race and class hatreds, who would straitjacket the American spirit? What indeed do they know of America—the America of Sam Adams and Tom Paine, of Jackson's defiance of the Court and Lincoln's celebration of labor, of Thoreau's essay on Civil Disobedience and Emerson's championship of John Brown, of the America of the Fourierists and the Come-Outers, of cranks and fanatics, of socialists and anarchists? Who among American heroes could meet their tests, who would be cleared by their committees? Not Washington, who was a rebel. Not Jefferson, who wrote that all men are created equal and whose motto was "rebellion to tyrants is obedience to God." Not Garrison, who publicly burned the Constitution; or Wendell Phillips, who spoke for the underprivileged everywhere and counted himself a philosophical anarchist; not Seward of the Higher Law or Sumner of racial equality. Not Lincoln, who admonished us to have malice toward none, charity for all; or Wilson, who warned that our flag was "a flag of liberty of opinion as well as of political liberty"; or Justice Holmes, who said that our Constitution is an experiment and that while that experiment is being made "we should be eternally vigilant against attempts to check the expression of opinions that we loathe and believe to be fraught with death."

There are further and more practical objections against the imposition of fixed concepts of loyalty or tests of disloyalty. The effort is itself a confession of fear, a declaration of insolvency.

The Ingredients of Patriotism

I admit that it is not easy to put your finger on what are the most meaningful ingredients of patriotism. Willingness to defend your country is only one of them and perhaps not the most important. From the Civil War, through two world wars plus Korea and Vietnam, the United States has never been in a major conflict without conscription.

The ingredients of patriotism which I would put first are these:

- Willingness to live by "government by the democratic consent of the governed."

- Total dedication to the freedoms without which free elections are meaningless—freedom of speech, freedom of peaceful assembly, freedom of religion.

- Devotion to giving unto others the freedom you wish to retain for yourself.

This, it seems to me, is the kind of patriotism we most need to cherish.

Roscoe Drummond, "Hurrah for Patriotism," *The Christian Science Monitor,* February 2, 1981, p. 23.

Those who are sure of themselves do not need reassurance, and those who have confidence in the strength and the virtue of America do not need to fear either criticism or competition. The effort is bound to miscarry. It will not apprehend those who are really disloyal, it will not even frighten them; it will affect only those who can be labeled "radical." It is sobering to recall that though the Japanese relocation program, carried through at such incalculable cost in misery and tragedy, was justified to us on the ground that the Japanese were potentially disloyal, the record does not disclose a single case of Japanese disloyalty or sabotage during the whole war. . . .

Who are those who are really disloyal? Those who inflame racial hatreds, who sow religious and class dissensions. Those who subvert the Constitution by violating the freedom of the ballot box. Those who make a mockery of majority rule by the use of the filibuster. Those who impair democracy by denying equal educational facilities. Those who frustrate justice by lynch law or by making a farce of jury trials. Those who deny freedom of speech and of the press and of assembly. Those who press for special favors against the interest of the commonwealth. Those who regard public office as a source of private gain. Those who would exalt the military over the civil. Those who for selfish and private purposes stir up national antagonisms and expose the world to the ruin of war. . . .

If our democracy is to flourish it must have criticism; if our government is to function it must have dissent. Only totalitarian governments insist upon conformity and they—as we know—do so at their peril. Without criticism abuses will go unrebuked; without dissent our dynamic system will become static. The American people have a stake in the maintenance of the most thorough-going inquisition into American institutions. They have a stake in nonconformity, for they know that the American genius is nonconformist. They have a stake in experimentation of the most radical character, for they know that only those who prove all things can hold fast that which is good.

The Ability
To Empathize

The ability to empathize, to see life and experience its joys and problems through another person's eyes and feelings, is a helpful skill to acquire if one is to learn from the life situation of others.

Consider the following situation.

The Flag Salute

Susan Russo, a high school teacher at Sperry High School in Henrietta, New York, was well qualified and impressed her principal when she was hired. As a teacher, just about everybody agreed, she did very well. She fared badly, nevertheless, because of "irreconcilable conceptions of patriotism." Each day her school began with the Pledge of Allegiance to the flag recited over the school's public address system. During the ceremony Mrs. Russo stood silently with her hands at her side. She made no issue of her refusal to say the pledge and place her hand over her heart; she merely didn't do it.

> I didn't agree with the wording of the Pledge, and it was a matter of my own personal conscience, and I couldn't be hypocritical about what I believed in. . .I am generally proud to be an American, but I object to saying the Pledge for basically two reasons. First of all, I don't think that anyone can demand the recitation of an oath of allegiance. I think loyalty is better proved through daily actions and the way you behave as an American citizen, but more importantly, I object to the actual wording of the Pledge, because the worlds "liberty and justice for all" are inaccurate, and I feel we are hypocritical in saying that as a truth.

Mrs. Russo was observed by her principal. When confronted with his disapproval she wouldn't reconsider her refusal and was asked to resign. When she did not, and since she was not tenured, she was terminated.*

The Pledge of Allegiance

I pledge allegiance to the flag of the United States of America and to the Republic for which it stands, one nation under God, indivisible, with liberty and justice for all.

*David Sanford, "In Conscience," *The New Republic,* June 22, 1974, pp. 24-25.

Instructions:

Try to imagine how the following individuals would react in this situation. What reasons might they give for their actions. Try to imagine and explain their feelings.

Susan Russo

school principal

Mrs. Russo's students

author of viewpoint 3 in this chapter

author of viewpoint 4 in this chapter

school board

local teacher's association

parents of Mrs. Russo's students

you

others

Periodical Bibliography

The following articles have been selected to supplement the diverse views presented in this chapter.

Gary L. Bauer — "Nothing Less Will Do," *The Saturday Evening Post*, November 1987.

Peter Berger — "Reflections on Patriotism," *Worldview*, July 1974.

Daniel J. Boorstin — "Can Patriotism Be Legislated?" *U.S. News & World Report*, February 13, 1989.

John Buell — "A Flag for Sunrise," *The Progressive*, July 1986.

Phillip Butler — "From Nationalist to Humanist," *The Humanist*, March/April 1986.

Christianity Today — "The Fourth of July: Time Out for Some Biblical Patriotism," June 26, 1981.

Harold Evans — "The Stuff of Patriotism," *U.S. News & World Report*, August 10, 1987.

Harry V. Jaffa — "Our Ancient Faith," *National Review*, November 29, 1985.

Robert Jewett — "Zeal Without Understanding: Reflection on Rambo and Oliver North," *The Christian Century*, September 9-16, 1987.

Lewis H. Lapham — "The New Patriotism," *Harper's Magazine*, June 1984.

Martin E. Marty — "Sailing Through Waves of Patriotism," *The Christian Century*, July 16-23, 1986.

Richard Neuhaus — "Is Patriotism a Virtue?" *The Religion & Society Report*, July 1987.

Thomas L. Pangle — "Patriotism American Style," *National Review*, November 19, 1985.

Michael Parenti — "Superpatriotism: The Importance of Being Number One," *The Witness*, December 1988.

Matthew Rothschild — "Put Out No Flags," *The Progressive*, July 1986.

TRB from Washington — "Blaming America First," *The New Republic*, July 29, 1985.

What Does America Need?

AMERICAN
V·A·L·U·E·S

Chapter Preface

Henry Steele Commager, an important American historian, has been teaching history for over sixty years. He had this to say about America's past:

> In the early years of our nation, our history was one of decency and honor and propriety. Hardly anybody cheated anybody. There were very few cases of impeachments for real crimes of any kind. Men took for granted that serving their country was enough reward. Jefferson was a bankrupt. His house, Monticello, was sold over his head before he died. Washington came back from the presidency practically bankrupt. John Adams had to go back and get in the hay, as it were, to keep his farm going. People didn't expect to make money in politics.

This description does not sound much like the Washington political scene that Americans read about today in their daily newspapers. Watergate and subsequent political scandals have forced some politicians to resign in disgrace. Others are leaving public office for more lucrative jobs in corporations, the lecture circuit, or private finance.

This complete disillusionment with public office points up the inability of the American people to admire their government with respect and as a source of ideals. The question this chapter asks, then, is what does America need to regenerate some of the feelings of sacrifice and commitment to justice and country in which the early presidents believed?

"We must revive and strengthen the central core of our national heritage, which is the legacy of liberty, tolerance, and moderation."

America Needs a Self-Examination

J.W. Fulbright

J.W. Fulbright was a senator from Arkansas until 1973 and chairman of the Senate Foreign Relations Committee, a post he held longer than any previous senator. He was first elected to Congress in 1943 after serving as president of the University of Arkansas. Currently an attorney in Washington, DC, he is the author of *Old Myths and New Realities*, *The Arrogance of Power*, and *The Price of Empire*. He will also be remembered for the program of international scholarships that bear his name, The Fulbright Scholarships. In the following viewpoint, Mr. Fulbright counsels Americans to avoid the dangers of hatred, bigotry, and moral absolutism that have been ever present in the country's history. He claims the remedy for these problems is for all citizens to recognize their own fallibility, while at the same time looking for merit in the views of others.

As you read, consider the following questions:

1. Why does Mr. Fulbright believe America needs a national self-examination?
2. In the author's opinion, how has Puritanism complicated American national life?

J.W. Fulbright, "The American Character," *Vital Speeches of the Day*, January 1, 1964, page 164-67. Reprinted with permission.

I believe that our society, though in most respects decent, civilized, and humane, is not, and has never been, entirely so. Our national life, both past and present has also been marked by a baleful and incongruous strand of intolerance and violence.

It is in evidence all around us. It is in evidence in the senseless and widespread crime that makes the streets of our great cities unsafe. It is in evidence in the malice and hatred of extremist political movements. . . .

A National Self-Examination

We must ask ourselves many questions about this element of barbarism in a civilized society. We must ask ourselves what its sources are, in history and in human nature. We must ask ourselves whether it is the common and inevitable condition of man or whether it can be overcome. And if we judge that it can be overcome, we must ask ourselves why we Americans have not made greater progress in doing so. . . . Finally, and most important, we must ask ourselves what we must do, and how and when, to overcome hatred and bigotry and to make America as decent and humane a society as we would like it to be.

I do not pretend to be able to answer these questions. I do suggest, however, that the conditions of our time call for a national self-examination although the process may be a long and difficult and painful one. I further suggest and most emphatically, that if such a national self-examination is to be productive it must be conducted in a spirit of tolerance rather than anger, serenity rather than guilt, and Christian charity rather than crusading moralism.

We might begin our reflections about ourselves by an examination of the effects of crusading self-righteousness, in the history of Western civilization and in our own society.

Moral Absolutism and the Spirit of Democracy

Moral absolutism—righteous, crusading, and intolerant—has been a major force in the history of Western civilization. Whether religious or political in form, movements of crusading moralism have played a significant and usually destructive role in the evolution of western societies. Such movements, regardless of the content of their doctrines, have all been marked by a single characteristic: The absolute certainty of their own truth and virtue. Each has regarded itself as having an exclusive pipeline to heaven, to God, or to a deified concept of history—or whatever is regarded as the ultimate source of truth. Each has regarded itself as the chosen repository of truth and virtue and each has regarded all nonbelievers as purveyors of falsehood and evil.

Absolutist movements are usually crusading movements. Free as they are from any element of doubt as to their own truth and virtue, they conceive themselves to have a mission of spreading

255

the truth and destroying evil. They consider it to be their duty to regenerate mankind, however little it may wish to be regenerated. The means which are used for this purpose, though often harsh and sometimes barbaric, are deemed to be wholly justified by the nobility of the end. They are justified because the end is absolute and there can be no element of doubt as to its virtue and its truth.

Thus it is that in the name of noble purposes men have committed unspeakable acts of cruelty against one another. The medieval Christians who burned heretics alive did not do so because they were cruel and sadistic; they did it because they wished to exorcise evil and make men godly and pure. The Catholic and Protestant armies which inflicted upon Europe 30 years of death and destruction in the religious wars of the 17th century did not do so because they wished anyone harm; on the contrary, they did it for the purpose of saving Christendom from sin and damnation.

In our time the crusading movements have been political rather than religious, but their doctrines have been marked by the same conviction of absolute truth and the same zeal to perpetuate it. Thus the German Nazis, with their fervent belief in a primitive racial myth, murdered 6 million Jews in their zeal to elevate mankind by ridding it of a race that they deemed venal and inferior. Similarly, the Russian Communists under Stalin, who as Djilas writes, was a man capable of destroying nine-tenths of the human race to make happy the one-tenth—killed millions of their own people and consigned countless others to the slave labor camps of Siberia in order to pave the way for a society in which all men should be equal and happy and free. . . .

The Impossible Contradiction

When a free nation embarks upon a crusade for democracy, it is caught up in the impossible contradiction of trying to use force to make men free.

J.W. Fulbright, *Vital Speeches of the Day*, January 1, 1964.

The strand of fanaticism and violence has been a major one in western history. But it has not been the only one, nor has it been the dominant one in most western societies. The other strand of Western civilization, conceived in ancient Greece and Rome and revived in the European age of reason, has been one of tolerance and moderation, of empiricism and practicality. Its doctrine has been democracy, a radically different kind of doctrine whose one absolute is the denial of absolutes and of the messianic spirit. The core of the democratic idea is the element of doubt as to the ability of any man or any movement to perceive ultimate truth. Accordingly, it has fostered societies in which the individual is left free to pursue truth and virtue as he imperfectly perceives them, with a different, and quite possibly superior, set of values.

Democratic societies have by no means been free of self-righteousness and the crusading spirit. On the contrary, they have at times engaged in great crusades to spread the gospel of their own ideology. Indeed, no democratic nation has been more susceptible to this tendency than the United States, which in the past generation has fought one war to "make the world safe for democracy," another to achieve nothing less than the unconditional surrender of its enemies, and even now finds it possible to consider the plausibility of total victory over communism in a thermonuclear war.

It is clear that democratic nations are susceptible to dogmatism and the crusading spirit. The point, however, is that this susceptibility is not an expression but a denial of the democratic spirit. When a free nation embarks upon a crusade for democracy, it is caught up in the impossible contradiction of trying to use force to make men free. The dogmatic and crusading spirit in free societies is an antidemocratic tendency, a lingering vestige of the strand of dogmatism and violence in the Western heritage.

The Influence of Patriotism

For a number of complex historical reasons, while most of Europe remained under absolute monarchs and an absolute church, England evolved very gradually into a pluralistic society under a constitutional government. By the time of the establishment of the English colonies in the New World, the evolution toward constitutional democracy was well advanced. The process quickly took hold in the North American colonies and their evolution toward democracy outpaced that of the mother country. This was the basic heritage of America—a heritage of tolerance, moderation, and individual liberty that was implanted from the very beginnings of European settlement in the New World. America has quite rightly been called a nation that was born free.

There came also to the New World the Puritans, a minor group in England who became a major force in American life. Their religion was Calvinism, an absolutist faith with a stern moral code promising salvation for the few and damnation for the many. The intolerant, witch-hunting Puritanism of 17th century Massachusetts was not a major religious movement in America. It eventually became modified and as a source of ethical standards made a worthy contribution to American life. But the Puritan way of thinking, harsh and intolerant, permeated the political and economic life of the country and became a major secular force in America. Coexisting uneasily with our English heritage of tolerance and moderation, the Puritan way of thinking has injected an absolutist strand into American thought—a strand of stern moralism in our public policy and in our standards of personal behavior.

The Puritan way of thinking has had a powerful impact on our foreign policy. It is reflected in our traditional vacillation between self-righteous isolation and total involvement and in our attitude toward foreign policy as a series of idealistic crusades rather than as a continuing defense of the national interest. It is reflected in some of the most notable events of our history: in the unnecessary war with Spain, which was spurred by an idealistic fervor to liberate Cuba and ended with our making Cuba an American protectorate; in the war of 1917, which began with a national commitment to "make the world safe for democracy" and ended with our repudiation of our own blueprint for a world order of peace and law; in the radical pacifism of the interwar years which ended with our total involvement in a conflict in which our proclaimed objective of "unconditional surrender" was finally achieved by dropped atomic bombs on Hiroshima and Nagasaki.

Throughout the 20th century American foreign policy has been caught up in the inherent contradiction between our English heritage of tolerance and accommodation and our Puritan heritage of crusading righteousness. . . .

A Strand of Intolerance and Violence

The mythology of the frontier, the moral absolutism of our Puritan heritage . . . have injected a strand of intolerance and violence into American life.

J.W. Fulbright, *Vital Speeches of the Day,* January 1, 1964.

The danger of any crusading movement issues from its presumption of absolute truth. If the premise is valid, then all else follows. If we know, with absolute and unchallengeable certainty, that a political leader is traitorous, or that he is embarked upon a course of certain ruin for the Nation, then it is our right, indeed our duty, to carry our opposition beyond constitutional means and to remove him by force or even murder. The premise, however, is not valid. We do not know, nor can we know, with absolute certainty that those who disagree with us are wrong. We are human and therefore fallible, and being fallible, we cannot escape the element of doubt as to our own opinions and convictions. This, I believe, is the core of the democratic spirit. When we acknowledge our own fallibility, tolerance and compromise become possible and fanaticism becomes absurd.

It is necessary to mention another major factor in the shaping of the American national character. That factor is the experience of the frontier, the building of a great nation out of a vast wilderness in the course of a single century. The frontier experience taught us the great value of individual initiative and self-reliance in the development of our resources and of our national economy. But the individualism of the frontier, largely untempered by social and legal restraints, has also had an important influence on our political life and on our personal relations. It has generated impatience with the complex and tedious procedures of law and glorified the virtues of direct individual action. It has instilled in us an easy familiarity with violence and vigilante justice. In the romanticized form in which it permeates the television and other mass media, the mythology of the frontier conveys the message that killing a man is not bad as long as you don't shoot him in the back, that violence is only reprehensible when its purpose is bad and that in fact it is commendable and glorious when it is perpetrated by good men for a good purpose. . . .

The mythology of the frontier, the moral absolutism of our Puritan heritage, and of course, other factors which I have not mentioned, have injected a strand of intolerance and violence into American life. This violent tendency lies beneath the surface of an orderly, law-abiding, democratic society, but not far beneath the surface. When times are normal, when the country is prosperous at home and secure in its foreign relations, our violent and intolerant tendencies remain quiescent and we are able to conduct our affairs in a rational and orderly manner. But in times of crisis, foreign or domestic, our underlying irrationality breaks through to become a dangerous and disruptive force in our national life. . . .

Suspicion and Hatred in America

It is not at all surprising that the underlying tendencies toward violence and crusading self-righteousness have broken through the surface and become a virulent force in the life and politics of the postwar era. They have not thus far been the dominant force because the Nation has been able to draw on the considerable resources of wisdom, patience, and judgment which are the core of our national heritage and character. The dominance of reason, however, has been tenuous and insecure and on a number of occasions in these years of crisis we have come close to letting our passions shape critical decisions of policy.

American politics in the postwar period have been characterized by a virulent debate between those who counsel patience and reason and those who, in their fear and passion, seem ever ready to plunge the Nation into conflict abroad and witch hunts at home. . . .

The voices of suspicion and hate have been heard throughout the land. They were heard when statesmen, private citizens, and even high-ranking members of the Armed Forces were charged with treason, subversion, and communism, because they had disagreed with or somehow displeased the Senator from Wisconsin, Mr. McCarthy. They are heard when extremist groups do not hesitate to call a former President or the Chief Justice of the United States a traitor and a Communist. They are heard in the mail which U.S. Senators receive almost daily charging them with communism or treason because they voted for the foreign aid bill or for the nuclear test ban treaty.

If I may, I should like to read a section of a letter which I received from a person called John Haller of Greenville, Pa., who writes on stationery carrying the letterhead, "In Defense of the Constitution." The letter is not atypical. It reads, in part, as follows:

> Just heard on the news that you are defending the wheat sale to Russia and are for giving them credit at the American taxpayers' expense.
>
> For some time now I have been checking your record and find that you would make a better Communist than you make an American. Any proposals that would protect America or our free-enterprise system are opposed by you and any proposals that would help our enemies are given your wholehearted support. Your famous memorandum is a disgrace and you are a traitor to the Constitution.

This malice and hatred which have become a part of our politics cannot be dismissed as the normal excesses of a basically healthy society. They have become far too common. They are beyond the pale of normal political controversy in which honest men challenge each other's motives and integrity. The excesses of the extremists in our country have created an intolerable situation in which we must all guard our words and the expression of an unorthodox point of view is an extraordinary act of courage. . . .

What We Must Do

What is to be done? What must we do to overcome hatred and bigotry in our national life? . . .

We will, and should, continue to have controversy and debate in our public life. But we can reshape the character of our controversies and conduct them as the honest differences of honest men in quest of a consensus. We can come to recognize that those who disagree with us are not necessarily attacking us but only our opinions and ideas. Above all, we must maintain the element of doubt as to our own convictions, recognizing that it was not given to any man to perceive ultimate truth and that, however unlikely it may seem, there may in fact be truth or merit in the views of those who disagree with us. . . .

Furthermore, if we are to overcome violence and bigotry in our national life, we must alter some of the basic assumptions of American life and politics. We must recognize that the secular puritanism which we have practiced, with its principles of absolute good, absolute evil, and intolerance of dissent, has been an obstacle to the practice of democracy at home and the conduct of an effective foreign policy. We must recognize that the romanticized cult of the frontier, with its glorification of violence and of unrestrained individualism, is a childish and dangerous anachronism in a nation which carries the responsibility of the leadership of the free world in the nuclear age.

Finally, we must revive and strengthen the central core of our national heritage, which is the legacy of liberty, tolerance, and

Reprinted by permission of The Minneapolis Star and Roy Justus.

moderation that came to us from the ancient world through a thousand years of English history and three centuries of democratic evolution in North America. It is this historic legacy which is the best and the strongest of our endowments. It is our proper task to strengthen and cultivate it in the years ahead. If we do so, patiently and faithfully, we may arrive before too long at a time when the voices of hate will no longer be heard in our land.

"We human beings are essentially social creatures, fully human only in our relationships to each other."

America Needs a Sense of Community

Frances Moore Lappé

Since writing *Diet for a Small Planet* in 1971, Frances Moore Lappé has written several books on hunger. In 1975, she co-founded the Institute for Food and Development Policy, a San Francisco organization that researches world hunger. In 1989, Lappé wrote *Rediscovering America's Values*. In the following viewpoint, an excerpt from that book, Lappé argues that the American values of freedom, democracy, and fairness can be most fully realized by promoting a sense of community and responsibility toward one another.

As you read, consider the following questions:

1. How does the liberal worldview portray human nature, according to the author?
2. What scientific ideas does Lappé contend have contributed to the liberal worldview?
3. How does Lappé's view of government differ from the view of Edmund A. Opitz, the author of the opposing viewpoint?

Francis Moore Lappé, *Rediscovering America's Values*. Copyright © 1989 by the Institute for Food and Development Policy. Reprinted by permission of Ballantine Books, a division of Random House, Inc.

Each of us carries within us a worldview, a set of assumptions about how the world works—what some call a paradigm—that forms the very questions we allow ourselves to ask and determines our view of future possibilities. It is our personal philosophy. Many of us aren't aware that we have a personal philosophy, especially if it is the dominant one of our society. It becomes like the air we breathe—so taken for granted as to be invisible. The question thus becomes: How do we make our personal philosophy conscious—accessible to our reflection—so that it frees rather than constricts?

Scrutinizing our philosophy is in part self-protection, for if we don't understand our own belief system, we leave ourselves vulnerable. Lacking a framework with which to weigh alternatives put before us, we can easily be manipulated, even against our own interests. More positively, such reflection is essential to our personal development: only if we know what we believe and why can we make real choices, including the choice to change. . . .

The Liberal Worldview

One voice expresses the dominant Liberal tradition, a powerful shaper of Western political and economic life since the seventeenth century. We won't let the term "Liberal" confuse us, however. This tradition actually shapes the thinking of today's free-market conservative more decisively than it does today's liberal, although both share many of its assumptions.

Briefly, let me sketch the value assumptions underpinning this mainstay of our common life:

In the Liberal tradition, freedom means individual autonomy. Its positive face is the celebration of individual integrity and expression, giving rise to the concept of inalienable human rights laid out in the founding documents of our nation.

And how is this autonomy to be achieved? Only by making sure that individuals are minimally circumscribed and constrained by society. Thus, to safeguard freedom, our link to one another must always be, in some sense, defensive. As classically expressed by philosopher Isaiah Berlin, freedom is

> the holding off of something or someone—of others, who trespass
> on my field or assert their authority over me . . . intruders or
> despots of one kind or another.

Berlin's statement is only a twentieth-century version of a long philosophic orientation, most often identified with philosopher Thomas Hobbes (1588-1679), who described our emergence from a primordial "war of each against all."

Hobbes's dictum *homo homini lupus* (human beings are like wolves toward one another) captured our essential nature: to be at each other's throats! . . .

Thus, in the dominant Liberal worldview, we cannot create a

good society. We can, however, attain the best of all *achievable* alternatives by building on the only trait of which we can be certain—self-centeredness. And we can do so most effectively by wherever possible reducing choices to market transactions, or to economic cost/benefit calculations. Of course, within the realm of the family, church, and community, compassion must be nurtured and expressed. But it is an inappropriate, indeed dangerous guide when applied in the public arena of the marketplace and government.

It's our individual self-seeking that turns the wheels of the economy to the ultimate benefit of everybody, and at the same time we are spared the terribly divisive process of debating *common* choices. Moreover, we can avoid the danger inherent in any process seeking consensus—that the few can impose their choices on the many.

But within this tidy, self-regulating system, don't the resulting extremes in reward—surfeit for some amid destitution for others—cast doubt on Liberalism's sanguine premises?

Here, Western religion has come to the aid of the Liberal tradition.

The Tendency To Cooperate

This tendency to cooperate, to work actively with rather than against others, has been found among toddlers and even infants. So-called "prosocial behaviors"—cooperating, helping, sharing, comforting, and so on—occur in almost every child, even though research in this area has been practically nonexistent until very recently. Regular examples of children under three years of age giving their toys to playmates, spontaneously taking turns in games, and so on must give pause to anyone who assumes competitiveness is the natural state of the human.

Alfie Kohn, *No Contest: The Case Against Competition*, 1986.

First, in what has become almost a civil religion, incorporating Judeo-Christian biblical images, the "Hobbesian brutes" of Liberalism are transmuted into decent, self-sacrificing entrepreneurs. Living in the image of God the Creator, entrepreneurs participate in creation through generation of new wealth. Their very success is evidence of their righteousness, since God rewards the righteous, increasing their bounty multifold.

A variant of the Protestant work ethic holds that work is distasteful and hard, but God rewards with prosperity those who stick to it anyway. The bargain is thus a private one between the individual and God, making it quite easy to determine who the economic failures are: they must be the unredeemed, those still caught in original sin who did not keep their bargain with God. The poor, the homeless, the hungry are thus victims of their own sinfulness—they are merely getting their just deserts.

The consequences for human sympathy are obviously profound.

The Mind/Body Dichotomy

The Liberal worldview has been further buttressed by Western religion's ready acceptance of the notion of the internally divided self, split between body and mind, as conceived by Thomas Hobbes's contemporary, René Descartes (1596-1650). This mind/body dichotomy eases the way for a parallel division in our lives. Our private lives become the realm of religion and transcendent values; in our political and economic lives, secular rules of the market and property appropriately take command.

In 1926, British historian R.H. Tawney observed this dualism in modern political thought, noting that matters of the soul and affairs of society are conceived as independent provinces. "Provided that each keeps to its own territory, peace is assured," wrote Tawney. "They cannot collide, for they can never meet."

Given these historical roots, it becomes easy to understand why morality today is believed to pertain almost exclusively to our sexual and interpersonal relationships, but not to our responsibility for the economic and political structures we support and live within.

Human Nature and Government

Since the nineteenth century, the Liberal worldview has also incorporated evidence from the biological sciences in its view of human nature. Pure Social Darwinism may be out of fashion, but a belief that the human personality has evolved through eons of competitive struggle (a permutation of Charles Darwin's theories) remains widely accepted. More recently, the emerging field of sociobiology, pioneered by E.O. Wilson's study of the biological determinants of human social behavior, has bolstered a view of essentially selfish human nature. The notion of a "selfish gene"— coined in Richard Dawkins's 1976 book by that title—only confirmed for many that individuals must be seen as calculating organisms, each out only for its own good.

Understandably, from this view of our nature grows a profound suspicion of government and the political process. Government is a necessary evil that restrains us from hurting each other; its power is best kept limited, lest self-seeking individuals use it for their private gain against the citizenry. Prospects for popular democracy appear dim, for democracy presumes citizens acting through government on behalf of the common good, while Liberalism doubts this possibility altogether. Democratic government is a means of protecting individual goods, not a value in itself.

In the Liberal view, the human essence is closely identified with possessions. It is thus acquisitive, and so to stifle individual accumulation is directly to thwart the individual's free development. This human characteristic has a fortuitous side effect for all, however. It drives us to work, to invent, to construct, to transform nature—all to the ultimate benefit not just of ourselves individually but of all humanity. . . .

In the Liberal tradition, private property and market exchange become sanctified as virtual natural rights, unqualified and absolute—so essential are they to human freedom.

What follows from these beliefs? On the one hand, the assumption that individual self-interest is natural while the community and government are artificial (though necessary) constructs. And on the other, that freedom for unlimited accumulation must be upheld at all costs. Once combined in a single worldview, a certain picture of society snaps into focus.

Civic Solidarity

Suppose that before acknowledging the primacy of the market early Americans envisaged a republic of virtue, its citizens united in the cultivation of common terrain—not dispersed to work exclusively on their private gardens. Imagine, too, that this republic were conceived as a political community, a polis—so that public life had its own morality, quite distinct from and even superior to the private sphere. We would possess the elements of a very different sort of American politics, in which rights and responsibilities were in more evident balance, in which civic solidarity counted for as much as the defense of property.

Norman Birnbaum, *The Radical Renewal*, 1988.

In it, individuals have prior claim to all goods as they are produced or exchanged, with nothing "left over" for society as a whole. The community has therefore no legitimate claim to resources needed to meet any general demand for economic or social rights—the right to earn a living or to health care, for example.

In the Liberal worldview, to tamper with these institutions is to threaten the very bedrock of individual freedom, which cannot be allowed in a free society. As long as they are intact, individuals must be left free to pursue their own private interests, out of which spontaneously will emerge a workable whole. In other words: Tend to the parts, and the whole will take care of itself. Certainly that process of conscious, group decision-making toward common goals, usually called "politics," is always suspect. By all means, it must be kept outside our economic lives, that sanctuary of individual, private decision-making.

In barest outline then, this is the dominant social philosophy that has long shaped America's search for solutions to its problems. Its striking coherency is in large part thanks to the influence of its most formative thinker, Isaac Newton (1642-1727). Once Newton's concept of universal laws governing the physical universe permeated society, the effect was immediate and indelible. In the eyes of social philosophers, human beings became like atoms of the material world, bouncing about in limited space.

Not surprisingly, the Liberal view is often termed "mechanistic" and "atomistic," because in it individuals become distinct social atoms, each maintaining only external relations with other insular egos. Out of the random collisions of these self-seeking atoms an orderly society takes shape. All human beings need do is discover what philosophers of the seventeenth century called the "gas laws" of human conduct, and fashion institutions according to these laws; everything else will then take care of itself.

Thus, the Liberal worldview—having provided the framework for social debate for three centuries—explains much of our willingness to accept economic and political laws as dogma beyond accountability to consciously evolving social values. Not surprisingly, the result has been increasingly widespread feelings of powerlessness, separateness, and fear. . . .

Let me be perfectly clear: The challenge before us is not to reject the Liberal tradition's evident and, to me personally, very precious stress on the value and sanctity of the individual. Rather, I want to build upon all that is most worthwhile in the Liberal worldview, while incorporating the richer, more relational understanding of human nature and society emerging today.

The Alternative Voice

What, then, is the alternative voice?

It is my emerging philosophy, nourished and inspired by a chorus of voices challenging the prevailing paradigm. It grows from my conviction that the framework I've just presented, if it ever did reflect social reality, is jarringly out of sync today; a conviction that unless we develop the insight effectively to challenge its core assumptions, we cannot envision a livable future.

Like the Liberal tradition, this emerging alternative is more than a collection of distinct value commitments. While it does not yet have a historical label, it is nonetheless an interacting and coherent set of assumptions, the roots of which go back many centuries.

First, we human beings are essentially social creatures, fully human only in our relationships to each other. In some sense, this view is even older than the Liberal tradition, identified, as it is, with Aristotle. But surprising to many today might be the discovery that in our philosophic heritage there has been no more eloquent proponent of this social understanding of our nature than Adam Smith (1723-1790). Adam Smith? Yes, the same Smith who is celebrated by today's business leaders for supposedly proving that individual self-interest alone can drive a productive economic system. In his *Theory of Moral Sentiments*, however, Smith describes in sensitive detail our moral ties to each other. He concludes:

> It is thus that Man who can live only in society was fitted by nature for that situation for which he was made.

Whereas in the classic Liberal tradition from Thomas Hobbes to Isaiah Berlin, the individual is poised defensively against society, Adam Smith perceived the individual's sense of self and worth embedded entirely *within* society. He thought it quite easy to identify universal human feelings, making possible our capacity to imagine ourselves in each other's shoes.

To Smith, not only do we need each other's approval, but we also need to feel deserving of this approval. All our strivings, according to Smith, whether for wealth or rank, boil down to the same need: "to be taken notice of with sympathy, complacency, and approbation."

Smith held that it is possible to talk sensibly about the well-being of the self only within society. He thus pointedly reconstructed the Christian precept to love our neighbors as ourselves, writing that

> It is the great precept of nature to love ourselves only as we love our neighbour; or, what comes to the same thing, as our neighbour is capable of loving us.

If self-love is dependent on community, as Smith so simply states, then surely the selfish and the selfless are impossible to sort out. From this point of view, Hobbes's "state of nature," in which fully formed human beings once lived as solitaries in a condition of a "war of each against all," is unthinkable. Not only is it impossible to imagine human beings having evolved in the absence of an intensely social environment, but it is inconceivable to consider a fully formed human "person" apart from a social milieu. In this paradigm a more vital sense of individuality emerges: a person's individuality is constituted, not in defensive protection against society, but in that unique mix of relationships she or he bears to family, friends, neighbors, colleagues, and co-workers. . . .

In this worldview, once the enveloping social context is perceived as an indistinguishable extension of one's self, it is impossible to think in terms of trade-offs between society's well-being and the individual's unfettered pursuit of happiness. The health of the social whole is literally vital to a socially constituted individual's well-being.

Note the implication: there are no external laws governing our lives together, as in the Liberal tradition; here, we have ultimate responsibility for society—because we *are* society. Suddenly, human beings are back *on* the hook!

From this very different vantage point comes a very different view of the role of government, private property, and market exchange. Since our nature is social, government is no artifice; it is an expression of our social nature. The democratic process of self-government is no longer simply a means but is prized *in its own right*: through it, we make and remake our social reality to ever better serve our needs, and, in the process, remake ourselves.

No longer are private property and market exchange absolutes that exist solely for protection of individual autonomy. Instead, they become mere tools. Removed from the mystique of "natural law," they become devices subordinated to our socially defined needs, including our need for justice. . . .

The Meaning of Work

In this vein, the meaning of work also changes. Whereas the Protestant ethic assumes that people labor for fear of punishment, this view suggests that human beings cannot live without work because it fulfills a need to partake in community life. The issue of work therefore becomes more than a debate about earning income: to deprive people of work is to deprive them of an essential rite—and right—of membership in the human family.

Although the dominant paradigm sees all our resources already legitimately claimed in individual "property" rights, the worldview I voice sees our resources differently: it perceives that most wealth generated today builds upon a common pool of knowledge, invention, and public works developed over countless generations. Thus, no individual or group alive today can legitimately take full claim; as human beings we each have inherited a share in the legacy. . . .

Ultimately, these contrasting worldviews lead to diverging opinions about the very possibility of change, as well as the agents of change. While the Liberal paradigm has presided over unprecedented quickening in the pace of technological change, its stance toward social change is firmly negative: What we have today, flawed as it may seem, is the best we can realistically hope for, we are told. Better not touch bedrock rules governing our social world or we will end up with something much worse.

In the alternative worldview, the opposite assumptions hold: there are no such external rules above human accountability. Accordingly, efforts to achieve broad social goals through government action need not be seen as necessarily coercive and illegitimate. Instead, they reflect traits embedded in our nature. For in every human family, organization, and enterprise, we set goals with others and harness resources to meet these goals. Such efforts by communities and by whole societies may go awry, but the process itself is not suspect; it is essential to fulfilling our nature.

Recognizing Ethnocentrism

Ethnocentrism is the attitude or tendency of people to view their race, religion, culture, group, or nation as superior to others, and to judge others on that basis. An American, whose custom is to eat with a fork or spoon, would be making an ethnocentric statement when saying, ''The Chinese custom of eating with chopsticks is stupid.''

Ethnocentrism has promoted much misunderstanding and conflict. It emphasizes cultural and religious differences and the notion that one's national institutions or group's customs are superior.

Ethnocentrism limits people's ability to be objective and to learn from others. Education in the truest sense stresses the similarities of the human condition throughout the world and the basic equality and dignity of all people.

Most of the following statements are taken from the viewpoints in this book. Some have other origins. Consider each statement carefully. *Mark E for any statement you think is ethnocentric. Mark N for any statement you think is not ethnocentric. Mark U if you are undecided about any statement.*

If you are doing this activity as the member of a class or group, compare your answers with those of other class or group members. Be able to defend your answers. You may discover that others will come to different conclusions than you. Listening to the reasons others present for their answers may give you valuable insights in recognizing ethnocentric statements.

If you are reading this book alone, ask others if they agree with your answers. You too will find this interaction very valuable.

E = *ethnocentric*
N = *not ethnocentric*
U = *undecided*

1. Business is today the most significant force shaping American life.

2. We Indians have a more human philosophy of life. We Indians will show this country how to act human.

3. Certain general but essential orientations of the Gospel way and the American way are contradictory.

4. America is the "new Israel"; a people chosen by God.

5. The United States has the best economic system in the world.

6. The United States has the most powerful military force in the world.

7. Communist countries undoubtedly have more absenteeism, alcoholism and plain loafing on the job than any advanced nation in the West.

8. In our Constitution, the Founding Fathers created a structure of government based on the separation of powers between President and Congress.

9. American democracy is a more workable system than communism as practiced in Russia.

10. Americans, as a direct result of the individual freedom specified by the Constitution and the Bill of Rights, have earned the greatest degree of security ever enjoyed by any people anywhere.

"Adopting a different fiscal policy is not just an economic desideratum but a moral imperative."

America Needs a New Economic Policy

Benjamin M. Friedman

Benjamin Friedman is professor of economics at Harvard University. Before joining the Harvard faculty, he worked in investment banking in New York City. He has written extensively on the economics of fiscal and monetary policies. The viewpoint that follows is taken from his book, *Day of Reckoning*, in which he claims that the new economic policy that was adopted in 1981 violated the basic moral principle that has traditionally bound each generation of Americans to the next: that men and women should work and eat, earn and spend, both privately and collectively, so that their children and their children's children would inherit a better world. Americans, he argues, have been living well by increasing their debts and selling off their assets. He warns of a coming day of reckoning and advises America to change its economic values.

As you read, consider the following questions:

1. Why does the author think America's current fiscal policy is inconsistent with traditional American values?
2. Why does he claim the country's current prosperity is an illusion?
3. What course of action does he recommend? Do you agree with his assessment and recommendation?

What can you say to a man on a binge who asks why it matters? Flush with cash from liquidating his modest investment portfolio and from taking out a second mortgage on the inflated value of his house, he can spend seemingly without limit. The vacation cruise his family has dreamed about for years, the foreign sports car he has always wanted, new designer clothes for his wife and even his children, meals in all the most expensive restaurants—life is wonderful. What difference does it make if he has to pay some interest? If necessary, next year he can sell his house for enough to pay off both mortgages and have enough left over to buy an even faster car. What difference does it make whether he owns a house at all? For the price of the extra sports car, he can afford the first year's rent in the fanciest apartment building in town. Why worry?

Americans Have Traditionally Planned for Descendants

Americans have traditionally confronted such questions in the context of certain values, values that arise from the obligation that one generation owes to the next. Generations of Americans have opened up frontiers, fought in wars at home and abroad, and made countless personal economic sacrifices because they knew that the world did not end with themselves and because they cared about what came afterward. The American experiment, from the very beginning, has been forward looking—economically as well as politically and socially. The earliest Americans saw this experiment as an explicit break with the past and devoted their energies to constructing the kind of future they valued both individually and collectively. The generations that followed accepted their debt to the past by attempting to repay it to the future.

Since 1980 the Tradition Has Been Broken

The thesis of this book is that the radical course upon which United States economic policy was launched in the 1980s violated the basic moral principle that had bound each generation of Americans to the next since the founding of the republic: that men and women should work and eat, earn and spend, both privately and collectively, so that their children and their children's children would inherit a better world. Since 1980 we have broken with that tradition by pursuing a policy that amounts to living not just in, but for, the present. We are living well by running up our debt and selling off our assets. America has thrown itself a party and billed the tab to the future. The costs, which are only beginning to come due, will include a lower standard of living for individual Americans and reduced American influence and importance in world affairs.

For many Americans, the sudden collapse of stock prices in October 1987 punctured the complacency with which they had ac-

Berry's World

"Sonofagun! Isn't that GREAT — THE DOW DID IT AGAIN!"

cepted a national policy based on systematic overconsumption. After all, the resulting economic environment had looked pretty appealing to the average citizen. Jobs were plentiful in most areas, inflation and interest rates were both down from the frightening levels that had marked the beginning of the decade, and taxes were lower. Plenty of foreign-made goods were still available at cheap prices despite the falling dollar. Most companies' profits were high and going higher. The business recovery that began at the end of 1982 had already become the longest sustained economic expansion in American peacetime history, and there was no recession in sight. The phenomenal stock market rally, with the average share price almost tripling in just five years, seemed both to reflect this prosperity and to foretell its permanence.

By now it is clear that this sense of economic well-being was an illusion, an illusion based on borrowed time and borrowed money. Jobs are plentiful and profits are high because we are spending amply, but more than ever before what we are spending for is consumption. Prices have remained stable in part because business was depressed at the beginning of the decade, and also because until recently the overpriced dollar delivered foreign-made cars and clothes and computers more cheaply than the cost of producing them in America. Our after-tax incomes are rising because we are continuing to receive the usual variety of services and benefits from our government, but we are not paying the taxes to cover the cost.

We Have Sold Our Children's Economic Birthright

In short, our prosperity was a false prosperity, built on borrowing from the future. The trouble with an economic policy that artifically boosts consumption at the expense of investment, dissipates assets, and runs up debt is simply that each of these outcomes violates the essential trust that has always linked each generation to those that follow. We have enjoyed what appears to be a higher and more stable standard of living by selling our and our children's economic birthright. With no common agreement or even much public discussion, we are determining as a nation that today should be the high point of American economic advancement compared not just to the past but to the future as well. . . .

America Needs a New Economic Policy

America needs a new economic policy, a policy that is based on realistic assumptions about our economy's strengths and about how taxes and government spending affect them, and that at the same time faces the new realities of excess debt and underinvestment left from the Reagan years.

The central requirement, if we are not merely to continue on our current path toward fiscal instability, is a combination of tax and spending policies that will once again allow our federal debt to grow less rapidly than our income—and without higher inflation. . . .

Reagan's first fiscal priority when he took office was to lower tax rates. That was easy. It took just six months for Congress to pass the Economic Recovery Tax Act packaging the Kemp-Roth across-the-board cut in personal income tax rates with a smaller collection of saving incentives for individuals and tax breaks for business. Once that was done, Reagan's fiscal agenda turned to cutting various nondefense programs—though not the largest of all, Social Security—while at the same time increasing military spending. . . .

We Must Make Hard Choices

We must not only resolve to change our fiscal policy, but go ahead to enact the necessary legislation, including a phased tax increase as well as whatever spending cuts we are going to make, in a form to which we shall then be just as committed as we were to Kemp-Roth when we started down the path that has led us to our present unhappy situation.

Canceling nondefense programs. Making Social Security or Medicare less generous. Spending less on defense. Paying higher taxes. These are obviously hard choices, and whichever route we choose, we will have to make real sacrifices.

Successfully addressing the problems that Reagan's fiscal policy has left us will therefore be possible only if Americans not only understand why the steps we must take are necessary but also see that they are fair in how they spread their impact. Whether we cut spending by shutting down military bases or letting inflation erode retirees' incomes or paying government employees lower salaries or eliminating food stamps or farm price supports altogether will make little difference in economic terms. But it will determine who makes the sacrifices. In economic terms, what kind of tax increase to implement is also distinctly secondary to the choice of whether to increase taxes and by how much. But because there will be no public support for a tax increase that Americans think is not fair, in the end what form any proposed tax increase takes will determine whether we increase taxes at all.

Tax and Spend To Borrow and Spend

The importance of these fundamentally political dimensions of the choices we now face means that there is still much to be done. But at least the basic outlines of what we need to do are clear. Unfortunately, so are the consequences of failing to do it. In his initial budget address to Congress as America's new president in February 1981, Ronald Reagan asked of those whom he identified with the tax-and-spend strategy of the past, "Are they suggesting that we can continue on the present course without coming to a day of reckoning?"

The irony is that the right answer would have been "yes" in 1981, but it is surely "no" seven years later. The old policy of tax-and-spend, as the president derisively labeled it, delivered budgets that were approximately balanced by today's standards. More important, apart from wars it always reduced federal debt in relation to America's growing income. The new policy of large tax cuts not matched by spending cuts has instead delivered record deficits and a debt that is rising compared to our income. As a result, our domestic capital formation has been eroded, and for a while our international competitiveness all but collapsed. The policy of tax-and-spend at least led along a trajectory that was not fundamentally explosive. The policy of spending without taxing points a course that is clearly unstable.

The Day of Reckoning

If the day of reckoning that our new fiscal policy has made inevitable were likely to be concrete, sharply visible, and tangibly cataclysmic, a political system like ours that responds mostly to crisis would be better able to deal with it. But except perhaps for occasional crises in the foreign exchange markets, the costs of the fiscal policy we have pursued in the 1980s are occurring and will occur both gradually and subtly.

Without economic growth, American society will ultimately lose its vibrancy, its dynamic sense of progress, its capacity to accommodate the aims and objectives of diverse groups within the population, its ability to offer such remarkable social mobility and individual opportunity. Without a strong and competitive economy, America as a nation will watch others take its place in the world order. These are the real costs of our current fiscal policy, and for the most part they will not even be perceptible from one year to the next. Even on the occasions when discrete events do occur, like the collapse of some industry or financial institution or our abdication of a major international responsibility, it will be impossible to identify them unambiguously as by-products of our fiscal imbalance.

A Moral Imperative

The best way to meet this challenge is simply to be clear about what is at stake. The issue in the first instance is one of economics. But it matters because its consequences affect more fundamental aspects of what America is about as a society and as a nation. Adopting a different fiscal policy is not just an economic desideratum but a moral imperative. If we do not correct America's fiscal course, our children and our children's children will have the right to hold us responsible. The saddest outcome of all would be for America's decline to go on, but to go on so gradually that by the time the members of the next generation are old enough to begin asking who was responsible for their diminished circumstances, they will not even know what they have lost.

"Building community should be the mark of a social ethic for today's world, not rugged individualism at home and chauvinism abroad."

America Needs a New Social Ethic

Raymond G. Hunthausen

Raymond G. Hunthausen, the Archbishop of the Roman Catholic Archdiocese of Seattle, is a constant spokesman for the cause of social justice. He became prominent on the American scene in 1981 when he called for unilateral disarmament based on a critical reading of the Gospel. In the following viewpoint, Archbishop Hunthausen calls for a new social ethic based on Biblical values of communal life and cooperation. He claims this new emphasis will be difficult for America to attain because of its traditional ideals of private gain and individual initiative.

As you read, consider the following questions:

1. What evidence does the author present to support his claim that America's social ethic is defective?
2. What role in building America's current social ethic does he attribute to John Locke?
3. On what three elements would he restructure America's social ethic? Do you agree?

Raymond G. Hunthausen, *Moral Aspects of Leadership in Private and Public Life*, a speech delivered before the 1988 Mansfield Conference at the University of Montana on May 23, 1988.

The ethics of public figures have become something of a national pastime. The revelation of extensive illegal trading practices in the most prestigious of New York brokerage firms brought ethics to the front pages of our newspapers. Editorials and in-depth reports followed. Business schools scurried to beef up long neglected ethics courses. Reporters began subjecting presidential candidates to particularly close scrutiny, and more than one of them has been forced from the race by scandal. Television evangelists have been disgraced. And *Time* magazine has wondered at length about the state of ethics in this nation. Despite the extent and seriousness of the incidents that have generated this attention, some would find encouragement in the public soul searching that has attended these events.

There is much to be said for the continuing discussion of ethics in the media and among the public. There is even more to be said for the response to these ethical concerns in terms of remedial actions on all levels. But, for all that is positive in this, I find it all a little off the mark.

America's Focus on Private Ethics

For, at the same time we as a nation have found Ivan Boesky, Gary Hart, Joseph Biden and a host of others wanting, we have failed to come to grips with the moral and ethical dimensions of the Iran-Contra scandal. While the unattributed use of another politician's speech drove Joseph Biden from contention for the presidency, the fact that Colonel North deliberately defied the law and deceived the Congress seems to qualify him as a patriot and as a potential candidate for the United States Senate.

This apparent lack of capacity for consistent ethical thinking is manifest in equally deep ways on a number of fronts:

- A high official of our State Department, Elliot Abrams, has persistently embroidered on the truth before Congress and the public in order to undermine every opportunity for peace in Central America. Why? Because the maintenance of low intensity conflict in the region is our policy—or at least his. Every month a thousand people die there in this continuing violence, ninety percent of them innocent civilians.

- In this decade, we have spent two trillion dollars on our own military and have been a major participant in the arming of the Third World. Worldwide, military expenditures have been $6 trillion during a decade when approximately five million people have died in war, 100 million have been threatened by famine, and one billion live in deep poverty.

- We continue to tolerate the development and proliferation of nuclear weapons. Well over 60,000 nuclear devices are now in the hands of twelve different nations; these are soon to be joined by five to ten others. This arsenal is enough to destroy the world hundreds of times over.

As we survey those contrasts in our ethical landscape, it becomes clear that our ethical sense begins to fail precisely at that point when we leave the sphere of private life and enter the social realm. We can grasp the implication of lying about one's private life, or violating an intimate relationship. But the grand lies of state, or the violation of entire nations, escape us. Our culture has so radically prized individualism and the private life, that it has left us without the social reference points necessary to the construction of an ethic adequate for this new moment of interdependence in human history. . . .

The Legacy of John Locke

What is most difficult about the task of building a truly social ethic for this nation is that the division between the private and the public spheres is deeply rooted in our political culture. It comes down to us from no less an authority than John Locke, and echoes through the philosophy which has so influenced our constitutional system. The myth of a "state of nature" where individuals existed outside of community, without political order, in a state of genteel bliss is a powerful one. It gives rise to the idea that political, indeed social life, is a human invention, a matter of convenience, contracted for by independent individuals in order to secure their private lives.

This way of thinking not only leads to the idea of limited government, it subtly limits all social possibilities. What is truly positive in our lives, this philosophy tells us, is found in our individual selves. Government and society is nothing more than a check—albeit necessary—on private excess and individual aberrations. In this perspective, government is essentially negative. Government is not even a good tool through which to realize the positive fruits of common endeavor, let alone a common ground on which we could come together to share our aspirations as a people. This narrow and limited view of political life is certainly a weak reed upon which to set the conceptualization of a social ethic.

The Social Ethic Taught in Scripture

The vision of social life found in scripture is in profound contrast with this perspective. The story of creation in Genesis sees us born not in cold isolation, but with the intimate touch of the Creator's hand. We are created together, husband and wife made for each other, and multitudinous generations to come. As the Lord told Jeremiah, this God knew us before we were formed in our mother's womb. Or as Matthew says, God numbers the very hairs of our head. In John's Gospel, the Genesis story is recast to emphasize that the entire human family is made heirs to the loving intimacy that is the spirit of God through the spiritual bonding of humankind in Christ. This radical intimacy that binds all of us equally to God and each other is summed up in the best known and most accessible of the passages in scripture, when Jesus teaches us to pray to God as "our Father," an acknowledgement that we are brothers and sisters with a common loving parent.

Drawing by W. Miller; © 1973 The New Yorker Magazine, Inc.

Just as the Biblical perspective of human community contradicts the idea of glorious solitude of the state of nature, the conclusions based on this perspective depart dramatically from the conclusions of John Locke and other philosophers of the Enlightenment. In fact, the Lord's Prayer is, itself, a good summation of these differences. For the first thing Jesus asks us to pray for is the coming of the Biblical kingdom of justice and peace. In pronouncing "Thy Kingdom come, Thy will be done" we are acknowledging that it is God's intention and hope for us that we build for ourselves the "shalom" community in which we all share the peace that comes from being "right" with ourselves, our neighbor, our environment, and our God. In Matthew 25, or in the story of Lazarus and the rich man, Jesus tells us in no uncertain terms that "being right" involves recognizing, affirming, and materially supporting the least among us. Time and again Jesus clearly articulates the religious perspective which makes him one with the prophets of the Hebrew scriptures. The Lord's Prayer continues by alluding to the "daily bread." Jesus uses this powerful image to underscore the immediacy of the plea for the coming of the Kingdom and for full participation in communal life. Far from viewing social life as a convenience and a tool to smooth the rough edges of our individual existence, the scriptures contemplate a social life that is at the very center of human existence, and the institutions of that life as a positive force in human relationships.

Finally, the prayer has a simple plea for reconciliation: "Forgive us our trespasses, as we forgive those who trespass against us." Yet this plea is a proposal for action of the first moment. It is a plea for that gift of vulnerability and openness, the will to bridge the abyss in order to gather in the other, the alien. It is the succinct statement of the Christian paradox: one finds oneself only by going outside of oneself, by putting oneself wholly at risk. It is the very antithesis of seeking security in control, of holding the other at arm's length.

It is ironic that the modern view of the Enlightenment philosophers seems quaint and out of touch, while the challenge of the scriptures is as ever fresh as it is discomfiting. The world has grown beyond the myth of an isolated individual. We are too obviously connected physically, socially, economically. The deeper we probe our biology, psychology, or anthropology, our human integration appears in ever more profound outline. The unique biological determinations carried in our individual DNA structures root us back through generations. They can be read as a personal history of our human community. We have discovered that our basic psychological make-up is formed in the womb through the experiences of our mother. Anthropology points to a common genesis, and a difficult, but steady development through collective effort. But, however antiquated, we cling to a social ethic that is the heir of the theories of the Enlightenment.

The Importance of Social Values Must Be Recognized

The radical separation of private life and social life, along with the denigration of the social order in preference for the individual, has caused us to concentrate on developing an ethic of private morality. This essentially private ethic has then been applied to social concerns to form a makeshift social ethic. At best, the virtues essential to one's private life—personal integrity, loyalty, honesty, forthrightness—are pressed into service as the paramount social virtues. At worst, social life is seen as life in the jungle, where the killer instinct becomes a virtue. Overall, the end result is an ideal where personal honesty, care for one's kind, and private charity is sufficient; thereafter the harder one strives after or fights for one's private interest, the better. To be combative, shrewd, competitive, to constantly strive to be number one, is good. This is, in short, an ethic of private struggle in a social milieu. Its virtues are the virtues of conflict; the figure of the public person is that of the warrior. A Colonel North manifests in his person what we collectively believe about our social life.

The reconstruction of social ethics demands the elevation of specifically social values in importance, and the integration of those values with the values associated with the private sphere. Most especially, it demands the establishment of new organizing principles for a renewed sense of social life. . . .

The Formation of a New Social Ethic

The movement toward a new social ethic turns then on three elements. First, there must be a recognition of interdependence as the critical fact of life in today's world. Second, the quality of the interdependence we experience must be measured by the norms of justice and human rights. Finally, we must cultivate and practice the virtue of solidarity.

The movement from the recognition of interdependence as ethically important to a critique of today's social order based on an understanding of human rights, is the essential step in conceiving a new social ethic. In Catholic social thought, human rights are derived from the understanding of the creative act. We are all made in the image of God. We are all made to realize together the full potential of our relationship with the divine. As St. Augustine says: "You have made us for yourself, oh Lord, and we are not at rest until we rest in you."

We all share equally in this inheritance, and in the gift of the resources of the earth to bring it to fruition. We, therefore, have a claim to all that is necessary to fulfill our own unique potential as persons. In practical effect, this means that we claim the broad range of those human rights incorporated in the United Nations Declaration on Human Rights: From the right to life to the right to food and shelter, from the right of freedom of thought to the right to organize and participate in social life, from the right to work to the right to a living wage, and a healthy and stimulating working environment. But since these rights are given to us all together, they are at the same time social obligations. We are obligated to recognize the rightful claims of all our sisters and brothers.

As St. John said:

> In this we have come to know His love, that He laid down His life for us; and we likewise ought to lay down our life for the brothers and sisters. The person who has the goods of this world and sees their brother or sister in need and closes their heart, how does the love of God abide in them? My dear children, let us not love in word only, but in deed and in truth.

I John 3:16-18

The human development based on the mutual recognition of rights and responsibilities can only be worked out in the social order, where the required mutuality can be organized and secured. Given the substance of human rights, human obligations, Catholic social thought is led necessarily to contemplate a positive role for government and, by extension, the public person. It is the primary responsibility of any public officer, then, from ordinary citizen to the highest executive, to foster human rights. It is the affirmation of this responsibility which should be the cornerstone of a renewed social ethic in this country.

The Virtue of Solidarity

It is one thing, of course, to affirm human rights intellectually and quite another to affirm human rights in concrete action. The affirmation of human rights in practice requires the virtue of solidarity; we all must be able to live out the reality of being one human family. To be in solidarity means that we envision our relationships so clearly that we see ourselves in the other; to know that what is good for one is good for all, and the pain of the least among us affects us all. This vision is especially incumbent on the public official. Not only must the public official be in solidarity with all the people, the public official must define and articulate for all the people what is common among us. It is the preeminent role of the public official to solidify the human family in all its ramifications.

Just as it is the primary responsibility of the public official to solidify the human family, our common responsibility is to build the foundation for that work. Solidarity does not come down to us from the powerful, it grows from the roots. It is our responsibility to cultivate the vision to see everyone as a brother and sister, so that we can collectively build and maintain an ethic of solidarity. We must, most of all, commit ourselves to fully participate in public life, in order to hold those who govern to account and to constantly renew our social possibilities. It is our social imagination, it is the social ethic that all of us together create, that both empowers and gives character to the leadership our public officials provide.

The primary responsibility of public life—the responsibility to foster human rights—leads inevitably to its corollary, the responsibility to build community. It is a responsibility we all share equally. I submit that living in solidarity, acting responsibly on behalf of human rights and building community should be the mark of a social ethic for today's world, not rugged individualism at home and chauvinism abroad.

The Problems We Face

- The growing gap between the wealthy industrialized nations and whole peoples struggling in poverty, weighed down by international debt

- Ongoing wars affecting the people of Central America, the Middle East, the horn and southern cone of Africa
- The arms race, which seems to continue of its own accord despite the good news of the treaty on medium range missiles

All speak to profound alienation; the alienation of ethnic groups and nations one from another and the alienation of the poor and the oppressed from the human community. Driven by our own fears and doubts, we allow ourselves to hate the Russians and to scapegoat the poor. It is these, and many other faces of alienation that challenge our social will and the social ethic upon which it is based. The recognition of human rights, solidarity and community all are necessary antidotes to alienation and its effects, but the will to overcome alienation is the will to reconciliation.

If we look back over the great span of history, we will discover that the great changes effected in its course did not come through cataclysmic and violent events. Rather they came silently. They came because someone or something broke the mold: thought new thoughts, or dreamed new dreams, and resolved the conflict between known truths, joined opposing forces, or united peoples in conflict. Greek civilization, the rise of scientific thinking, the development of our constitutional system, the civil rights movement in this country—much more, the Christian revolution—all were changes that speak to the power of reconciling opposites. It is the will to effect these kinds of reconciliations that is needed most in today's world.

We need the collective courage to question our conventional wisdom, to put aside our security and self-interest, and above all, to risk failure in order to seek out and embrace that which is opposed. "Forgive us, as we forgive," Jesus said.

"Moral education is essential in a democratic society because government by the people requires that the people be good."

America Needs Moral Education in Its Schools

Association for Supervision and Curriculum Development

The Association for Supervision and Curriculum Development (ASCD) is America's largest non-political professional leadership organization in education. Its 112,000 members include school superintendents, school principals, and other educational professionals. The following viewpoint is taken from an ASCD commissioned panel that was asked to examine critical issues such as morality and religion in public schools. In addition to making specific recommendations for strengthening moral education in the country's schools, the panel claims that failure to do so threatens the survival of American democracy.

As you read, consider the following questions:

1. What evidence does the ASCD present to support its claim that America needs moral education?
2. What six characteristics does it attribute to the morally mature person?

ASCD Panel on Moral Education, *Moral Education in the Life of the School.* Reprinted with permission of the Association for Supervision and Curriculum Development. Copyright © 1988 by the Association for Supervision and Curriculum Development. All rights reserved.

Moral education is whatever schools do to influence how students think, feel, and act regarding issues of right and wrong. American public schools have a long tradition of concern about moral education, and recently this concern has grown more intense.

One reason for this increased concern is the substantial, long-term increase in emotional problems among young Americans. Figure 1 shows three disturbing trends: notable increases in the rates of adolescent death by homicide and suicide, and of out-of-wedlock births. The data focus on whites—our more advantaged population—to emphasize that these shifts are unrelated to racial discrimination or poverty. As the graph indicates, the rates of male adolescent death by homicide and suicide increased by 441 percent and 479 percent, respectively, between the mid 1950s and 1984. Both rates have decreased slightly in the recent past, but the overall rise in homicides and suicides remains alarming. During roughly the same years (1940-85), the rate of out-of-wedlock births to adolescents rose by 621 percent. At different times in the last decade, all of these rates peaked at their highest points in history (Wynne and Hess 1986).

Nor are these the only indications that something is awry. National surveys disclose that, in 1969, only 21 percent of high school seniors admitted to ever using marijuana (Bachman et al. 1978); in 1980 and 1985, the comparable figures were 60.2 percent and 54.2 percent (Johnston et al. 1987).

It is still true that there are millions of well-adjusted American adolescents. But these data indicate that, by some measures at least, young people show more self-destructive and other destructive behavior today than they did two or three decades ago.

In addition, young people's moral development has implications for their participation in the workplace. Such apparently simple actions as coming to work regularly and on time; being polite to co-workers, customers, and superiors; obeying legitimate authority; and working diligently all have strong moral elements. Together, such attitudes and actions make up the American work ethic—an ethic that many believe is in decline. . . .

Contemporary Issues

Issues that have confounded moral education over the past century are intensified today: How do we respond to disagreements about the proper methods of moral education? How does the school balance common values with pluralistic beliefs? What should be the relationship between religion and moral education in the public schools? What is the relationship between private and public morality? Should moral education emphasize indoctrination or reasoning? . . .

In earlier times, American schools did not find such questions troubling. The predecessors of today's public schools were founded under a Massachusetts law passed in 1647, twenty years after the first settlers landed. The law, which stated "that old deluder Satan" flourished on ignorance, was aimed at establishing schools that would deliberately foster morality. The academic learning transmitted in such schools was inextricably bound up with religious doctrine.

Indeed, until the middle of the 19th century, public schools were

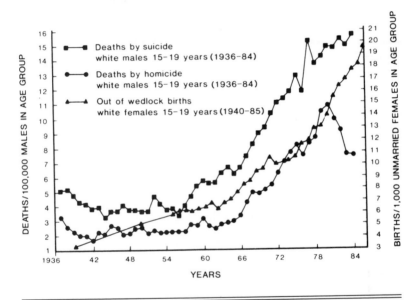

Figure 1
Changes in the Rates of Youth Homicide, Suicide, and Illegitimate Births

typically pervaded with a strong, nonsectarian Protestant tone, which was reflected in Bible readings, prayers, ceremonial occasions, and the contents of reading materials. (In some communities where one sect was dominant, a more sectarian tone prevailed.) As Roman Catholic immigration proceeded, conflicts arose over moral and religious education. These disputes were circumvented by the creation of parochial schools.

By the end of the 19th century, public schools increasingly adopted a purely secular form of moral education, often called "character education" (Yulish 1980). The character education movement identified a body of activities and principles by which moral education could be transmitted in a secular institution. The approach emphasized student teamwork, extracurricular activities, student councils, flag salutes and other ceremonies, and common-sense moral virtues like honesty, self-discipline, kindness, and tolerance. . . .

Morality and Religion

Religion is a major force in the lives of most Americans. Indeed, international studies continually report a comparatively high level of religious practice among Americans. Because religion is, above all, a meaning system, it naturally speaks to its adherents about right and wrong, good and bad. For many Americans, the first and foremost moral guide is their own religion.

While the theological doctrines of religions differ substantially, there is a great deal of overlap in moral theologies, particularly in their everyday application. Broad areas of consensus exist regarding concern for our fellow human beings, honesty in our dealings with one another, respect for property, and a host of other moral issues. These same issues are fundamental to the rules our nation has chosen to live by; in practice, the dictates of one's religious conscience and the precepts of democracy tend to reinforce each other.

There are many Americans, however, in whose lives religion does not play a significant role. There are others who, for a variety of reasons, are antagonistic to religion. For them, moral education based on religion and appeals to religious principles to solve moral issues are serious affronts. On the other hand, some religious people are equally affronted by public schools teaching students to look outside their religious tradition for moral guidance.

Public schools, committed as they are to serving all Americans, must approach this question with understanding, sensitivity, and willingness to compromise. Educators need to be sensitive to students' religious beliefs and respect their legitimacy, yet must not promote such beliefs in the classroom. Teachers should stress the democratic and intellectual bases for morality, but they should also encourage children to bring all their intellectual, cultural, and religious resources to bear on moral issues.

Appreciating the differences in our pluralistic society is fundamental to the success of our democracy. And tolerance must begin in the schools: If we are to survive as a nation, our schools must help us find our common moral ground and help us learn to live together on it.

Moral education is not only inevitable in schools; it is essential. Human beings vary tremendously and are enormously adaptable, and our broad potential requires that we teach the best of our inherited culture. That teaching begins, of course, in our families, but it must be supported by other agencies. A common morality should be developed while a society's future citizens are still

America's Core Values

Public opinion surveys show that Americans have two top priorities for the public schools: first, to teach basic skills, and, second, to instill basic values. . . .

What we need to do is first decide upon the core of values that we share as a people and, second, determine the most effective methods for instilling these values. And that is the debate we are having now.

Each of us has an important contribution to make. Those on the right have emphasized the moral dimension of values—the essentials of personal behavior that most of us have learned in our homes and churches and synagogues. At a time when so many lives have been damaged by teenage pregnancy and by drug and alcohol abuse, it is time for us to remember these home truths.

Those on the left, for the most part, have emphasized the civic values, the principles that express our obligation to each other and to our communities and to our nation.

At a time of lawlessness in government and on Wall Street, rising racial and religious intolerance and declining voter turnouts, it is also important for us to remember the basic principles of participation, of respect for the rule of law and for other people's rights.

In a sense, both sides of the debate are correct. We need to teach the moral and civic values that we the people share, because we Americans do share core values about the good life and the good society and we can pass those values on to the next generation.

In the sphere of moral values, the vast majority of us, Protestants and Catholics, Jews and even secular humanists share the belief in certain values: honesty, courage, integrity, compassion, for instance. For most of us, these values are rooted in our religious heritage, but in truth, they are universal. We can teach them in our public schools in a nonsectarian way without offering a religious explanation.

Similarly, in the sphere of civic values, the vast majority of us, Democrats, Republicans, civil libertarians, socialists, share a belief in basic principles: majority rule, the rule of law respecting the individual, and racial and religious justice. Not just in the civics classes, but throughout the curriculum, we can teach these principles without propagandizing people in any one ideology.

Anthony T. Podesta, president of People for the American Way, speech of March 22, 1987.

children—before misdirected development leads them to harm themselves or others.

To accomplish this important task, all societies have public systems to help develop moral principles in children. In America, schools are a central part of that system. Our schools thus cannot ignore moral education; it is one of their most important responsibilities. . . .

The Morally Mature Person

What kind of human being do we want to emerge from our efforts at moral education? What are the characteristics of the morally mature person?

A moment's reflection tells us that moral maturity is more than just knowing what is right. The world is full of people who know what is right but set moral considerations aside when they find it expedient to do so. To be moral means to *value* morality, to take moral obligations seriously. It means to be able to judge what is right but also to care deeply about doing it—and to possess the will, competence, and habits needed to translate moral judgment and feeling into effective moral action.

We submit that the morally mature person has six major characteristics, which are derived from universal moral and democratic principles. These characteristics offer schools and communities a context for discourse about school programs and moral behavior. The morally mature person habitually:

1. *Respects human dignity,* which includes
   - showing regard for the worth and rights of all persons,
   - avoiding deception and dishonesty,
   - promoting human equality,
   - respecting freedom of conscience,
   - working with people of different views, and
   - refraining from prejudiced actions.
2. *Cares about the welfare of others,* which includes
   - recognizing interdependence among people,
   - caring for one's country,
   - seeking social justice,
   - taking pleasure in helping others, and
   - working to help others reach moral maturity.
3. *Integrates individual interests and social responsibilities,* which includes
   - becoming involved in community life,
   - doing a fair share of community work,
   - displaying self-regarding and other-regarding moral virtues— self-control, diligence, fairness, kindness, honesty, civility— in everyday life,
   - fulfilling commitments, and
   - developing self-esteem through relationships with others.
4. *Demonstrates integrity,* which includes
   - practicing diligence,
   - taking stands for moral principles,

- displaying moral courage,
- knowing when to compromise and when to confront, and
- accepting responsibility for one's choices.

5. *Reflects on moral choices,* which includes
   - recognizing the moral issues involved in a situation,
   - applying moral principles (such as the golden rule) when making moral judgments,
   - thinking about the consequences of decisions, and
   - seeking to be informed about important moral issues in society and the world.

6. *Seeks peaceful resolution of conflict,* which includes
   - striving for the fair resolution of personal and social conflicts,
   - avoiding physical and verbal aggression,
   - listening carefully to others,
   - encouraging others to communicate, and
   - working for peace.

In general, then, the morally mature person understands moral principles and accepts responsibility for applying them. . . .

Conclusion

Education for moral maturity is also education for democracy. Thomas Jefferson argued that moral education is essential in a democratic society because government by the people requires that the people be good—that they have at least a minimal understanding of and commitment to the moral values on which a democracy rests.

In order to educate our children to be morally mature individuals who will work to create a morally mature democratic society, we must provide moral education that is broad and deep. It must be systematic, planned, theoretically grounded, and conscientiously sustained. It must embrace both the formal curriculum of academic subjects and the "human curriculum" of rules, roles, and relationships that make up the moral life of the school. Only moral education of this magnitude can meet the challenge before us. . . .

The moral education we call for is part of the living legacy of our nation. It is at the center of our evolving tradition as a national community. Our vision of the moral education children need is one that is basic to the survival of our culture, building on the past while preparing young people to deal with the moral challenges of the future.

> "Every American child should be taught the
> fundamental skills for living successfully in
> a multicultural world."

America Needs
Multicultural Education
in Its Schools

Marlene A. Cummings

By the year 2000, one-third of the US population will be nonwhite.
In the following viewpoint, Marlene Cummings argues that
American education must be reformed to reflect this demographic
change. Traditional education has devalued the contributions of
blacks, Hispanics, and Native Americans to American culture, she
maintains, and thus promoted bitterness, a poor self-image, and
low self-esteem among minority children. To truly integrate
America's schools, she contends, teachers must recognize and
teach the contributions of all of America's diverse peoples. Cummings is the author of *Individual Differences* and the secretary of
the Wisconsin Department of Regulation and Licensing, a state
agency in Madison, Wisconsin.

As you read, consider the following questions:

1. Why does the author dislike the term "minority"?
2. How are schools failing to help black, Hispanic, and
   Native American children, according to Cummings?
3. How does Cummings respond to the idea that the US is
   a melting pot?

Marlene A. Cummings, "Education for a Pluralistic, Democratic Society," *Education and
Society*, Summer 1988. Reprinted with permission.

To understand what is required in terms of education for a pluralistic, democratic America, we need to examine where we stand today and what the requirements will likely be for tomorrow.

Some predictions about tomorrow's population profile may be drawn from today's statistics. The baby-boom generation has reached maturity. Its members, 38 years old or a little younger, now have children of their own in school and some of their children are already out of school. Both parents in these families must work to earn a decent living that does not, however, meet the escalating cost of higher education for their children.

They are not so different as a group, but they number 78 million, approximately one-third of the nation's population. They have been likened to a hearty meal moving toward a snake. They are the 1960s flower children, the "me" generation, the hippies, yippies, and now yuppies. Their protest helped to end the Vietnam War because of their numbers.

They are the most powerful population group in America. They have been that since they were born and will continue to be that until they die. They were the catalyst for the boxed and disposable diaper industry, baby food, convenience stores, school district growth and, of late, the closing of schools.

At every point in their aging, their numbers alone will enable them to have the ultimate say in how things go. They have typically had fewer children than their parents and consequently have a smaller backup generation. They know about the good life, and in many instances they live it by dint of harder work. They hope to preserve the quality of life to which they have become accustomed.

Demographic Changes

Children born to a smaller group of people—people labeled *minorities*—on the other hand are themselves a growing force. Along with newer immigrants from Asia and South America, they will emerge from minority status to become the majority in 53 major American cities and the state of California. Nationally, those now labeled minorities will change the profile of the nation, and one of three persons will be nonwhite.

Let us consider for a moment this term 'minority'. This term, perhaps more than any other, has contributed to disrespect for the cultural, racial, and religious pluralism of this country during this century. 'Minority' is seldom used to signify number; it has been used rather to denote such social phenomena as welfare, illiteracy, busing, affirmative action programs, discrimination, and dependency on government. The truly tragic impact of the term has been felt by children of blacks, Hispanics, and Native Americans.

How can one acquire a healthy self-respect and respect for one's roots if those roots bear the label 'minority'? Is it any wonder that these children who will make up most of the work force of the future, who will deliver the services of the future, will not be ready unless early commitment is made to take radical steps to remedy an urgent situation?

It is not the word 'minority' alone that causes hardship, but rather all the accompanying social institutions the word betokens. Consider just one of the so-called minorities—black children.

Ian McNett, principal researcher for *Demographic Imperatives: Implications for Educational Policy*, reported that black children are twice as likely to have an adolescent or single mother, to have an unemployed parent, to be unemployed themselves as teenagers, and to not go to college after high school graduation. They are five times as likely as white children to become dependent on welfare, to become pregnant as teenagers, and four times as likely to be placed in an educable though mentally retarded class, to be murdered before reaching one year of age, or to be incarcerated as a teenager between 15 and 19 years of age.

A Bridge-Building Process

The concept of ethnic studies, with its focus on the cultural demands of racially oppressed people in the United States, has always involved, along with its challenge to racism in our own educational system, a bridge-building process inviting us to identify with the struggles and accomplishments of oppressed people of color around the world. While we have recognized the bonds linking us to Africa, Asia, the Caribbean, the Middle East, and Latin America as having been wrought by our respective racial and cultural heritages, we must be equally cognizant of the fact that these ties have been enormously strengthened by our common pursuit of dignity and freedom.

Angela Davis, *Women, Culture & Politics*, 1989.

The school is one institution that teaches children generally and therefore minorities. Minorities become whatever excuse can be found for the failure of school districts to do little more than discipline children and move them along with such rationalizations for failing to help them as that they are disadvantaged, products of broken homes, undernourished, undisciplined, alienated from learning, mobile, and lacking in motivation to learn. And, employing the currently fashionable expression, we should remember to assert that children are "at risk." It is rather, however, schools and society that are at risk when so many of the nation's children with similar characteristics are failing and being failed by the institutions that should be saving them.

The label 'minority' gives rise in society to the expectation that prisons are going to be filled by blacks, Hispanics, and Native Americans. Seldom are the reasons sought for the fact that half the prisoners in state correctional institutions are made up of minorities. If there existed any genuine appreciation for the history, culture, and diversity of all the American people and the human family generally, instead of this attitude toward the plight of the poor among the black, Hispanic, and Native American populations, perhaps more people would seek reasons for the percentages of the impoverished and imprisoned. They would not assume that poverty and crime are adequately explained by mere membership in a minority. . . .

What Then About Education?

Every American child should be taught the fundamental skills for living successfully in a multicultural world. That must start with a good sense of self and progress to an acknowledgment, understanding, and respect for the differences of others. Wherever American people work with American people, they should be expected and be able to exhibit skills and behavior that reflect *multicultural* literacy along with cultural literacy.

We need to teach our young people to celebrate and to glory in our diversities. That we are all characterized by sameness is an illusion and a delusion belied by the rich reality of our differences. We are a nation of nations. None of us were ever really melted down by the melting pot. Nor will we melt during the 21st century either. That is neither the way we are nor the way we began.

We are going to have to set aside our ethnocentrism and cultural arrogance and parochialism and work together as individual Americans to eliminate the gap in educational achievement. It is a large order.

We black Americans have gone from *colored*, to *Negro* to *black* and back again to *colored* by another name—minority. We have asked to be called *black*. Who has ever asked us what we want to be called, whether we want neighborhood schools, what input we want into staffing the schools, how we want to be taught the basic skills, and what we think and feel about the way history depicts our ancestors?

Promoting Integration

We did not create the segregated neighborhoods by redlining and other devices designed to polarize people by color. We want and value quality education for our children because that is the only way true integration ever takes place. Gordon Allport, noted psychologist, said that true integration is possible only when all those integrating can make equal contributions. We believe this is possible, given the right opportunities.

If all the specious reasons why children of minority groups can't learn were set aside and we retained only the principle that all groups are equally endowed with the ability to learn, learning would then take place. If it did not, we should have to acknowledge our own failures but not blame the children. . . .

Ethnocentrism

The curriculum in traditionally White, mainstream environments reinforces ethnocentrism and ignorance of nonwhites' cultural and intellectual creativity.

Black and progressive educators have long recognized that the cultural battleground is absolutely decisive in the broader political and economic empowerment of oppressed people. The values taught to our children largely determine their behavior.

Manning Marable, *The Witness*, March 1989.

So many children in the 21st century, if we can effect the necessary changes, will be able to live in a world that belongs to a harmonious human family, instead of a world occupied by this group, that group, and a multitude of other mutually hostile subgroups. Not only will they participate effectively in the world marketplace, but we may hope that they will achieve world peace.

The Control of the Oppressor

Carter G. Woodson, historian and founder of the Institute for the Study of Black History that led to the commemoration of Black History Week, wrote:

No systematic effort toward change has been possible; for taught the same economics, history, philosophy, literature and religion which have established the present code of morals, the mind of the Black child has been brought under the control of the oppressor. The problem of holding Blacks down is easily solved.

When you control a man's mind, you do not have to tell him to stand here or go yonder. . . . "He will find his proper place and stay in it."

You do not need to send him to the back door. He will go without being told.

In fact, if there is no back door, he will cut one for his special benefits.

His education makes it necessary.

These are great and urgent challenges; wisely conceived and carefully designed foundational work must be laid for the new superstructure we hope will rise in the 21st century.

Recognizing Stereotypes

Step 1.   The class should break into groups of four to six students. Working individually each student should fill in the blank spaces below, placing the names of groups in America he or she think best fit the descriptions on the right side of the page. Add any groups and descriptions, not included, that are commonly used by others.

1. _____ are good students

2. _____ are emotional

3. _____ have rhythm

4. _____ all look alike

5. _____ are aggressive and pushy

6. _____ are shrewd business people

7. _____ are lazy

8. _____ are hot tempered

9. _____ are _____

10. _____ are _____

Step 2.   After individuals have finished step 1, a member from each small group should read aloud the following definition of a stereotype.

*A **stereotype** is an oversimplified or exaggerated description. It can apply to things or people and be favorable or unfavorable. Quite often stereotyped beliefs about racial, religious and national groups are insulting and oversimplified. They are usually based on misinformation or lack of information.*

Step 3.   The Small groups should next discuss the following questions:

1. What stereotypes did different class members use in the statements in step 1?
2. What stereotypes were added by individuals in the blank spaces 8 through 10?
3. Which stereotypes were based on reason? Which were based on emotion?
4. What kind of situations tend to stereotype people?
5. Why does stereotyping exist?
6. What are the effects of stereotyping?

Periodical Bibliography

The following articles have been selected to supplement the diverse views presented in this chapter.

William J. Bennett	"In Defense of Our Common Culture," *USA Today*, March 1987.
Lester R. Brown	"The Need for New Values," *Christianity and Crisis*, November 30, 1981.
James M. Campbell	"Affirming a New Public Philosophy," *The Witness*, April 1982.
Porter Crow	"Finding Our Moral Compass," *Vital Speeches of the Day*, August 15, 1974.
Louis DeBakey	"Our National Priority," *Vital Speeches of the Day*, June 1, 1987.
Educational Leadership	Entire issue on "School, Parents, and Values," May 1989.
Chester E. Finn Jr.	"Giving Shape to Cultural Conservatism," *The American Spectator*, November 1986.
Claude S. Fischer	"Finding the 'Lost' Community: Facts and Fictions," *Tikkun*, November/December 1988.
Norman C. Gaddis	"Our Survival As a Nation: Our Moral and Spiritual Values," *Vital Speeches of the Day*, May 15, 1974.
Georgie Anne Geyer	"Is Your Generation Doomed To Live in a Second Class America?" *Vital Speeches of the Day*, August 1, 1988.
John Glenn	"A Blueprint for America's Future," *USA Today*, July 1983.
Ed Grady	"The Premium on Our Survival Insurance," *Vital Speeches of the Day*, May 15, 1981.
Arthur G. Hansen	"A New Sense of Purpose and Pride," *Vital Speeches of the Day*, July 15, 1976.
Jeffrey R. Holland	"The Value of Values," *Vital Speeches of the Day*, January 15, 1982.
Richard D. Lamm	"Decline of the West," *Chronicles*, February 1989.
Norman S. Rean	"The Crisis of Our Age," *The Freeman*, February 1980.
Vincent A. Sarni	"The American Dream," *USA Today*, May 1985.

Organizations To Contact

The editor has compiled the following list of organizations concerned with the issues debated in this book. All of them have publications available for interested readers. The descriptions are derived from materials provided by the organizations themselves.

American Atheists
PO Box 140195
Austin, TX 78714
(512) 458-1244

American Atheists is an educational organization dedicated to the complete and absolute separation of state and church. It opposes religious involvement in public schools. Its purpose is to stimulate freedom of thought and inquiry concerning religious beliefs and practices. It publishes *American Atheist* magazine and numerous books and reprints.

American Civil Liberties Union (ACLU)
132 W. 43rd St.
New York, NY 10036
(212) 944-9800

The ACLU champions the rights set forth in the Declaration of Independence and the US Constitution, including freedom of inquiry and expression, due process of law, a fair trial for everybody, and equality before the law. It publishes a monthly, *Civil Liberties Alert*, and a quarterly magazine, *Civil Liberties*. It also publishes policy statements, a handbook, reprints, and pamphlets.

American Conservative Union (ACU)
38 Ivy St. SE
Washington, DC 20003
(202) 546-6555

The ACU promotes conservative interests, such as limited government, strong national defense, and anticommunism. It maintains a speakers' bureau and its publication, *New Freedom*, appears quarterly.

American Humanist Association
7 Harwood Dr.
PO Box 146
Amherst, NY 14226-0146
(716) 839-5080

The Association's members are devoted to humanism as a way of life. They do not acknowledge a supernatural power. The Association opposes school prayer and government aid to religion. It favors education in ethics as an alternative to religious training for the young. It publishes *The Humanist* magazine bimonthly.

American Vision
PO Box 72515
Atlanta, GA 30328
(404) 988-0555

American Vision is a Christian educational organization working to build a Christian civilization. It believes the Bible ought to be applied to every area of life, including government. It publishes a monthly newsletter, *Biblical Worldview*.

Americanism Educational League
PO Box 5986
Buena Park, CA 90622
(714) 828-5040

The League is concerned with free enterprise, America's heritage, and traditional values. It is also interested in promoting constitutional principles and reducing the size of bureaucratic government. It publishes numerous brochures, pamphlets, and tracts.

Americans for Democratic Action (ADA)
815 15th St. NW, Suite 711
Washington, DC 20005
(202) 638-6447

ADA formulates liberal domestic and foreign policies and tries to put them into effect through the political process. It publishes *ADA World* bimonthly.

Americans for Religious Liberty (ARL)
PO Box 6656
Silver Spring, MD 20906
(301) 598-2447

ARL is an educational organization working to preserve religious, intellectual, and personal freedom in a secular democratic state. It opposes school prayer and any government involvement with religion. It publishes the newsletter *Voice of Reason* and numerous pamphlets.

Americans United for Separation of Church and State
8120 Fenton St.
Silver Spring, MD 20910
(301) 589-3707

This organization's purpose is to protect the right of Americans to religious freedom. It opposes the passing of both state and federal laws which threaten the separation of church and state. Its many publications include brochures, pamphlets, and a monthly newsletter, *Church and State*.

Association for Supervision and Curriculum Development
125 N. West St.
Alexandria, VA 22314-2798
(703) 549-9110

This professional association of educators is interested in school improvement at all levels of education. It promotes professional development in curriculum and supervision. Its magazine, *Educational Leadership*, is published eight times a year. It also publishes numerous books and pamphlets.

Common Cause
2030 M St. NW
Washington, DC 20036
(202) 833-1200

Common Cause is a national citizens' lobby devoted to making government at the national and state levels more open and accountable to citizens. It publishes a bimonthly called *Common Cause Magazine*.

Democracy Project
215 Park Ave. S., Suite 1814
New York, NY 10003
(212) 674-8989

Democracy Project is a nonprofit institute founded in 1981 to critique conservative public and political policy and to develop progressive alternatives. Although it has no newsletter or periodic publication, in 1989 it published *America's Transition: Blueprints for the 1990s*. The book is an anthology of recommendations by 58 of America's most prominent progressives.

Eagle Forum
PO Box 618
Alton, IL 62002
(618) 462-5415

Eagle Forum supports pro-family and conservative policies. It promotes traditional morality, private enterprise, and national defense. It publishes a monthly newsletter, *Phyllis Schlafly Report*.

Ethics Resource Center (ERC)
1025 Connecticut Ave. NW, Suite 1003
Washington, DC 20036
(202) 223-3411

ERC is committed to increasing public trust in America's institutions by strengthening their ethical foundations. It sponsors research and conferences on ethics-oriented issues. Its newsletter, *Ethics Resource Center Report*, is published quarterly.

Foundation for Economic Education (FEE)
30 S. Broadway
Irvington, NY 10533
(914) 591-7230

FEE promotes the study of private ownership, free market theory, open competition, and limited government. It publishes a monthly magazine called *The Freeman*.

Freedom from Religion Foundation (FFRF)
30 W. Mifflin, Suite 801
Madison, WI 53701
(608) 256-8900

FFRF is a politically active organization of "free thinkers." Its purpose is to promote separation of church and state and combat fundamentalism. Its extensive publications include books, brochures, pamphlets, and the monthly newspaper, *Freethought*.

The Heritage Foundation
214 Massachusetts Ave. NE
Washington, DC 20002
(202) 546-4400

The Foundation is a public policy research institute dedicated to the principles of free competitive enterprise, limited government, individual liberty, and a strong national defense. It publishes a weekly bulletin, *Backgrounder*, a monthly magazine, *National Security Record*, and many other books and research papers.

Josephson Institute for the Advancement of Ethics
310 Washington St., Suite 104
Marina del Rey, CA 90292
(213) 306-1868

The Institute is a nonprofit educational and leadership training organization which seeks to increase the nation's awareness of ethical issues and to provide individuals with the skills to make their behavior more ethical. It works with decision makers in government, journalism, business, law, and the nonprofit community through workshops, presentations, and publications. It publishes a quarterly magazine, *Ethics: Easier Said Than Done*, and a newsletter for law students called *The Good Lawyer*.

Moral Re-Armament (MRA)
1707 H St. NW
Washington, DC 20006
(202) 872-9077

MRA is a worldwide program based on fundamental Christian values that aims to advance the Christian religion by bringing about a transformation of character and motive in people and nations. MRA has programs operating in many countries. It publishes *World News* biweekly and *Breakthrough* monthly. It also publishes books, pamphlets, and cassettes.

People for the American Way (PFAW)
2000 M St. NW, Suite 400
Washington, DC 20036
(202) 467-4999

PFAW is comprised of religious, business, media, and labor figures committed to reaffirming the traditional American values of tolerance, pluralism, diversity, and freedom of expression and religion. In addition to issue papers, reports, and books, it also publishes a quarterly newsletter, *PFAW Forum*.

The Rockford Institute Center on Religion and Society
152 Madison Ave., 24th Floor
New York, NY 10016
(212) 532-4320

A division of the Rockford Institute, this interreligious research and educational organization focuses on issues of culture and change in the contemporary world. It seeks to address the role of religion and religious values in society. It publishes a monthly newsletter, *Religion and Society Report*, and a quarterly journal, *This World*.

Williamsburg Charter Foundation
1250 24th St. NW, Suite 270
Washington, DC 20037

The Foundation is a private nonprofit, nonsectarian organization, concerned with the place of religion in American public life. Although it has no periodic publication, in 1988 it published a survey on religion and public life in America. It can be purchased for $15.

Annotated Book Bibliography

Mortimer Adler

We Hold These Truths: Understanding the Ideas and Ideals of the Constitution. New York: Macmillan, 1987. A popular philosopher illuminates the ideas and ideals that form the core of the Declaration of Independence and the Constitution.

ASCD Panel on
Moral Education

Moral Education in the Life of the School. Alexandria, VA: Association for Supervision and Curriculum Development, 1988. A policy analysis by the nation's largest educational leadership organization, presenting a case for improved moral education in America's schools and giving specific recommendations for attaining it.

Robert N. Bellah

The Broken Covenant. New York: Seabury Press, 1975. A description of America's "civil religion" by the popularizer of the term.

Robert N. Bellah, et al.

Habits of the Heart. Berkeley: University of California Press, 1985. Scholars from several disciplines interview over 200 Americans to examine their values, goals, and attitudes. The authors conclude that excessive individualism has harmed American culture, and that Americans must look to their roots and cultivate community to be made whole.

Patrick J. Buchanan

Right from the Beginning. Boston: Little Brown & Co., 1988. A prominent conservative journalist and commentator presents his views on a number of issues confronting American democracy.

Vine Deloria Jr.

God Is Red. New York: Grosset & Dunlap, 1973. A native American calls for a complete cultural change, recommending that America's Judeo-Christian tradition be replaced with a new religious outlook based on the values of native tribal religions.

Betty Sue Flowers, ed.

Bill Moyers: A World of Ideas. New York: Doubleday, 1989. In 1988 Bill Moyers interviewed 41 extraordinary men and women in a public television series, asking them how American values are changing and how these values affect America in an increasingly global culture. These valuable interviews are made available in this book. If you read only one book in this bibliography, read this.

Benjamin M. Friedman

Day of Reckoning. New York: Random House, 1988. The author claims that the economic policy adopted in 1981 violates the basic moral principle that has traditionally bound each generation of Americans to the next.

Herbert J. Gans

Middle American Individualism: The Future of Liberal Democracy. New York: The Free Press, 1988. The president of the American Sociological Association claims that middle class Americans have developed an individualistic value system that alienates them from corporate America and involvement in American government.

Lee Iacocca	*Talking Straight.* New York: Bantam Books, 1988. Chrysler Corporation's chief executive officer gives an insider's evaluation of the current state of America's business values with recommendations.
Alfie Kohn	*The Case Against Competition.* Boston: Houghton Mifflin, 1986. This well researched study argues that America's love affair with competition is destructive. The author urges Americans to replace competition with cooperation which he claims will strengthen society by building character and self-confidence.
Lewis H. Lapham	*Money and Class in America.* New York: Weidenfeld & Nicolson, 1988. A witty and penetrating analysis of America's preoccupation with wealth, a trait the author refers to as America's real civil religion.
Frances Moore Lappé	*Rediscovering America's Values.* New York: Ballantine Books, 1989. The author, in dialogue with great thinkers from the past and present, explores America's basic values, and attempts to bring into focus a path Americans can follow to successfully deal with the cultural and social problems it now faces.
Sidney Lens	*Permanent War: The Militarization of America.* New York: Schocken Books, 1987. A liberal journalist and activist describes an American economy that is dedicated to permanent war, weakening the country's legal and moral values and endangering its democratic foundations.
Herbert McClosky and John Zaller	*The American Ethos.* Cambridge: Harvard University Press, 1984. A study of the political culture of the United States, examining its principal values, their sources and historical development, and the extent of popular support they enjoy today.
Martin E. Marty	*Religion & Republic: The American Circumstance.* Boston: Beacon Press, 1987. A survey of contemporary American religion, with commentary on its political and social roots, by perhaps the most influential interpreter of the subject.
Robert Nisbet	*The Present Age: Progress and Anarchy in Modern America.* New York: Harper & Row, 1988. A critical analysis of modern America, identifying three problem areas: the prominence of war since 1911, the Leviathan-like presence of national government, and the number of Americans who are only loosely attached to groups and traditional values and are so plainly governed by a cash nexus.
Norman Ornstein, et al.	*The People, the Press, & Politics.* Reading, MA: Addison-Wesley, 1988. An extensive survey by the Gallup Organization, commissioned by the Time Mirror publishing company, examining public attitudes and values on social and political issues.

A. James Reichley

Religion in American Public Life. Washington, DC: Brookings Institution, 1985. A historical examination of the foundational values in which American political and religious traditions are jointly rooted.

George Roche

A World Without Heroes. Hillsdale, MI: Hillsdale College Press, 1987. A conservative observer laments the absence of authentic heroes in modern American culture.

Anne Wilson Schaef

When Society Becomes an Addict. New York: Harper & Row, 1987. The author argues that American society has the same characteristics as an alcoholic or addict, and is deteriorating at an alarming rate.

Studs Terkel

The Great Divide: Second Thoughts on the American Dream. New York: Pantheon Books, 1988. The author, a roving interviewer, catalogs the observations of Americans from many walks of life. He discovers that the country is divided by Americans who subscribe to different sets of values.

Cal Thomas

The Death of Ethics in America. Waco, TX: Word Books, 1988. A journalist examines the moral health of American society, claiming that the widespread decline of ethics and integrity endangers the democratic health of the nation.

Alexis de Tocqueville

Democracy in America. New York: Harper & Row, 1966. Edited by J.P. Mayer. The classic description of American values and character by a visiting French historian and political theorist in the 1830s.

Touche Ross

Ethics in American Business: A Special Report. New York: Touche Ross & Co., 1988. An analysis of the current state of business ethics in America, sponsored by a national accounting firm. Available from Touche Ross & Co., 1633 Broadway, New York, NY 10019.

Paul L. Wachtel

The Poverty of Affluence. Philadelphia: New Society Publishers, 1989. In this examination of America's insatiable desire for growth, the author contends that the country's desire for consumption and profits has failed to replace its greater need for community.

John Kenneth White

The New Politics of Old Values. Hanover, NH: University Press of New England, 1988. In showing how President Reagan's successful presidential politics were based on traditional American values, the author claims the country's basic values have changed little since colonial times. Then, as now, he argues, these values are liberty, freedom, and equality of opportunity.

Daniel Yankelovich

New Rules: Searching for Self-Fulfillment in a World Turned Upside Down. New York: Random House, 1981. An analyst of social trends claims Americans are casting off traditional social values and searching for a new social ethic.

Index

312